The
Accidental
Prime
Minister

Also by Annika Smethurst

On Secrets

The Accidental Prime Minister

ANNIKA SMETHURST

hachette
AUSTRALIA

Published in Australia and New Zealand in 2021
by Hachette Australia
(an imprint of Hachette Australia Pty Limited)
Level 17, 207 Kent Street, Sydney NSW 2000
www.hachette.com.au

A catalogue record for this
book is available from the
National Library of Australia

ISBN: 978 0 7336 4694 2 (hardback)

Cover design by Luke Causby/Blue Cork
Cover photograph courtesy of Louie Douvis
Author photograph courtesy of Sam Ruttyn
Typeset in Adobe Garamond Pro by Kirby Jones
Printed and bound in Australia by McPherson's Printing Group

MIX
Paper from
responsible sources
FSC® C001695

The paper this book is printed on is certified against the
Forest Stewardship Council® Standards. McPherson's Printing
Group holds FSC® chain of custody certification SA-COC-005379.
FSC® promotes environmentally responsible, socially beneficial
and economically viable management of the world's forests.

This book is affectionately dedicated to Byron and Merv,
for their unwavering love and support

Contents

Author's Note

For this first-ever biography of Australian Prime Minister Scott Morrison, I have drawn on interviews with Scott Morrison, senior Cabinet ministers, staffers, parliamentary allies and rivals, as well as colleagues, close friends, and friends from school and university. Many of the more than seventy subjects interviewed for this book were prepared to be quoted only on the condition that they not be identified by name, as they feared blowback from the powerful thirtieth prime minister. With an election due before May 2022, the interviews and research took place between September 2020 and April 2021, ahead of the federal poll.

– Annika Smethurst, July 2021

Introduction

It will come as no surprise to learn that former Australian prime minister John Howard used to lean on a sporting analogy to describe the highs and lows of political life. Howard would tell colleagues that on good days – like those that followed each of his four election wins – it felt like the start of the perfect game of golf: the sun is out, the sky is blue, putts drop and drives sail down fairways with ease. On bad days, you're on the eighth at two under par and chipping onto the green to line up a birdie putt when you shank it – the ball charges out low and to the right, landing in a deep bunker. It should be a simple shot out of trouble and you can get back on track. If you're lucky, you might even walk away with par. But as all those who play it know, golf is a mental game. When you're under pressure to return to form and your head is filled with bad thoughts, your score will suffer.

Howard, whose career seemed all but over in 1987 when he lost the federal election to Bob Hawke, knows a thing or two about survival. He would use the golf analogy to calm nervous colleagues who feared the wrath of the public over the latest political scandal. This analogy could never be used to describe Scott Morrison's career, but it perfectly sums up his prime ministership.

In becoming prime minister, Morrison unexpectedly fell over the line in a leadership ballot that would make last-man-standing Olympic skater Steven Bradbury blush. He was then predicted to be one of Australia's shortest-serving leaders, but he took advantage of a Labor Opposition that made itself a huge target at the May 2019 federal election. His unanticipated victory, a miracle of sorts, appeared to guarantee him years in the top job. It elevated his status to that of Liberal Party legend. However, within months things started to unravel. Like a golfer making air shots, Morrison repeatedly swung and missed.

In December 2019, he refused to cancel a family holiday in Hawaii despite the bushfires raging in Australia's eastern states. When he did finally return home, his qualified apology for holidaying abroad and his spontaneous defence that 'I don't hold a hose' were early signs that he is prepared to dig in when under pressure, that he becomes defensive when he feels he is under attack.

Landed with a global pandemic in early 2020 when his strong leadership appeared to be waning, Morrison seemed to learn the lessons of his past mistakes. Initially, he was calm and rational and positioned himself as a capable centralist as he embraced massive pandemic spending in a U-turn from the Coalition's preferred policy of fiscal restraint. The pandemic also allowed Morrison to lean on a favoured tactic: framing issues as trivial when he feels that he is being unfairly treated. With COVID-19 dominating the news cycle, Morrison deflected questions and downplayed minor scandals that threatened his government.

In many ways, he became a victim of his own success. With COVID-19 largely under control in Australia in early 2021, his deflections stopped working. On the eve of the long-awaited vaccine rollout, for which the federal government initially wanted to take credit, the allegation that former Liberal staffer Brittany Higgins had been raped by a colleague in Parliament House in March 2019 rocked the government and triggered a wider debate about the treatment of women in Canberra. Morrison, who married his childhood sweetheart and has resisted the salacious side of political life, was one of just a handful of MPs who might have successfully moralised on the issue, potentially turning a political hit into personal gain. But his response to the growing public anger further fuelled his government's problems – he invoked his daughters in response to the rape allegations, and subsequently suggested that the thousands of women who attended the March4Justice rallies should be thankful they were not 'met with bullets'. Like a golfer stuck in a bunker, his great day on the course was taking a turn for the worse.

* * *

As a politician, Morrison is a master communicator. He has perfected the art of the political attack, which ultimately has helped him attack the Opposition and its policies. When under pressure, Morrison also hits back – sometimes it works, other times it fails spectacularly. Embracing the false belief that he has wooed certain sections of the media or that he will be saved by his savvy marketing prowess, Morrison is also prone to overreach. It's almost as if, lacking any strong factional backing in Canberra, he has made the middle-class, tabloid-reading mums and dads of Australia his factional bosses and tries to please them with every pitch. Seasoned politicians who see the world through factional prisms are cynical about Morrison's endless need to pitch to punters. But it is perhaps the key to his success.

Throughout his political career, Morrison has been more willing to answer to newspaper editors than to factional heavyweights. Internally, he was once known as the 'Tabloid Treasurer'. But it's an example of his pragmatism and endless pursuit of power. Of course, factions do play an important role in Canberra, whether the Prime Minister likes it or not. Shared ideologies act as a political compass that guide the direction of policy. Without them, it can be difficult to make tough decisions and you can find yourself adrift when scandals hit. Morrison's decision-making resolutely is not based on ideology but on research and focus groups and newspaper editors that help him understand what the public is thinking. His lack of a strong belief system has been met with caution in Canberra but it has perhaps allowed him to better represent Australia than more ideological prime ministers in the past.

Unlike former prime ministers Turnbull and Abbott, Morrison isn't a Rhodes scholar. He has been unassuming and often underrated by those who know him, work with him and compete against him on the political battlefield. Writing about Donald Trump after his November 2020 US election loss, *Wall Street Journal* columnist Peggy Noonan described how Trump hadn't been changed by his time in the White House. She said it was almost an achievement to have been 'untouched by the grandeur, unchanged by the stature and history of the office'. Morrison's supporters insist that he is much the same, in that, so far, the role hasn't altered him. He has tried, sometimes unsuccessfully, to focus on service delivery to middle Australians and not be beholden to the country's thinking class. He knows who the voters and colleagues who have helped him succeed are and is determined to deliver for them.

Critics have repeatedly underestimated Morrison's political nous and overplayed the impact of his missteps. But Morrison seems to understand, more than most, what gets through to mainstream Australians and what they ignore.

The Organisation for Economic Co-operation and Development considers almost 60 per cent of Australians as middle class. Morrison has dedicated much of his adult life to understanding this voting group, trying to replicate their lifestyle and representing them in Canberra. He is mocked for playing up his daggy dad persona and suburban style, but it works.

By throwing on a cap and speaking frankly, he has been able to get through to voters who other politicians largely ignore. He may ham it up, but those closest to him believe it's an accurate representation of what this unpretentious prime minister is like behind closed doors.

At times, his devout Christian family man image seems at odds with the ambitious, poll-obsessed politician. So too, his ability to largely ignore jibes from the political and cultural elite while simultaneously proving himself susceptible to a bruised ego.

His political ascendance can be attributed to a powerful mix of hard work and unbridled ambition, aided by a devotion to data and polling and the consistent underestimating of his ability by political opponents.

Scott Morrison's rise to the prime ministership, his unexpected victory in a supposedly unwinnable election and his initial success in fighting the coronavirus has elevated him to status within the Liberal Party.

But his tin-eared response to the treatment of women, the bushfires and the all-important vaccine rollout, coupled with a propensity to blame-shift, chart a course that has the potential to unravel his prime ministership.

Chapter One

Moulding the National Character

Five months before Scott Morrison was born, an unimaginable and tragic incident occurred at Cheviot Beach on Victoria's Mornington Peninsula.

On the afternoon of Friday 15 December 1967, Australia's prime minister, Harold Holt, arrived in the coastal village of Portsea. According to Doug Anthony, the then deputy leader of the Country Party and the last politician to see Holt alive, the prime minister was 'not a happy soul'. He had been facing sustained media pressure over the alleged misuse of planes, his Cabinet was leaking, and there were rumours of a looming leadership spill. He was also haunted by the war in Vietnam and his Labor rival Gough Whitlam was proving to be a tougher opponent than he had anticipated. Having wrapped up his final Cabinet meeting for the year, Holt had left his wife, Zara, and their children in Canberra and headed for the family's Portsea holiday home. Back in those days, not only were prime ministers permitted to take a holiday over the summer, they didn't require the security detail and restrictions that more recent prime ministers have had to contend with.

Australia didn't know it at the time, but Holt had planned to spend a few days in Portsea with his secret lover, Marjorie Gillespie, who was also on the Mornington Peninsula that weekend. It was a windy morning at Cheviot Beach on Sunday 17 December when Holt, Marjorie, her daughter Vyner and two of their friends arrived for a swim. Even on the most perfect summer day, winds whip up the surf on the peninsula's back-beaches, sending waves smashing into the shore. Few dare to swim at Cheviot Beach, which was named in honour of the SS *Cheviot*, a cargo ship that had been bound for Sydney when it sank off Point Nepean in 1887, taking with it the lives of thirty-five of its crew. But neither that tragedy nor the blustery conditions were enough to deter Holt, who was a confident swimmer and avid spearfisherman. He waded into the raging sea about midday while the others remained onshore and within minutes the heaving waters of Bass Strait had engulfed him. He did not reappear.

Police divers and search and rescue teams scoured the turbulent waters off the beach as helicopters swept the wild coastline from above. By Sunday evening, hope had faded that Holt would be found alive, but the search for his body continued for several weeks before officially being called off on 5 January 1968. His body was never found. The authorities concluded that Holt had accidentally drowned, but his death, which occurred at the height of the Cold War, proved a magnet for conspiracy theories, including claims that he had defected to Russia, had been abducted by a submarine, and had taken his own life.

In politics, when death or tragedy unexpectedly end a career, there is little time to mourn. With Holt lost to the sea, attention quickly turned to deciding on his permanent replacement. Deputy prime minister John McEwen was temporarily sworn in as Australia's new leader until the Liberals could elect a successor. As the leader of the Country Party, McEwen was never going to get the top job. But he made it clear he would not serve in a government led by the divisive Liberal William McMahon, threatening to withdraw his party from the Coalition in protest should McMahon get the nod. To preserve the Coalition's fragile unity, McMahon pulled out of the leadership race, and on 10 January, Sir John Gorton, a senator and compromise candidate, became prime minister. Due to factional rivals threatening to split the already divided government, Gorton essentially fell into the prime ministership. He was forced to resign from the

Senate in February 1968 and contest a by-election in the seat of Higgins, which had been left vacant by Holt's death. The unusual path Gorton took to the prime ministership saw him take on the mantle of 'the accidental prime minister'.

Half a century on, in August 2018, Scott Morrison also found himself unexpectedly grasping the country's leadership, the beneficiary of more divisive opponents. He was appointed prime minister when a factional split meant he was viewed as the most palatable option by the warring moderate and conservative wings of the Liberal party.

It wasn't quite as unanticipated as a drowning, but few politicians or pundits had predicted that the socially progressive Liberal prime minister Malcolm Turnbull would be challenged by his home affairs minister, the conservative Queenslander Peter Dutton, that week. The major flaw in Dutton's attempted takeover was that he was considered unpalatable by a significant number of Liberal MPs, who feared the party would be destined to lose the next election should he become leader. The other prominent contender, the moderate Julie Bishop, would never be accepted by the party's hard-right faction, and so a consensus candidate emerged. Morrison – who, if you believe his version of events, put his campaign together at the last minute – defeated Dutton by forty-five votes to forty, even though Dutton had plotted his attack for months.

Scott Morrison has been keen to cultivate the image of the 'accidental prime minister' since taking on the role.

But while the timing of his rise was somewhat accidental, his rise to the top job seemed somewhat inevitable from the moment he landed in Canberra. Colleagues describe a man who spent years manoeuvring himself into the perfect position to take the prime ministership at the most opportune time. These suspicions were fuelled by the fact that, while Morrison impressed his peers with his analytical approach and strong work ethic, few trusted him. Parliamentary colleagues have observed that every decision he took in Canberra was geared towards improving his chances of one day becoming Australia's leader. As one long-serving Liberal minister commented: 'I thought he always wanted to be the prime minister from the first moment he entered politics.

In some ways, this is not unusual. It's often said that every single politician who arrives in Canberra wants to become prime minister. While that may be the case, it is a dream achieved by very few. In Morrison, veterans of Parliament House saw a determination that few others had displayed. At his worst, he was calculating and manipulative. At his best, he was incredibly focused and hardworking, always answerable to the people rather than to the factional heavyweights.

* * *

If it's true that every member of parliament dreams of becoming prime minister one day, then it is probable that most potential candidates dream of taking over in a bloodless transition, with a strong majority in both houses and the backing of their colleagues and the wider public. But this also is rarely the case.

When Scott Morrison become Australia's thirtieth prime minister on 24 August 2018, conditions could be best described as suboptimal. Morrison was the Liberal Party's third leader in five years and represented the sixth change of prime minister in Australia in eleven years. A bitterly divided Coalition was struggling in the polls and an election was due within months. Things looked grim. But this was Canberra, and you didn't turn down the opportunity to ride around in the prime ministerial vehicle with the numberplate 'C1', which stands for 'Commonwealth 1', because that opportunity was unlikely to ever present itself again.

The coup that snatched the prime ministership from Malcolm Turnbull had far greater consequences than simply a change of leadership. Turnbull had made it clear that, should he ever lose the prime ministership, he would resign from politics, which is exactly what he did. As such, Morrison's first big test would be a by-election in October 2018 in the seat of Wentworth, which takes in many of the most affluent suburbs in Sydney's inner east. Based on the average tax return of its wealthy resident voters, Wentworth should be an ultra-safe Liberal seat. But it has become an exemplar of the phenomenon known as 'doctor's wives', a clumsy political phrase that attempts to describe a voting bloc that is so well off that its members put social conscience ahead of financial self-interest. This switched-on cohort was angry about what had happened to Malcolm Turnbull and it was determined to seek revenge at the ballot box.

Julie Bishop, the popular foreign minister – at least in the eyes of the public – also resigned from the frontbench, creating a headache for Scott Morrison and his party, which was widely viewed as being anti-female, even in those early days. Following the leadership spill, the first-term MP Julia Banks also quit the Liberal Party, citing bullying and intimidation by her colleagues, further fuelling the narrative that the Liberal Party does not support women.

Two weeks into the job and with his party haemorrhaging public approval, Morrison skipped an international talkfest in Nauru and opted instead to travel to the regional NSW city of Albury to deliver his first major speech as prime minister. Expectations were high. Like Gorton, Morrison had emerged as a consensus candidate, a man who was tolerated by both his party's warring moderate and conservative factions but who was favoured by few. His ascendance may have offered the Liberal Party the hope of a fresh start, but few of his colleagues really knew or trusted the man who would lead them to the next election.

Just as Barcaldine in Queensland is regarded as the birthplace of the Australian Labor Party, Albury, located on the New South Wales–Victoria border, is where the modern Liberal Party was established under Sir Robert Menzies in December 1944. The party had been registered in Canberra a few months earlier, but Menzies chose the Riverina city as the place where he would outline his vision for a broad centre-right political party. Morrison wanted to follow in Menzies's footsteps. With the Liberals all but broken after years of leadership tension, he wanted to put an end to the factional bitterness, just as Menzies had done for centre-right politics in Australia towards the end of World War II. In those early days of his reign, Menzies wasn't necessarily popular, but he was the only person considered capable of leading this new party – a predicament mirrored by Morrison's.

And so, on 6 September 2018, at the Mirambeena Community Centre in Lavington, Albury's largest suburb, Morrison made his pitch to his colleagues, who were still somewhere between the mental paralysis and stunned mullet stages. Knowing that both the moderate and conservatives wings of the Liberal Party trade on Menzies's name, Morrison latched onto Sir Robert's legacy, desperately hoping that the city in which Australia's longest-serving prime minister whipped up the Liberal Party framework would somehow inspire his shattered team to put aside their differences and focus on winning the next election:

This is an important ritual, for us to come here today where Robert Menzies came all those years ago. To come here and pledge to that legacy, to that heritage … To show the things that we believe in today are the things that he believed in then and the things we will always believe in as a Liberal Party … [1943] was a horror election

for what were known as the non-Labor parties. They were wiped
out. You'd think after a big election loss like that ... 'it's all done',
'it's all finished', that 'the Labor Party will run the country forever',
it 'was all doomed', all that sort of thing. But Robert Menzies
at that time, seventy-five years ago, almost to this day, it was in
August 1943, he wrote to the president of what was called the
Australian Council of Retailers, a fellow called Mr Lamp. And he
said this to him in his letter ... 'There is a great opportunity if we
are ready to seize it' ... fifteen months later, here in Albury, not far
as you've just heard, they were putting the final touches and bringing
together the formation of the Liberal Party, which has been the most
successful political party at a federal level of any party.

With his delivery veering to evangelical, Morrison preached
the gospel of Menzies to his lost parishioners, vowing to focus
on the value and virtue of all Australians:

He [Menzies] understood that for the individual to be successful in
life, and to be able to realise what they wanted ... they needed some
very important things. If they were fortunate enough, they would
have a family that loved them, and not all Australians have that ...
they would have a family and the family would support them. That
is the first building block of any successful country, community,
society, is family.

Morrison not only needed to win over his war-weary colleagues
but also his greater constituency, who were largely confused as

to why a new prime minister had been installed. He called for healing, unity and prayers. And he would need them. The following month, the independent candidate Kerryn Phelps would go on to win the Wentworth by-election, with a swing of almost 20 per cent away from the Liberals.

* * *

Albury was the perfect place for Morrison to unite his lost Liberals, but the town's surrounds also held great personal significance for the new Prime Minister and his family. In the late 1870s, Scott Morrison's great-great-aunt Mary Cameron attended school in the bush settlement of Bungowannah, which lies less than 20 kilometres to the north-west of Albury. Bungowannah would be one of many towns in the area where Mary lived and later taught. The daughter of a farmer who emigrated from Scotland, Mary would go on to become one of Australia's most famous poets, writers and radicals under her married name, Dame Mary Gilmore. However, to the Morrison household, she would always be Aunt Mary.

Mary spent much of her childhood in southern New South Wales, moving between the farming towns of Wagga Wagga, Cootamundra and Yerong Creek as her father chased work. She proved to be a gifted child and in 1890 moved to bustling Sydney to begin teaching at Neutral Bay Public School. It was there that she struck up a friendship with another writer and poet, Henry Lawson. While the nature of their relationship remains unclear, some – including Scott Morrison – believe they were unofficially engaged for a brief time. What is clear is that the two talented authors forged a strong emotional bond centred on a mutual interest in social reform and a shared mission to improve conditions for maritime workers and shearers. In addition, introversion fuelled their connection. Dame Mary wrote in 1922:

> *The young Lawson and I were both retiring almost to the extent of the recluse, so that when we met fellowship was perhaps the deeper and the greater. Lawson never had any secrets from me.*

Through her writing, Morrison's great-great-aunt fought for the rights of workers, from farm labourers to seamstresses, and her progressive views allowed her to mix with many famous radical thinkers of the day. One of her friends was the firebrand journalist and trade unionist William Lane, who sold Mary on the idea of leaving Sydney for a new utopian settlement in South America known as the New Australia Movement. In 1895, Mary made the brave yet utterly naive decision to resign from her teaching job and sail across the Pacific to join Lane's socialist settlement deep in the jungles of Paraguay. It perhaps comes as no surprise to learn that, for Mary, the reality of this utopian existence was far from the idyllic life Lane had promised. Still, when the community dissolved, Mary followed Lane to a new colony 70 kilometres south of New Australia, which was called Cosme. It was there, while working as a teacher and editing the handwritten newspaper *Evening Notes*, as well as a printed publication called *Cosme Monthly*, that she met and married fellow settler William Alexander Gilmore. She also gave birth to her only child, a baby boy called William – known as Billy. When the Cosme socialist experiment also failed, Mary and her son were forced to move to the slums of Buenos Aires while William travelled across Argentina shearing sheep to make enough money for the journey back to Australia.

Mary and her family eventually made their way back home and in 1902 settled on a property in Casterton in western Victoria, where her husband's family had farmed. From her rural farmhouse, Dame Mary lobbied the editor Henry Lamond for a column in the union-affiliated newspaper *The Worker*, to which she contributed poetry, political analyses and recipes, but in the main continued her fight for equality. She used those column inches to campaign for social and economic reforms that included voting rights for women, an old age pension, improved children's welfare and better treatment of Indigenous Australians. She would also play an instrumental role in helping Labor secure the federal seat of Wannon in Victoria in 1906 and again in 1910 – although it is now one of the safest Liberal seats in Australia.

With Mary's literary influence growing, the Gilmores made the decision to leave Casterton in 1912. Mary moved to Sydney so that Billy could attend secondary school, while her husband joined his brother in Cloncurry, Queensland, where they established the first of the family's properties. As Australia grappled with the outbreak of World War I in 1914, Dame Mary used her writing to help her country process the devastation of the battles being fought abroad. She explored the horrors of war in a book of verse titled *The Passionate Heart* (1918), which included the evocative battlefield poem 'Gallipoli'. Her popularity continued through to the next world war, when she produced the defiant 'No Foe Shall Gather Our Harvest' (1940) and 'Singapore' (1942).

It's easy to assume that, were she alive today, this heroine of the labour movement would despise the views of her conservative nephew and the party he leads. But this radical socialist was a contradictory character. She was an observant Christian and revered the British monarchy. Her writing was patriotic, but having lived abroad she also considered herself a fierce internationalist. Dame Mary was considered a prominent pacifist yet her stirring verse was widely read and quoted in times of conflict – 'No Foe Shall Gather Our Harvest' even received a commendation from US general Douglas MacArthur. She was a radical feminist who fought for the rights for women, but she also extolled the virtues of married life and domestic duties, using her columns to provide hints and tips for Australian housewives. In 1937, Mary was appointed Dame Commander of the Order of the British Empire, the first Australian to be granted the award for services to literature. She remains the face of Australia's $10 banknote.

Scott Morrison acknowledges that his political views vary greatly from those that were held by Dame Mary, and that a gaping political divide has developed in his family over recent generations, but he believes her radical outlook was symptomatic of her generation's fight for a better life. He also believes her views, like those of many Australians, cannot be so easily defined. 'She was a big nationalist, and a patriot,' Morrison says during an interview for this book. 'You never know, in her time maybe my views may have been more like hers.' This seems unlikely, but it is clear that Morrison is incredibly proud of the achievements of this Australian icon.

While perceptions of her may differ, it's impossible to deny the influential role that Dame Mary Gilmore played in shaping modern Australia. She was such a champion for the rights of workers that she became the first female member of the Australian Workers' Union. In 1942, on her seventy-seventh birthday, then prime minister John Curtin said Dame Mary had 'helped mould the national character'. Curtin had just made his first train trip to Perth as Australia's leader, along with his wife, Elsie, who used the long journey across the Nullarbor to knit a pair of Russian-style woollen bed socks for Dame Mary.

While 1945 brought the end of World War II, it also brought great personal grief for Mary. In February of that year, an innocuous scratch from barbed wire turned septic before her husband William could reach the hospital in Cloncurry; his arm was amputated in an effort to save him but he died shortly after the surgery. At the time of his death, Mary had long been separated from her husband, but she nonetheless wrote that there had never been a day she hadn't thought of him. While grieving William's loss, Mary received a letter from her son, now married and with a family of his own, and living east of Cloncurry in Julia Creek. Billy assured his mother he was coping with his father's untimely death, but in reality his life was spiralling out of control as he battled alcoholism and bouts of depression. Five months after his father passed away, Billy died after drinking 'benzine by mistake', according to postmistress Nell Green, who detailed his final day in a letter to Mary Gilmore dated 30 July 1945. Scott Morrison's paternal grandmother Noel – Mary's niece – passed on the tragic news to Dame Mary; Billy's wife Dorothy and her young son, also called Bill, had spent time living with Noel in Sydney, so that Bill could begin school.

Dame Mary died in 1962, six years before Scott Morrison was born, meaning she never met the great-great-nephew who would go on to lead Australia's centre-right Liberal Party. In Mary's later years, Morrison's father John would visit his aunt in her modest flat on Darlinghurst Road in Sydney's inner east while he was patrolling the streets of Kings Cross as a young policeman. Taking a break from penning her weekly column for the Communist newspaper *The Tribune* – a task she performed until several weeks before her death – she would regale John with stories, recite poetry and offer him some of the homemade jam which she always seemed to have on the boil.

Scott Morrison's paternal grandparents kept a bust of Dame Mary in the front of the 1920s bungalow they rented in Bronte, right across the road from the home where Scott Morrison was raised. According to Morrison, he and his brother Alan would often go and eat breakfast with their grandparents on mornings when their parents had to work, the terrifying bust glaring at them as they crossed Evans Street. As Scott and Alan got older, the dramatic artwork prompted the boys to ask their grandparents questions about the woman who had helped to shape not only their family but Australia. 'There was an enormous pride,' Morrison says.

In 2012, while standing in the Federation Chamber in Canberra's Parliament House, about 100 kilometres south of the town of Cotta Walla, where Mary was born, Morrison paid tribute to his great-great-aunt. After referring to his daughters' high opinion of Dame Mary, he said:

Even to this day they look on the $10 note with great pride. She was an immensely talented and compassionate woman of fierce conviction and heart. She may well not agree with everything I agree with today, but she was a ... great Australian. With her words, Dame Mary challenged a nation to its core, but she also helped to heal the grief of a war-torn people.

* * *

While Scott Morrison feels tremendous pride in Dame Mary, there is little doubt that one of the greatest influences on his life was his father. John Douglas Morrison was born in Waverley in Sydney's east on 2 December 1934 to Douglas Charles John Morrison (1900–77) and Gwendoline Noel Webster (1902–79). In 1953, John was called up for National Service, the program introduced by the Liberal and Country Party alliance which required eighteen-year-old men to do six months of military training within Australia. This sparked in John a passion for community service, prompting him not only to remain in the Citizen Military Forces (now the Australian Army Reserve) but also to join the NSW Police Force. John, as a man of faith, further embraced his community through his involvement with the church. He also showed his commitment through sport – at twenty years of age he joined the Randwick District Rugby Union Football Club, where he played sixty-seven graded games. He hung up his rugby boots in 1962, the year before he married twenty-year-old Marion Elsie Smith. Scott Morrison describes his father as 'larger than life' and the 'knockabout bloke', adding that 'everyone knew who Dad was'.

Marion was born in the suburb of Surry Hills, just outside Sydney's CBD, on 14 January 1943. Her father, labourer Leslie John Smith, who went by the name of Sandy, had moved to Australia from New Zealand as a child. Sandy was a gunner in World War II, serving in Sir Roden Cutler VC's 2/5th Field Regiment as part of the Second Australian Imperial Force

7th Division fighting in the Middle East, Papua New Guinea and Borneo. Prior to the war, Sandy married a woman called Mardie and settled in a house on Victoria Street in Waverley. Morrison keeps a photo of Sandy, his maternal grandfather, in his office at Parliament House.

As children, Scott Morrison's parents briefly lived on the same street, but it would be years before a romantic relationship bloomed. John and Marion's courtship started when she was still a teenager, while he was almost a decade older. Marion invited John to be part of the Bondi Theatrical Society, and slowly their friendship and mutual passion for the stage transformed into love. They married in 1963. Money was tight in those days, but thankfully John's Aunty Frank (Francis) invited the couple to move into her large home on a corner block – 27 Evans Street – in Bronte. Francis was the sister of Scott Morrison's grandmother and so was another niece of Dame Mary. She had married late in life but her husband had died shortly after the wedding and she never had children of her own. She had inherited the house on Evans Street, which was laid out in such a way as to effectively allow the Morrisons to have the privacy craved by all newlyweds. That said, as part of the deal, the Morrisons agreed to live with Toby, a cat who came with the property – Toby loved Aunty Frank and seemed to tolerate the rest of the family.

As a child, Scott Morrison had wanted a dog, but that wasn't an option for a family that had been warmly invited into the home of an archetypal cat lady. Still, in the lead-up to the 2019 election campaign, that fact didn't stop Labor from latching onto a rumour that the Morrisons had had a dog with the offensive and anachronistic name 'Nigger'. Despite the obvious untruth of the story, it was soon swirling around the Canberra press gallery with a not-so-gentle nudge from Shorten's office. Eventually, a diligent journalist thought it was best to ask Morrison's media team about it, and the story was flatly rejected.

It was just one the many odd accusations the prime minister has been forced to deny – and that embarrassed staff have had to ask him about. Another was a story about Morrison suffering an unfortunate toilet incident at a McDonald's restaurant in the southern Sydney suburb of Engadine after his beloved NRL team, the Cronulla Sharks, lost the grand final in 1997. While there is no truth in the story, Morrison's staff say that the prime minister is amused by the rumour which started on Twitter.

In their first five years of marriage, John and Marion welcomed two sons, with their firstborn being Scott's older brother, Alan. Scott John Morrison was born in Waverley on 13 May 1968, which would eventually make him Australia's first generation X prime minister. On the day of his birth, a Monday, the Duke of Edinburgh was attending a Commonwealth conference at the University of Sydney. Heavy autumn rains were lashing central and eastern Australia, breaking a longstanding drought – rising waters had even isolated some Queensland towns and cut off Alice Springs. Abroad, American and North Vietnamese negotiators were kicking off peace talks in Paris after years of bloody warfare. Indeed, 1968 was a year of rapid social and political change across the globe – in the United States alone, it saw the election of Richard Nixon and the assassinations of Martin Luther King Jr and Robert F Kennedy. In Australia, meanwhile, John Gorton had just become prime minister in unusual circumstances, his predecessor Harold Holt having been lost to the sea. And after decades of conservative rule, radical politics was on the rise as anti-Vietnam War demonstrations gathered momentum.

But such events, whether local or global, were rarely discussed at 27 Evans Street. The Morrisons were compassionate but somewhat insular folk. Scott Morrison says of his parents: 'They weren't political. My parents voted Liberal but it wasn't talked about, it was just sort of known.' Rather, says Morrison: 'We were very community orientated. It was the rugby club and the church.' The Morrisons appeared to live by the proverb that charity begins at home.

When appraising Australia's thirtieth prime minister, it would seem that this inward-looking approach rubbed off on the young Scott Morrison. While recent predecessors such as Kevin Rudd and Malcolm Turnbull enjoyed the global stage, Morrison has always preferred domestic policy. He explained this while attending the G7 (Group of Seven) summit in the French coastal town of Biarritz in August 2019: 'I'm not one that rushes to the plane to attend summits. As Australia's prime minister, I always prefer to be in Australia dealing with issues on the ground domestically.' That may be the case, but Morrison also understands there are few votes to be won in attending overseas summits. It's also likely that many Australians embrace and perhaps share this more inward-looking perspective.

Bronte has long been an affluent family-friendly suburb with leafy streets and a beautiful beach. But when the Morrisons lived there in the 1970s and 1980s, it wasn't quite as prestigious as it is today. There were also space issues in Evans Street. The family had benefited from the generosity, and perhaps the loneliness, of their Aunty Frank, who permitted them to stay in her home – Morrison believes his parents would have been forced to move to western Sydney if it wasn't for Frank's gracious offer. But Scott and Alan still had to share a bedroom for their entire childhood and teens, even after Alan began attending university. At one point, their parents agreed to swap rooms so that their growing sons could have more space.

Morrison's maternal grandfather, Sandy, whom he called Pop, lived nearby on Victoria Street and would take his grandsons on the Bondi to Bronte walk and for swims at the Bronte Bogey Hole, a natural rock pool that appears when the tide goes out. 'It was a great childhood,' says Morrison. 'We played footy and went to the beach all the time.'

The Morrisons remained a close-knit and civic-minded family. John rose through the ranks of the police force and ran the local branch of Christian youth organisation the Boys' Brigade. Not long after Scott's first birthday, Marion went back to work as a school bursar while juggling her commitments to her family, her local theatre group and the Girls' Brigade. The Reverend Dr John Squires, who served at the same ministry as John and Marion, described them both as 'striking personalities' and 'devoted and committed church people'.

Morrison describes his mother as a 'woman of great and practical faith'. He adds: 'Life is about what you contribute, not what you accumulate. That's what Mum and Dad have taught me. It's about serving others, because in life, it's people that matter.' In those days it was unusual for women to enter tertiary education: Marion had married young and was mother to two young boys by the time she reached her mid-twenties. Morrison firmly believes that had she been born in a different era, she would have attended university: 'She's really intelligent and in a different time would have gone to university ... but her time didn't enable that for her.'

Again as was the case with many women of that era, Marion never voiced regret about her life – she loved her family, was a dedicated mother and threw herself into her local community. But eventually she did complete an entry-level business qualification that allowed her to be paid at the same rate as a man, a significant achievement at the time. However, when Marion came home to proudly show off her certificate and explain her new pay rate, John failed to realise the significance of his wife's achievement. He was somewhat dismissive, leaving Marion perturbed. Witnessing the exchange, Scott's brother Alan counselled his father, who then reflected on Marion's accomplishment and put things right.

Marion's clerical work helped the family save money, but musical theatre was her true passion, one that she shared with John and which, in turn, they instilled in their children. John was first drawn to the stage in the 1950s, when he took a short break from rugby, and he would go on to star in such productions as *Oliver*, *My Fair Lady* and *The Pirates of Penzance*. Marion, meanwhile, would direct and otherwise orchestrate more than a dozen plays, even choreographing the musical numbers. Scott Morrison believes he has a greater knowledge of musical comedies than any other straight man in Australia: 'It was part of our family life. I used to love watching Mum and Dad perform.' In Morrison's opinion, his mother, while a strong actress, was a better director, but his father loved the limelight – he had natural comic timing which he showed off in humorous operettas like *The Pirates of Penzance* and *HMS Pinafore*.

One year, the whole family took parts in the local church production of *Oliver*. Scott Morrison played the role of the Artful Dodger, the young pickpocket who introduces Oliver to a thieving gang. As his name suggests, the Artful Dodger is an untrustworthy and cunning thief who is willing to sell out his own friends in order to save his own skin. He is also charming, skilled and a convincing leader. The irony of Morrison playing this polarising character is not lost on many of his political colleagues, who see parallels between Morrison, the tricky but talented politician, and the character he once portrayed on stage.

The role launched what would be a short-lived but profitable acting career for the future prime minister, who acquired an agent and starred in several television commercials. A rumour that has long-circulated in Canberra is that Morrison is the young blond boy in pyjamas who appears in a well-known 1970s commercial for Vicks VapoRub. Morrison denies it's him but admits he was in a different commercial for the same product, with the jingle 'Vicks'll lick a ticklin' throat'. He was also in the first ever antipodean Burger King ad when the franchise hit Australia's shores in the early 1970s. 'We got to eat a lot of fast food,' Morrison recalls of the experience. He was also among the singers in a *Sun-Herald* commercial for Tibby the Lion, a character the newspaper dreamed up to ensure children hounded their parents to buy a copy of the paper each week.

* * *

While the Morrisons weren't focused on the politics of Canberra, John did put his hand up to run for Waverley Council in the late 1960s, shortly after a change in the law meant that police could run as candidates. His politics are best described as conservative, but at the time John was driven more by a desire to curb the huge developments popping up in Sydney's east than any ideological bent. He was elected as an independent alderman in 1968, one of two policemen to achieve the feat that year. Still, while he was an independent on paper, he almost always voted with the Liberal-aligned councillors. John's father, Douglas, had supported Menzies. According to Scott Morrison, his grandfather believed Menzies to be 'the finest person to ever walk the earth', and that credence rubbed off on Douglas's son and grandson.

Despite his obvious political allegiance, John maintained he was the 'only true independent' on the council when others described him as a yes-man for the Liberal majority. In 1987 he told the *Sydney Morning Herald*:

> *That doesn't worry me … I have voted both ways in my time on the council. I'm disappointed at the political fighting that goes on within council – and that goes for both sides. With the rise of party groupings in Waverley I had to decide which side I was more inclined to. The problem is people think if you're not for them you're against them.*

According to Scott Morrison, his father didn't like the extension of partisan politics into local councils and wanted to remain an independent, even if it was in name only. The younger Morrison would later shift between the conservative and moderate factions of the Liberal Party, never really finding a natural home.

Towards the end of his two decades on the council, in 1986 and 1987, John Morrison served as mayor of the Municipality of Waverley. But his elevation caused a stir as he was simultaneously rising through the ranks of the police force. In January 1986, the *Sydney Morning Herald* claimed John was the first person to be appointed police inspector of the same municipality of which he was mayor. John denied there was a conflict of interest, telling the newspaper that such a circumstance 'would only come with a confrontation, and I'm not expecting any disagreements between the council and the local police'.

The mayoral promotion was eventually overturned after an appeal by a senior police officer who was backed by a local Labor politician. At the time, John said he would not stand down. But eighteen months later, in September 1987, he resigned from Waverley Council after having served it for nineteen years, which happened to match the age of his youngest son. 'After all those years, it's time to look at yourself and ask how much more you have to offer,' he said at the time.

It's hard to deny the impact John Morrison's career in local politics had on Scott Morrison. While Alan showed little interest in his father's council duties, Scott treated those years as early political training. He would answer the phone at home after school and allow constituents to vent their concerns. Without the backing of a political party, funds were tight, so Morrison and his dad would make canvas signs in lieu of modern-day corflutes, using spray-paint and stencils to promote John ahead of polling day. 'I got to spend time with Dad if I campaigned with him,' Morrison says. 'I got exposed to it [politics] and I saw what he did and how much he liked it.'

As well as his 45-year involvement in the local Boys' Brigade, John was a long-term member of the Bronte RSL, the Bondi Junction Rotary Club and the Eastern Suburbs Memorial Park group, and later he worked at Claremont College as a bus driver while continuing to coach up-and-coming theatre stars. Professionally, John remained a dedicated policeman and by 1979 he had joined the Criminal Investigation Branch to work with the fingerprint division. That year, late on the evening of 9 June, one adult and six boys aged from four to thirteen perished when a fire tore through the Ghost Train ride at Sydney's Luna Park, despite the efforts of attendants who desperately tried to free people as carriages emerged from the dark tunnel. John helped establish the names of the young victims, who were of a similar age to his two sons. Four of the boys were students at Waverley College, located just blocks from the Morrison's Evans Street home. Like many emergency service workers, particularly back then, John didn't speak of the grim scene that met him at the amusement park, but it had an impact on him. Scott Morrison recalls: 'Those boys were the same age as my brother and me. They came from the community we grew up in. It was my father's grim task to identify those bodies.'

Theatre fortunately played a therapeutic role in John's life. Years later, when his eldest son Alan announced that he wanted to join the ambulance service, John encouraged him to have an outlet to balance the darker side of the job. 'In his line of work, you had to have other parts of your life,' Scott Morrison says. '[Theatre] was an escape for him, something that was completely different than the horrors of identifying brutally tortured bodies.'

* * *

In 1973, a young Scott Morrison set off for nearby Clovelly Public School dressed in a tie and a pair of Bata Scout shoes that had a lion paw-print tread, a detail that was very impressive to a boy who was yet to turn five. Morrison has since recalled the impact his teachers – Mrs Hitching, Miss Gould and Mrs O'Connor – had on him in those early years. Like the Morrisons themselves, the school encouraged a love of music – in one year, teacher Freda Katzmann took her student choir all the way to the Sydney Opera House for the Combined Primary Schools' Choral Concert. But it was still the 1970s and teachers dished out tough punishment to 'Cloey kids' who stepped out of line. Mary O'Connor, the infants' mistress who taught a young Scott Morrison in Year Two, organised the carols every Christmas and kept students in check with a small paddle that she carried. After school, Morrison would visit his paternal grandparents across the road from his house. Mardie also doted on her grandchildren, crocheting them what Scott, Alan and their cousins all referred to as 'Mardie rugs'. Her husband Sandy died when Morrison was just thirteen.

Like many Sydney families at that time, the Morrisons holidayed in the Blue Mountains to the west of Sydney. In the early 1970s, after years of staying in modest hotels and units, John and Marion had saved up enough money to purchase a small holiday home at Blackheath. Over time, members of the larger Morrison clan followed John and Marion to the area, buying properties nearby.

In 1980, aged twelve, Scott travelled with his brother to visit their Uncle Bill and Aunty Robin at Greenwood Station, 30 kilometres east of Cloncurry, which had been purchased by William Gilmore and his brother in the lead-up to World War I. For the two boys from inner Sydney, this was a big trip. Morrison describes it as his first real excursion into the bush and says he was blown away by what he saw: 'I recall being completely in awe of the landscape of this great country. Growing up on Sydney's beaches, I was very used to seeing a horizon on water. I had never seen one on land.'

It was also the first time the boy from Bronte had interacted with Indigenous Australians. 'There was a large Indigenous family working on that property ... they were skilled stockmen,' recalls Morrison.

I had almost no interaction with Aboriginal people at this time in my life, and my first reaction as a young boy was to withdraw. They

*were beautiful, kind and generous people but certainly different
from any I had ever known ... Uncle Bill sensed my unease. He
approached me to provide reassurance and said that, above all, I
must treat my new friends with the utmost respect and that, while
in so many of our ways we were different, we were in fact the same.
We too often withdraw when we don't know or don't understand.
My uncle ... helped me to connect, to see and to appreciate and
understand. During the days that followed, I came to learn about
their deep connection to land and country ...*

While in Cloncurry, Morrison's uncle took him to an open-air cinema to see a western movie starring Rock Hudson. 'I wish we had gone back more often, but we couldn't afford it,' Morrison says.

Morrison's youth was largely shaped by his parents, the church and his local community. The values he absorbed impacted his approach to politics, particularly as a campaigner. From an early age, he seemed to understand how religion had unified his own family and community and the power of bringing people together behind a common belief.

His boyhood wasn't one of struggle, nor was it grand in any sense. His parents worked hard to provide their children with considerable opportunities. They instilled a strong sense of community in their children, with less regard for the concerns of the wider world.

Chapter Two

School, Sport and Spin

Until Scott Morrison became Prime Minister, John Howard was the only Liberal PM to have been entirely educated in Australia's public school system. Morrison's non-private education provided him with a convenient narrative as he sought to distance himself from toff-spawning institutions such as the Melbourne and Sydney Grammar schools, which each boast three prime ministers among their former pupils. Weeks ahead of the May 2019 election, Morrison gave a speech which leaned heavily on his apparently basic start in life, one that was straight from the Howard playbook:

We went to public schools, like Jenny and her older sister and her brother did. My family story is not uncommon in our country. Australians quietly going about their lives with simple, decent, honest aspirations. Get an education. Get a job. Start a business. Take responsibility for yourself, support others. Work hard.

Scott Morrison wasn't born into immense wealth. But like Howard, who attended Canterbury Boys' High School in Sydney, Morrison went to a selective-entry institution that would be somewhat unrecognisable to Australians who were educated at more modest state schools of the same era. In 1980, aged twelve, Morrison was accepted by Sydney Boys High School in Moore Park, one of the best schools in the NSW public sector. It was 'public' in designation only. In reality, it churned out as many highly accomplished men as any private school, including the actor Russell Crowe; filmmaker George Miller; Australia's eleventh prime minister, Earle Page; High Court justice and former Labor attorney-general Lionel Murphy; Australia's only winner of the Nobel Prize in Chemistry, John Warcup Cornforth; and ten Rhodes scholars.

Back then, Sydney Boys High was zoned, meaning that while there were academic requirements for entering the school, young men who lived outside Sydney's eastern suburbs had no hope of being accepted. While his academic abilities may have got him through the front door, friends of Morrison from that time describe him as 'middle ground' when it came to schoolwork. And all contend he showed no signs of becoming a prime minister. 'There were a few high flyers at school ... you know, people that did sort of stand out as all-rounders, but Scott was in the middle,' says one former classmate.

Morrison played the saxophone in the Concert Band and later in the Stage Band. He also performed in various school musicals, including *Oliver, Joseph and the Amazing Technicolor Dreamcoat* and *The Pirates of Penzance* – although in the latter it was his brother Alan who starred as the Pirate King. Around the schoolyard, though, Morrison was best known for his sporting prowess. In Year Seven he was introduced to rowing and progressed steadily to the First VIII by Year Twelve. He was equally talented on the rugby field, making the First XV in Year Twelve, having started playing in the under-six team at the Clovelly Rugby Club. Those closest to him in those days say the teenage Morrison was easygoing and loyal, and while he could be fun, he wasn't funny. 'He was actually someone you could probably poke a bit of fun at, the way that Australian males tend to take the piss out of each other,' says one schoolfriend. 'He was slightly goofy and a bit unco, but he was a good sport.' Other classmates report that Morrison had a healthy ego, with one claiming he was a 'fairly arrogant and self-important kid'.

Another former classmate, who played rugby and rowed alongside Morrison at Sydney Boys High, has been shocked by Morrison's transformation since then. 'We were probably the sporting jocks to tell you the truth,' he says. 'For rugby we were probably training five days a week ... and rowing up to six days a week, then you'd go on rowing camps on the weekend. It was a pretty tight group'. He then adds that Morrison 'was a good kid [and] we both shared a strong faith, which I found hard to reconcile years later when he took on the role of immigration minister'.

That view is shared by many of Morrison's contemporaries, who say that they were shocked to see him implement the Coalition's tough border policies, which they saw as conflicting with the moral obligations of Christians. In early 2015, when Morrison was no longer in the immigration and border protection post but was still a minister in the Abbott government, he was invited to speak at a Sydney Boys High fundraising event. More than 300 alumni wrote a scathing open letter opposing the talk, claiming that Morrison had been complicit in advocating offshore immigration detention policies that violated the United Nations Convention against Torture – signatories included former Supreme Court judge Hal Wootten and journalist John Pilger. In response, Morrison tweeted: 'Everyone is entitled to their opinion. That is what I learnt at Sydney Boys High School. Feel free to send [a] cheque in lieu of attendance.'

* * *

It was during his first year at Sydney Boys High that Scott would meet his future wife, Jenny Warren. She was not attending the prestigious Sydney Girls High next door to

Morrison's school; Jenny was raised in battler territory in Sydney's south. The pair actually met on a church youth group trip to Luna Park. Jenny has since described the young Scott Morrison as 'really confident' and 'good looking', with big hair that resembled that of a member of Spandau Ballet, the English synth-pop band that had just exploded onto the Australian music scene. On his part, Scott thought Jenny was a 'pretty good sort', and on the way home from the church trip he asked her for her phone number. She gave it to him but he never called her, and while he would see her on subsequent church trips, he rarely mentioned her to friends.

Former classmates say Morrison was never a ladies' man but instead was focused on sporting success. In Year Nine, Morrison wrote in his school yearbook – *The Record* – that, as captain of his rowing crew, he had been the 'brains' of the outfit that year and was responsible for plotting the race strategies. 'There was a great deal of loyalty between the crew members, which I led,' he wrote. By Year Ten, he'd made it to the Second VIII, where he was affectionately called 'Cigas', which was apparently a reference to his muscular calves, or so he claimed. Not one classmate recalls Scott Morrison being called 'ScoMo', a nickname he appeared to give himself as he hit the frontbench; instead, he was known as 'Scotty'.

In 1983, Morrison was playing rugby in a school tournament when a student from Saint Ignatius' College Riverview was seriously injured on the field. The young man was so badly hurt that he ended up losing the use of his arms and legs and was confined to a wheelchair. Inspired by a forty-hour famine fundraiser they had taken part in through their church, Scott and his friend Drew Tuckwell suggested the Sydney Boys High team organise a 24-hour 'rugby-a-thon' to raise funds for the Saint Ignatius boy. Tuckwell was the one who came up with the concept but he says Morrison should take credit for all the fundraising: 'He picked up the ball and was the real driver behind raising some money.' The two boys, helped by their team, persuaded local businesses and individual donors to support the game, which raised $3000 for the injured player.

While mostly well behaved, Scott and his mates still pushed the boundaries just like most teenagers – albeit they did so gently. In his final two years of school, Morrison and his rowing friends would sneak into local pubs like The Windsor Castle and Paddos. One of the school's rowing coaches, Wayne Williams, was also a local publican and would let the teenagers hang out at his bar on a Saturday night and have a drink. 'If we're going to go to a pub and drink, I guess he thought it's better for us to go and drink at his pub where he could keep an eye on us,' one rowing friend of Morrison says. 'We'd go on a Saturday night and get a pizza somewhere and go and have a beer and play some pool at the pub … it was pretty innocuous.' According to some of his mates, the most trouble Morrison got into during these drinking sessions was one night when he began to choke on a hot dog after trying to eat it too quickly.

Ahead of his final year of school, Morrison offered to run a campaign to get his best mate Scott Mason elected school captain – he'd crunched the numbers and thought he could deliver the captaincy to his friend. But the campaign failed. Morrison had banked on the rowing crew voting as a bloc, but they were split in their choices and Mason ended up coming a close second. Morrison thus learned a valuable lesson about allegiances and the importance of shoring up your support, one that would help him many years later.

Morrison failed to take home any academic awards in his last year at Sydney Boys High, although he did make the First VIII in rowing and the First XV in rugby. Every morning he would arrive at rowing training at 6.30 am to work out with Williams. His political ally and rowing captain Scott Mason describes it as a 'disappointing but enjoyable season' which saw the crew finish sixth overall. If his mornings were dominated by rowing, Scott Morrison's afternoons were dedicated to his other sporting love. School rugby master Mr Barnett believed Morrison's team was above average when compared with other rugby cohorts at Sydney Boys High. Morrison lacked size but his teammates report that he made up for it in mobility and a 'desire to secure possession at any cost'.

Academically, the members of the Sydney Boys High class of 1985 were told by staff that they were weaker than other years, collectively struggling in science, music and languages, although making up ground in English and social sciences.

The theft of examination papers and a markers' strike increased the stress of Morrison's final year of school, but eventually, on 13 January 1986, he and 37,554 other NSW students received their Higher School Certificates. Two weeks later, he received a first-round offer to study at the University of New South Wales (UNSW).

It was also in that final year of school that Morrison started dating the woman who would become his wife. Jenny Warren grew up in Peakhurst, in the St George district in Sydney's south, and she used to mock Scott for growing up in affluent Bronte. 'When you come from the eastern suburbs, people make assumptions,' Morrison says, assumptions which he rejects: 'In my case they weren't well founded.' The pair shared their first kiss during a church camp over Easter at Lake Munmorah on the NSW Central Coast. Faith had brought them together and the joint Waverley–Oatley Christian youth group trips gave them the chance to get to know one another. Their love grew throughout their late-teenage years as they travelled to the Blue Mountains and revisited the Central Coast with their Christian community.

Scott was struck by Jenny's looks but he was also blown away by her kindness, and like the Morrisons, the Warren family was tight-knit. When Scott would visit Jenny at home, her father would always ensure that every one of his guests had the chance for seconds at mealtime, even if it meant he went without. Morrison describes his father-in-law as 'probably the most generous and kindest person I have ever met', and he believes his two daughters have inherited their maternal grandfather's generosity.

* * *

After finishing school, Jenny – who is two months older than Scott – was accepted into a costume and theatre design course but deferred to study nursing instead. Morrison undertook a Bachelor of Science in Applied Economic Geography at UNSW. He also stopped attending the Protestant church where his parents worshipped in favour of the Christian Brethren church where his future wife, Jenny, and his brother, Alan, prayed. Unlike most future politicians, he wouldn't be drawn into campus life and despised student politics; rather, his social network was centred on his church. 'I wasn't in my university Liberal club, it was just never my scene,' he says. 'I hadn't run around in branches in my teens, stacking branches for faction bosses or anything like that.' For Morrison, politics would be a lifelong interest, but he never craved the all-consuming social life that comes with youth-dominated political movements.

One of his university mates, Arthur Ilias, says Morrison never spoke about politics during the early years of their friendship at university. However, in Morrison, Ilias recognised a certain natural leadership and competitiveness. Around classes, Arthur and Scott often found time to play a few holes at the Eastlake Golf Club, which is a five-minute drive from the main UNSW campus in Kensington. After a few months of regular games, Morrison suggested the pair start keeping a head-to-head score. When Morrison finally inched ahead of his mate, seventeen to sixteen, he stopped playing, steadfastly refusing to risk losing his title. To this day, the friends have not played another game of golf.

Morrison's acceptance by and subsequent experience with a church community had a profound impact on his life and led to him studying geography, more specifically the role of communities, as part of his bachelor's degree. He added an extra year to his studies, which he spent researching the Christian Brethren assemblies of Sydney between 1964 and 1989 for an honours' thesis. To Morrison, this was simply about gaining a better understanding of the dynamics of a social community:

> I was quite interested in the functioning life of communities and how they operate, and how they sustain. I could have done it [the thesis] on the rugby union community or the netball community or whatever community you want to pick.

Scott Morrison's thesis, which is permanently housed in the Christian Brethren Archive at the University of Manchester, was effectively an assessment of how the church could boost its numbers and increase its reach. Mirroring his future approach to conservative politics, Morrison pointed out that one of the church's shortcomings was that it had failed to engage with large sections of the community, in particular blue-collar workers, those without tertiary qualifications and those born overseas. It was an early incarnation of Morrison's 'quiet Australians', perhaps, and it provides an insight into his approach to politics.

In January 1990, a few months before his graduation ceremony, Scott married Jenny on a humid day at the Oatley Gospel Chapel. Beforehand, Scott hit the golf course with his groomsmen while Jenny got ready for the big occasion. She wore an off-the-shoulder dress and a baby's breath flower crown, which was the style at the time. 'She was radiant,' Morrison recalls.

The wedding was held a few months after Morrison finally popped the question. The couple had met up in the city, with Scott buying Jenny a bunch of flowers, as he often did. It was as they were sitting on a bench at the top of Martin Place that he asked her to be his wife. The rather unromantic proposal caught Jenny by surprise and initially she laughed, thinking it had to be a joke: there was no bent knee, no diamond ring. Morrison admits: 'It was impulsive. We had been going out for five years, we both knew we were going to get married. It was pretty pathetic, really.' The impetuous nature of the proposal also meant that Morrison hadn't asked Jenny's father for his daughter's hand in marriage, which nowadays is increasingly seen as an outdated tradition but nonetheless is one he wishes he had abided by.

* * *

In the early days of their marriage, Scott and Jenny dreamed of moving overseas. Morrison inquired about studying theology at the prestigious Regent College, a graduate school of Christian studies in the Canadian city of Vancouver. He also looked at several theological schools in America's Midwest. Jenny was likewise keen to move to North America. Together they would deepen their Bible studies and take that knowledge to the islands of the Pacific, where they would spread the word of the Lord. However, with Scott now a married man, his father John had other ideas. 'I would've loved to [study theology] ... but Dad wasn't very keen on that idea,' Morrison says. 'He wanted me to go and get a job and look after my family. That was my responsibility and my duty.'

With theology off the table, a career in business seemed like the next best thing for Morrison. But in July 1990 the Australian economy plunged into a severe recession, making work difficult to come by. It was an experience that had a profound impact on Morrison, who, shortly after he was elected prime minister, said that one of his main objectives was to ensure future generations of Australians never lived through such dire economic circumstances.

The year before the 1990 recession, Morrison and his mate Arthur Ilias opened up the *Yellow Pages* and chose about thirty large corporate firms they would write to seeking work in that final year of university. Morrison was the first to receive a response, from retail developer Kern Corporation, which subsequently interviewed him and offered him a job. At the same time, residential developer Delfin Property Group, which would later be taken over by Lendlease, also offered him work. Morrison, acting as a middle man, called his friend Arthur to see if he would be interested in the residential developer gig – Arthur was, and more than three decades later he's still with Lendlease.

Morrison didn't last long at Kern. At the end of 1989 he jumped to the Property Council of Australia, where he worked until 1995. He may not have studied marketing at university, but the young Morrison soon showed flair for spin. Peter Verwer AO, the man who gave Morrison the job at the Property Council, has said his employee had a 'unique capacity to communicate ideas in a persuasive and telling manner'.

In the early 1990s, the Property Council launched a campaign to try to streamline Australia's planning laws by ridding the country of duplicate local, state/territory and federal regimes. Morrison hatched a plan to physically weigh hardcopies of the duplicate laws across all jurisdictions as a way of bringing the community on board. The legislation weighed in at 28 kilograms and the trick transformed a boring policy debate into a much more mainstream concern. It was an early incarnation of 'Scotty from Marketing'.

Morrison also led the property industry's response to John Hewson's election centrepiece, Fightback!, an economic plan which included a proposed goods and services tax (GST) which was expected to negatively impact the construction sector. Morrison, who wasn't a member of the Liberal Party at the time, says it wasn't about politics: 'I just worked my arse off.' Indeed, by 1995 he had made enough money to buy a two-bedroom Californian bungalow at 7 Lugar Brae Avenue in Bronte with his wife.

* * *

By the time he bought the new family home in Bronte, Scott Morrison had made a name for himself at the Property Council of Australia but was looking for a new challenge. Two years earlier, in September 1993, Australia had erupted in celebration when International Olympic Committee president Juan Antonio Samaranch announced that Sydney would host the 2000 Olympics. It was clear that tourism had become the main game in town and Sydney was the place to be. So Morrison took a job at the Tourism Task Force (TTF), a lobby group chaired by former Labor tourism minister John Brown.

Brown had been a member of federal parliament for thirteen years and had held various ministerial portfolios, including arts, sports and the environment. But tourism was his passion. He had been a member of the Sydney Olympics bid committee and was a founding director of the Sydney Olympic Games Organising Committee. He had also overseen the famous 'shrimp on the barbie' Australian

Tourism Commission ad featuring comedian Paul Hogan, which came to define Australia in the eyes of the world. He was a powerful figure in the industry and he understood marketing. Brown's taskforce, which later became the Tourism and Transport Forum, was set up in 1989 as a voice for the tourism sector following the airline pilots' strike that year. It represented the corporate side of the industry and needed to be seen as apolitical. Morrison wasn't a member of the Liberal Party but neither was he known to be a Labor supporter. And so, not yet thirty, he was offered the role of deputy chief executive in order to balance the more Labor-leaning lobby group.

John Brown claims he hired Morrison based on a recommendation from his son Chris, a decision which remains a sore point between the pair. Due to Brown's lengthy career in Canberra, he'd become used to managing the egos and office tensions of Parliament House. But he was ill-prepared for the arrival of Scott Morrison. Brown recalls: 'We brought him in there to try and balance the lobby group but he was very unpleasant and I didn't like his attitude towards staff.' The relationship deteriorated to the point that it was unworkable. Up until he met Morrison, Brown, who had hired staff in politics and tourism for more than four decades, had only ever sacked one employee, a young woman who simply wasn't up to the job. When he broke the news that her services were no longer required, Brown gave her three months' notice and helped her find a new role. But Brown says that things were different with Morrison: 'I wanted to sack him almost from the start. But he beat me to it and quit. Everyone in the office was very relieved when he said ta-ta.'

Morrison, displaying little in the way of loyalty to Brown and his taskforce, had in fact defected to the Tourism Council Australia (TCA), a rival group run by former state Liberal minister Bruce Baird. There, he was given the lofty title of national manager. According to Baird, Morrison had suggested meeting over a coffee while he was still working at the Tourism Task Force in 1996, then asked Baird directly if he had a job for him. 'He said he'd like to work for our organisation, so I snapped him up,' Baird says, adding that he'd been made aware of Morrison's credentials and strong work ethic and thought he'd give him a shot. Morrison tells a different story, claiming he was poached. But Baird asserts that while he was always on the hunt for 'good people', this definitely wasn't a case of poaching.

Outwardly, Baird's TCA, which was largely a trade organisation, and Brown's TTF, a private lobby group, showed few signs of rivalry. But in those pre-Olympics years, the two groups were constantly tussling for relevance and lucrative tourism dollars. In June 1996, John Howard's newly appointed tourism minister, John Moore, learned about this rivalry the hard way when he accepted invitations to speak at a TCA breakfast and a TTF luncheon on the same day. Liberal heavyweight Baird had pitched the TCA event as the first formal address given by the minister to the tourism sector, which was quite a coup. When he learned of the scheduling clash, he bumped the breakfast forward by a fortnight to scoop his rivals at the TTF.

Tourism operators, backed by the major airlines, started to question why Australia's number one export industry needed two lobby groups with such big fees. Yet when a merger was floated, it was inevitably rejected – the two groups each batted away accusations of tension or rivalry as merely healthy competition. Given all this, it's not surprising that Morrison's defection caused such a stir. But his move from the TTF to the TCA wasn't just about a new job. There are those who believe that, in the mid-1990s, Morrison already harboured political ambitions. In Baird, who at that stage had only recently retired from state politics, Morrison saw a man who could help him launch a political career. In fact, it was Baird who suggested to Morrison that he join the Liberal Party, which is what he did in 1995.

Chapter Three

Opportunities Either Side of the Ditch

New Zealand and Australia have long enjoyed a healthy rivalry, whether competing at cricket, rugby or as a tourism destination. In those years just before the 2000 Olympics, however, Australia was the destination of choice for travellers seeking fun and major events, while across the Tasman – the 'Ditch' – New Zealand tourism was in chaos. By 1998, Auckland had secured the America's Cup yacht race, as well as the next Asia-Pacific Economic Cooperation forum that was due to be held in September 1999. These were big international occasions, but New Zealand was still struggling with its national marketing and also lacked much of the infrastructure needed to host such major affairs.

Then tourism minister Murray McCully coveted Australia's booming events sector, which had Sydney gearing up to host the next Olympics and Melbourne being transformed into a sporting and major events hub. McCully had meticulously researched Australia's success in this area, with a strong focus on Victoria. Melbourne had beaten the NZ capital Wellington for the right to host the 2006 Commonwealth Games, and McCully firmly believed that Victoria had succeeded in its bid by bringing together government responsibility for sport and tourism in the same portfolio. In New Zealand, on the other hand, tourism was run out of the Ministry of Commerce, while sport was an arm of Internal Affairs – the Commonwealth Games bid had been undermined by a clunky bureaucracy. In addition, Kiwi tourists were flocking to Melbourne for sporting and cultural experiences and McCully wanted to win back those tourism dollars.

In April 1998, McCully was ready to launch a new unit known as the Office of Tourism and Sport. Spruiking the plan in a press release, he said the new policy unit would assist domestic marketing in moving towards 'major events–related tourism activities. Upcoming events such as the America's Cup and the World Golf Cup are just as much tourism events as they are sports events so it makes sense for one Government policy unit to straddle both.' Of course, the new unit would need a leader, and who better than a young Australian who was working in Sydney's booming tourism sector in those pre-Olympics years.

At thirty, and with four years' experience at one of Australia's leading tourism lobby groups, Scott Morrison was headhunted to lead the new New Zealand Government department. Wellington Tourism boss Trevor Hall, one of those who interviewed the hopeful candidates, described Morrison as an 'outstanding applicant' who possessed a strong knowledge of tourism coupled with an equally strong understanding of politics. In his interview, Morrison also argued for more tourism funding, which he promised to deliver if given the job. It was exactly the kind of candidate McCully had been looking for.

On 20 May 1998, McCully announced that Scott Morrison would be the inaugural director of the Office of Tourism and Sport, starting in July. New Zealanders were told they were fortunate to have obtained the services of the Australian, that his experience and achievements in Sydney meant he was 'ideally suited' to the new role. McCully told his fellow Kiwis: 'I place a high priority on the contribution that tourism and sport make to New Zealand's economic development, and the advantages which they bring to New Zealanders. This is an important and growing sector which will benefit from a person of Mr Morrison's calibre.'

* * *

Jenny and Scott packed up their Bronte home and made the move across the Ditch to Wellington. With their earlier plan to live on a Pacific island having been derailed, a stint in New Zealand was an attractive new opportunity. The Morrisons quickly embraced their new home, promptly joining the Elizabeth Street Chapel, a Christian Brethren church where they were warmly welcomed by the congregation.

It's unlikely that Morrison knew exactly what he was in for when he arrived in Wellington in July 1998. According to NZ Government sources, over time McCully had become increasingly suspicious of the New Zealand Tourism Board (NZTB), which had been set up in 1991 to promote New Zealand overseas. After he was appointed the minister for tourism, McCully made a series of new board appointments, including designating Bryan Mogridge as the chair and selecting Michael Wall as Mogridge's deputy. One of the revamped board's first tasks was to undertake a strategic review of NZTB's priorities, the results of which were duly rubber-stamped in 1998. This meant that, as the minister accountable for the proposed reforms, McCully was now under pressure to make them happen.

Perhaps predictably, McCully's relationship with the NZTB began to deteriorate. The minister would tell the Office of the Auditor-General in 1999 that there was a gap between what the board had promised and what it delivered. By contrast, the board reported that the minister's expectations had been unrealistic, especially given the tight timeframe that had been imposed. There was also ongoing tension over the restructure that had created Morrison's role. By the time Morrison came on the scene, the relationship between minister and board had worsened significantly and it became clear that McCully wanted further changes to the newly revamped board. In fact, in the months following Scott Morrison's arrival in Wellington, the tourism saga would dominate New Zealand politics and trigger multiple resignations. Many of the players from that time remain unwilling to speak, publicly at least, about the dramatic events of 1998. Those events would eventually be the subject of a probe by the New Zealand auditor-general.

Although Morrison arrived in the middle of a brawl between the tourism minister and a high-profile board, Morrison understood the power of politics. Board members describe the young Morrison as highly ambitious. He had been appointed to the role as a senior public servant but he was answerable to the minister, who was a member of New Zealand's conservative National Party. He wanted to impress McCully and set about enforcing the minister's policies, which in turn involved placing pressure on the board.

Three months after starting his new role, Morrison met with auditors PricewaterhouseCoopers (PWC) to commission a review of the NZTB's overheads. Outwardly, McCully and Morrison told colleagues they were concerned that the board's costs were unacceptably high, especially when compared with similar bodies in other countries. Board members saw it differently, privately accusing the pair of a 'witch hunt'. One former NZTB member even suggested there was a desired outcome driving their actions. Multiple board members believe Morrison never even attempted to work constructively with them. They believe instead that the probe was designed to give the minister cover to sack inflexible board members, and that Morrison was eager to please his new boss.

On 20 October 1998 Scott Morrison emailed the board's chief executive, Paul Winter, to provide an update on the review:

> In order to fulfil my responsibilities to the Minister and the process that has been agreed between the Minister and the Board I have decided to commission PricewaterhouseCoopers (PWC) to conduct a management review of the Board to provide independent advice on the cost structure currently employed within the Board and make recommendations for change that will boost the productivity, cost efficiency and performance of the Board. I intend that this review be undertaken quietly and discreetly. I believe that such a report will greatly assist the task we have been given and will ensure we are dealing with facts and experienced advice, rather than arbitrary judgements.

Given little choice, the board reluctantly accepted the review process in the hope they would be given a fair hearing by the auditors. That week, Morrison met with a PWC partner to discuss the terms of the review, which were outlined in a letter on 2 November. It was agreed that the review would exclusively examine the board's cost structure, with a particular focus on overhead costs. But within days of that initial meeting, the terms of the review were expanded to also include any governance, decision-making, contract management and administration issues. PWC representatives later told the NZ auditor-general that they were also instructed not to interview any board members, essentially denying those members a right of reply. This arrangement would be described rather euphemistically by the auditor-general as 'problematic' when it later became clear that the findings would be critical of the board.

PWC's report was finalised and handed to Morrison on 20 November 1998. It criticised the NZTB's communication and governance and accused it of 'operating in a tactical rather than a strategic way'. Five days later Morrison sent copies of the report to the board. He also wrote to his minister, encouraging him to take 'direct and immediate action' to rectify the governance issues. In a move that many board members believed overstepped the mark, Morrison also recommended that the NZTB chairman be given just seven days to justify why he should continue in that position – if he failed to provide a satisfactory response, suggested Morrison, he should be sacked.

A year later, the Office of the Auditor-General would admit that it was surprised by the 'vehemence and timing' of Morrison's advice. PWC consultants had told the auditor-general that the report did not justify dismissing the NZTB chair, and they'd also alleged that they had made every effort to brief board staff on the contents of the report before its release but that those consultations were blocked by Morrison's office. By contrast, Morrison had access to drafts in the course of the report's preparation. The audtior-general believed that:

> *Mr Morrison was aware that the Board's directors (including the Chairperson) had deliberately been excluded from the review process, as part of the terms of reference. He was also aware that the report had not been shown to either the staff of the Board or to the members in draft form.*

The auditor-general also found Morrison had made both written and oral comments which 'influenced the shape of the report'. And it accused Morrison of misrepresenting the findings in the report – whether deliberately or not – when briefing McCully. The board members were justifiably furious that their performance had been questioned without any opportunity to defend their actions.

The board arranged to meet with PWC on 16 December to discuss the findings. Two days before that meeting, McCully sent a letter to board members reiterating the criticisms. He demanded a response before Christmas, adding:

> *In preparing your response you should be aware that due to the seriousness of issues raised in the report I must be prepared to*

consider all options to ensure that these issues are addressed by the Board if, in my view these issues are valid and of sufficient importance. These options must include all authorities available to me under the New Zealand Tourism Board Act 1991 *including clause 2(1) of the First Schedule to the Act to remove members from office for neglect of duty.*

But that wasn't the end of Morrison's intervention. On 15 December, Morrison's office advised McCully of a second potential breach by the board that might provide grounds for its dismissal. Two months earlier, when its funding was being released by the minister on a monthly basis, the board had renewed the lease for its Hong Kong office without explicit approval. After seeking advice from the Crown Law Office and a human resources firm, Morrison formed the view that the board had breached its terms. He advised McCully that the allegations were 'sufficiently serious for him to give immediate consideration to removing members from office'.

During a series of hastily organised meetings, it was agreed that board chairman Mogridge and deputy chair Wall would step down, a decision that would cost NZ taxpayers hundreds of thousands of dollars in payouts. Most board members felt the Hong Kong lease renewal was a small breach but nonetheless agreed that perhaps the only way to end the dispute was for Mogridge and Wall to resign without accepting any culpability. 'You had an ambitious young Australian who thought he knew everything there was to know, advising an egotistical minister, and they wound them up,' one former board member says.

However, the remaining board members did not back away from the fight, maintaining they had a right to respond to the criticism levelled at them in the PWC report. Their argument was strong enough to convince the auditors to reclassify the report as a draft and to continue working on the document over the summer break. Several drafts were circulated over the subsequent summer and board members were given the right to respond.

Finally, in February 1999, seven months after Scott Morrison arrived in Wellington, PWC delivered what would be its final report into the matter — although not before a third senior executive, chief executive Paul Winter, had resigned. At the time, Morrison maintained that he had told PWC to consult with the board during the process and he had assumed that had been the case when he'd written to McCully recommending immediate action. But an audtior-general report would later find there was never any clear direction about Scott Morrison's role and responsibilities as director of the Office of Tourism and Sport, and there was little doubt that Morrison had crossed a line.

When board director Gerry McSweeney became the fourth high-profile resignation in six weeks, McCully, as the minister, was under mounting pressure to stand down. Mogridge, Wall and Winter had received hefty payouts collectively worth about NZ$900,000 and signed confidentiality clauses preventing them speaking about events at the NZTB. But McSweeney did no such thing — he accused the minister of constant interference, which he said created impossible working conditions for the board. McCully wrote to the auditor-general inviting an investigation into the executive payouts, and he publicly described the portrayal of the payouts as hush money as 'scandalous and absolutely wrong'. But leaks continued to dog the embattled minister, with new claims soon emerging that he had taken a taxpayer-funded trip to Brazil, Chile and Argentina despite being told by the NZTB that those countries were not target markets.

Two months later, in April 1999, the auditor-general cleared McCully of corruption over the payouts but found the minister should have sought legal advice before offering money to the resigning board members. A week later, Murray McCully, the man who had brought Scott Morrison to New Zealand, chose to walk away. McCully denied his resignation had anything to do with his soured relationship with the tourism board, instead citing the relentless campaign against him by journalists and the Opposition. As for Morrison, in the wake of the NZ tourism minister and four NZTB board members all falling on their swords, he told journalists he was keen to stay on, though he admitted that lessons could be learned from the affair.

* * *

In the small city of Wellington, Morrison himself was now under pressure. But if there is one thing Scott Morrison understands, it's the power of the media. Those who have observed him as a politician can testify that he is the master of the narrative reset – with ease, he can make it seem as if the things journalists obsess over are a distraction to his work. And so, true to future form, by May 1999 Morrison had agreed to be profiled in a weekend feature in Wellington's *Dominion* newspaper, which was considered the voice of the conservative element in the city's politics.

In the feature, in between humanising banter about his passion for trashy thrillers and rugby union, Morrison tried to explain his side of the NZTB story. He was clearly attempting to resuscitate a damaged career that was currently on life support. Not quite one year into a three-year contract, Morrison wanted to minimise his role in the scandal, and so he maintained that the advice he'd initially offered McCully had been followed by advice that recommended 'a much more moderate response'. He went on to say: 'I'm not interested in New Zealand politics. I'm not interested in people's views on my nationality … I know what I need to do. I take lessons from what happened over the last nine or 10 months. I will continue to do my job.'

Easier said than done: the scent of scandal that had started in the tourism portfolio was now permeating New Zealand's conservative government in an election year. Prime minister Jenny Shipley was facing intense pressure over her relationship with advertising chief executive Kevin Roberts from the firm Saatchi & Saatchi. The ad agency had won a NZ$30 million contract to market New Zealand to the world the previous year. Shortly after the contract was awarded, Roberts and Shipley had dined together. When the get–together was exposed in early 1999, Shipley initially denied the dinner altogether before admitting it did happen but asserting that tourism was not discussed. Then she said tourism had been discussed but not Saatchi's contract. To make matters worse, Roberts's 'New Zealand on the Edge' tourism campaign was considered a 'flop', according to NZTB members at the time. By March 1999, Saatchi & Saatchi had been sacked by the tourism board, with its campaign viewed as ineffective and too costly.

It was a blessing in disguise. Rival advertising agency M&C Saatchi had been watching the unfolding drama and contacted the NZTB to pitch an idea for a new campaign. Art director Alan Morden had coined the tagline '100% Pure New Zealand' on a flight between Queenstown and Wellington, and it turned out to be an advertising masterstroke that saw visitor numbers jump 10 per cent and spending rise 20 per cent by the end of June 2000. That same ad agency would later be hired by Tourism Australia, by that time under Scott Morrison, and would come up with the far less influential but equally famous 'So where the bloody hell are you?' campaign.

NZ tourism insiders still mock Morrison for trying to link himself with the '100% Pure New Zealand' campaign, which was a catalyst for huge tourism growth. As head of the Office of Tourism and Sport, he certainly played a part in ticking off the campaign as well as substantially reforming tourism marketing, research and forecasting for the sector. But as one former board member says, 'I think he might have over-egged the omelette in terms of his involvement.'

* * *

In March 2000, Morrison resigned from the NZ Office of Tourism and Sport with a year left on his contract as director, after landing a job at KPMG in Sydney. At the time, a spokeswoman for the Internal Affairs Department said he would not receive any severance payout on leaving his job early. Indirectly, the move back across the Ditch would lead to a life-changing opportunity.

A year earlier, the NSW Liberal Party had suffered an embarrassing loss at the state election. Ballots were still being counted when a row erupted in the party's ranks over the Coalition's worst electoral defeat since 1981. The Victorian premier, Jeff Kennett, called for NSW Liberal leader Kerry Chikarovski to resign, while prime minister John Howard said a policy agenda had been missing in action. The former NSW Liberal leader Peter Collins, who had been spectacularly dumped only months before polling day, held a press conference where he blamed the result on 'the backroom boys of Riley Street', including state director

Remo Nogarotto who, Collins claimed, had orchestrated a coup to get rid of him. The only thing most Liberals agreed on was that the federal organisation and John Howard needed to intervene before the bitterness in Sydney infected the broader party. Nine months later, Nogarotto was gone and the hunt was on for a new state director.

In May 2000, the NSW Liberal Party advertised the role, with corporate headhunting group KPMG handling the application process. Michael Yabsley, who was working as the Liberal Party's corporate fundraiser and leading the search for a fresh face, hit the phones. He kept hearing good things about Morrison, who it turned out was miserable over how his career gamble in New Zealand hadn't paid off and willingly agreed to a meeting. According to Morrison, Yabsley rushed through the small talk before turning to him and asking, 'Would you like to run the NSW division of the Liberal Party?' Morrison claims he responded with 'That sounds interesting' or something to that effect. In reality, it was a far more gruelling selection process. Yabsley, who had served as NSW tourism minister in the early 1990s, knew that Morrison was a marketing guru who was looking for a new gig. But he also knew that Morrison had corporate knowledge, a strong understanding of politics, and most importantly, no political baggage.

As Yabsley put it, the Liberal Party was going through a 'very difficult time'. Once a broad church, the party's membership had narrowed, especially in marginal seats. The

NSW division was heavily factionalised, with its members at loggerheads over efforts to streamline decision-making. The new state director needed to build up the base, heal the war wounds and find a way to replenish the party's accounts, which were $3.5 million in the red. At thirty-two, Morrison had only been a member of the party for five years, two of which were spent in New Zealand. Normally this would be viewed as detrimental in politics, where the apprenticeships often start in school. But the Liberal heavyweights in Canberra wanted someone with a clean pair of hands. 'I hadn't come from either faction and no-one knew who I was other than Bruce [Baird],' says Morrison. Howard's emissaries, including one of his closest advisers, Grahame Morris, were sent to suss out Morrison.

Yabsley believes Morrison's relative inexperience in party politics was his most appealing trait. As one Liberal puts it, things had become so bad that there was little to no resistance to some of the more dramatic changes being proposed for the Liberal Party. Another source says: 'He was a cleanskin not only in terms of not having a factional background ... he didn't have any baggage and that's an unusual thing in political circles. The party was keen to embrace professional change.'

In mid-July 2000, Morrison – having passed the initial tests – flew to Brisbane to meet with prime minister Howard, who still needed to sign off on the appointment. There in his hotel suite, Howard apparently could see the ambition dripping off Morrison. 'He called me out,' Morrison recalls, quoting Howard as saying, 'Clearly, I reckon you've got an ambition to go into politics yourself.' Morrison adds: 'He told me to do the job I am in and the next job looks after itself.' A few months later, in September, during the Sydney Olympics, the appointment was confirmed. Scott Morrison's political career officially started on 3 October. That advice, to focus on the job you have, later guided Morrison in Canberra. It didn't rid him of ambition for his next career step, but it taught him to embrace every committee role, portfolio and Cabinet position to his advantage.

Up until that point, few of Morrison's friends or colleagues would have thought he'd harboured political aspirations. But the new kid on the block wasn't fooling the more senior members of the party. As one long-serving NSW Liberal says: 'I don't buy coincidences. Becoming state director is like placing a Z on a triple-word score [in Scrabble]. It gives you a huge boost up the ladder and from there he could schmooze and see opportunities and plan his path into parliament.'

* * *

At that time, the NSW Liberal Party was indeed shambolic. Attendance at annual general meetings in safe Liberal seats was so low that some, including one held by then financial services minister Joe Hockey, were unable to reach a quorum. Morrison ordered a membership audit to check whether

75 per cent of members lived in the state electorate of their branch or nearby, as they were required to do, and it saw more than twenty branches dissolved. Meanwhile, the sale of the Liberals' head office helped boost the party's coffers, but things were still tight. In February 2001, Morrison made a controversial call not to field a candidate in the Campbelltown by-election as the costs involved would be a drain on precious resources and could not be justified in the lead-up to the November federal election.

Days after that by-election, Morrison addressed NSW Coalition frontbenchers to walk them through pages and pages of private research he had commissioned, showing the policy areas that he wanted the party to prioritise. The NSW Liberals had previously prosecuted issues like hospital waiting lists and transport, but these concerns weren't seen as the most important in marginal seats. The voters in those seats were instead worried about a lack of values in society — they were highly aspirational and feared there would be fewer opportunities for the next generation.

The data from these early focus groups seem to have shaped much of Scott Morrison's political philosophy. His campaigns, both as state director and as prime minister, haven't targeted the interests of corporate or affluent Australia — few describe him as a friend of big business. He has instead trod into Labor territory, pitching to ambitious middle-class Australians who seek opportunities but fear social change. At the 2001 federal election, a focus on those aspirational 'battlers' in western

Sydney helped deliver Howard his third term in office. Morrison managed the NSW elements of the campaign and the swing to the government in that state was higher than the national average. Across Sydney, there was a 3.7 per cent swing against Labor, which was strongest in the west.

To the re-elected Howard, one of Morrison's great strengths was his ability to mobilise people around a common objective. 'He was somebody who I recollect as being very energetic and personable, and I had the impression that he was a person with quite definite views about what's good for the party,' says Howard.

Thinking back on their early interactions, Howard also recalls Morrison as having sound political judgement. In 2002, Howard canvassed opinions on whether or not the Liberal Party should run a candidate in a by-election for the seat of Cunningham. The sitting Labor MP, Stephen Martin, had resigned in August of that year, triggering an election in a NSW South Coast seat that had always been held by Labor. Howard recalls summoning Morrison to talk strategy: 'I remember having a conversation with Scott Morrison at Kirribilli [House] and he was emphatically opposed. He saw it as waste of resources. In the end I went along with that and it was the right decision. The Labor Party lost the seat to the Greens.'

It was around this time that future prime minister Malcolm Turnbull first met the man who, almost two decades later, would replace him. Turnbull, a dedicated student of contemporaneous notes, said that Morrison approached him about replacing Chikarovski – someone was spreading rumours about Turnbull entering state politics as a way of reviving the party's chances. Turnbull joked to Morrison at the time that the idea of him entering state parliament was 'particularly attractive to federal politicians who didn't welcome my joining them in Canberra'.

As Turnbull remembered it, Morrison pitched his idea at Turnbull's Point Piper home. He said he would ensure Turnbull was preselected into an upper house seat, become the leader of the Opposition, then switch to a lower house seat at the next NSW election, scheduled for 2003.

According to Turnbull, he challenged Morrison's plan, suggesting Labor would attack him for his wealth and for being out of touch with the average NSW voter. But Morrison came prepared, having already commissioned polling in Western Sydney which revealed that suburban voters didn't resent Turnbull's wealth but, rather, admired his success. 'It's all about aspiration. Australians don't want class wars,' Morrison is said to have said.

Such data and research became vital to Morrison's every decision as he climbed through the political ranks. Almost everyone who has worked alongside him, in tourism or politics, speaks of his unrelenting hunger for polling and research. 'He is an utterly political person, and very poll driven,' says one long-serving Cabinet minister. 'He is pathologically obsessed with research.' More generous colleagues describe him as incredibly analytical. All agree that he rarely makes a decision without checking what voters think.

In March 2002, not long after Turnbull rejected Morrison's plan for him to enter state politics, Pittwater MP John Brogden announced he would challenge embattled Liberal leader Kerry Chikarovski for the top job. He won. In politics, bad blood between the leader's office and that of the state director can be electorally disastrous. Morrison knew that if the Liberals wanted to avoid a repeat of the humiliation of the 1999 election, Brogden would need a good team around him. So he called former Liberal staffer David Gazard, who was working at Westpac, and asked him to lunch. It was eleven months out from election day and the polls all pointed to a Labor win, but Morrison told Gazard that the Liberals were a 'really big chance' to defeat the incumbent premier Bob Carr. He said that while Labor might currently be in front, there was a 'huge soft vote' in play, meaning voters might consider changing their minds closer to polling day.

It wasn't true of course. Morrison simply wanted Gazard to be Brogden's chief of staff and he had to sell the role. In this, Morrison was successful. Gazard agreed – he even paid for the lunch.

Few commentators – or Liberal politicians for that matter – gave the Coalition any chance of stopping Labor's Carr from securing an historic third term at the March 2003 NSW election. But Morrison was ambitious. Howard had told him that his next job in politics hinged on him working hard in his current role and he wasn't about to give up. From his office on Williams Street he could see the NSW Parliament, and as he worked late into the night on the campaign, he would see Opposition MPs going home. Morrison vented his frustration about this to Brogden's office, making it clear that Coalition staff and MPs had to work harder, especially in an election year. 'He was at it twenty-four hours a day and often overwhelmed people with his effort,' says one Liberal staffer. 'He just laboured hard with a little amount, given the lack of resources,' says another.

Brogden was a hard worker but voters were sceptical of the new Liberal leader due to his relative youth (he was thirty-three). And the party was still suffering the effects of a destabilising period in NSW politics. On election night, Labor lost one seat but picked up an extra two, with an overall swing to the ALP of 1.6 per cent. The Liberals suffered a swing against them of 0.4 per cent but picked up a seat on the South Coast. It was a defeat, but an admirable one.

John Howard believes that Morrison's time in the Liberal Party's head office has given him an edge when it comes to campaigning: 'He entered politics from the side, so to speak. He didn't come up through the party organisation.'

* * *

The job of state director rarely involves making friends. You end up having to say no to a lot of MPs, colleagues and would-be candidates who think they know better. And then there are the factional fights.

Malcolm Turnbull famously declared that the Liberal Party wasn't run by factions, which was ironic given it was the hard-right members of his own government who plotted his downfall. Where Turnbull is correct is that, unlike the Labor Party machine which has long forced its members into union-aligned factions early on, Liberal Party factions originated in the 1980s and 1990s when the more progressive MPs who favoured bigger government were loosely defined as being in the wet faction, while the more socially conservative free-marketeers were known as the dries – terms popularised by and stolen from former UK prime minister Margaret Thatcher who used the labels to describe her internal opponents who were against her economic policies and her cuts to public spending (wets) compared to those who favoured tight fiscal restraint (dries). More recently, Liberal Party factions have been based on social and environmental policy areas, with the moderates pushing for action on climate change and same-sex marriage, and the conservatives united by a need to do more to protect religious freedoms and reject ambitious greenhouse gas targets. Other factors such as age, home state, faith and personality have also come into play, making it easier for some MPs to shift their allegiances in parliament.

With an eye to the future, Morrison didn't want to limit his chances of securing a safe seat in politics while he was state director. So for the most part, he avoided factional fights.

Many of his contemporaries thought he was moderately aligned due to his friendship with Bruce Baird, but he has never really shown any strong allegiances and has dodged any factional battles that would reveal his stripes. 'He wasn't factional and that was a plus,' says Baird. 'He was bright and personable and new, and he didn't have a track record of clashing with people or stacking branches.'

However, while party officials ideally should operate above factional loyalties, such allegiances do provide a structure that political types understand. Think of it as their guiding principles or rules of engagement. Staying faction-free, as Morrison was back then, can bring its own problems because neither faction trusts you and both sides assume you are working against them. This situation frustrated Brogden, who was a moderate, and who couldn't bend his state director to his will.

Each year during the Liberal Party's Federal Council, the party's more moderate members get together for the Black Hand dinner, once described by Christopher Pyne, the former long-serving member for Sturt in South Australia, as an irreverent night of good-humoured speeches and fun poking. The tradition was started in the late 1980s by moderate Liberal MPs who felt oppressed by the conservative figures dominating their party. The dinner's name is borrowed from the secret Serb nationalist society that sponsored the attack on Austrian archduke Franz Ferdinand, which kicked off World War I. At one of these dinners, the then Queensland senator and leading moderate George Brandis was addressing his factional allies when Scott Morrison tried to slip into the function – Morrison had just spent time with leading conservatives, including Howard's right-hand man Bill Heffernan, at a Lyons Forum dinner that brought together socially conservative Christians in the Coalition. According to Bruce Baird, one of the many moderates there that night, Brandis stopped mid-speech and challenged Morrison about where he might have been earlier that night: 'Have you perhaps been to another dinner?' Laughter ensued. To this day, Morrison is believed to be the only Liberal to pull off such an audacious stunt.

While practical and decisive MPs are needed in every government, those who enter the waters of politics without an ideological anchor often find themselves adrift when things get tough. Morrison's ability to navigate the factions may have helped him woo supporters across the party, but it is viewed with suspicion by some of his colleagues. There is a view that lacking a faction means you lack commitment to any principles and exist purely for power. 'He is completely pragmatic,' says one Liberal MP. 'Winning is the only thing he believes in.' A former Liberal minister who once served with Morrison says the Prime Minister lacks conviction and has not been passionate about any policy area except for his fierce opposition to same-sex marriage. Other Liberals, however, view Morrison's pragmatism less cynically. 'In Australian politics, people do gravitate to the centre, middle of the road, fair dinkum, no carry-on candidates. He is that, but he is also smart,' says one senior party figure.

According to his long-term friend and confidant David Gazard, Morrison's guiding political philosophy is to deliver what the 'mob' wants, which in Gazard's view makes him a better leader than more ideologically driven politicians. 'You live in a democracy so you have to think about what the electorate is thinking,' Gazard says. 'You've got to synthesise it in a way that is palatable and acceptable and know when to back your own judgement and when to listen to other people. It's quite a skill and he's got that.'

* * *

The months leading up to the 2004 federal election were nerve-racking for the Liberal Party. John Howard was seeking a rare fourth consecutive term in office but the gloss of his prime ministership had well and truly worn off. Mark Latham had taken over from Kim Beazley as leader of the Labor Party in December 2003 and the Opposition was ahead in the polls. Then, in February 2004, Malcolm Turnbull made his foray into federal politics, challenging sitting Liberal MP Peter King in the plum seat of Wentworth in Sydney's eastern suburbs. Both candidates spent months frantically recruiting new members in an effort to build their support base ahead of the preselection vote. As state director, Scott Morrison knew that more members meant more money with which to campaign in target NSW seats like Eden-Monaro, Dobell and Greenway, but he still didn't want to become involved in the tussle for Wentworth. Nonetheless, he found himself in the middle of the brawl when he struck out a number of membership applications from King's Rose Bay branch. That decision meant King lost two seats on the preselection panel to Turnbull, potentially tipping it in his favour. The NSW right viewed this intervention as the strongest sign of Morrison's allegiances – it was a case of, 'If you're not with us, you're against us.' To this day, many more conservative NSW MPs have not forgiven Morrison for his intervention.

On 28 February, the preselectors met at the Swiss Grand Hotel on Bondi Beach to decide who would be the Liberal candidate for Wentworth. Both King and Turnbull were confident they had the numbers. After the votes were cast, Turnbull was deemed the winner by a margin of eighty-eight to seventy; he kicked off his campaign the next day. It was going to be a tight contest. King planned to run as an independent and refused to direct preferences to the Liberal Party. Morrison commissioned polling and the results weren't good: it looked as if the Liberals might lose the seat.

It was far from the only drama the party had to endure that year. In August, during an interview with *Good Weekend* magazine, conservative MP Ross Cameron revealed he had cheated on his wife. The confession not only had personal consequences for Cameron but put him at risk of losing the marginal seat of Parramatta, which he held by a margin of just 1.2 per cent. To John Howard's credit, he continued to campaign alongside Cameron in the lead-up to polling day, despite state and federal party officials advising him against it. Again, the results of polling convinced Morrison to keep Cameron in the seat, despite Cameron's offer to stand aside.

Ahead of the 2004 election, Morrison also had a realisation concerning the power of Christian congregations. Acting on this, he helped convince Louise Markus, a social worker who managed the Hillsong Emerge Centre – a not-for-profit organisation helping victims of domestic violence – to run for the seat of Greenway. Just like Cunningham, Greenway, in western Sydney, was considered a safe Labor seat, and Markus had no political experience. But Morrison could see a path to success with the backing of party headquarters and Australia's biggest congregation. He had studied religious communities as part of his geography degree and he knew the power of such a loyal community united by God. Labor also was running a new candidate in the seat, former branch secretary Ed Husic, following the retirement of Frank Mossfield.

In late August 2004, John Howard took the bold step of announcing an October poll and kicked off a rare six-week campaign by asking, 'Who do you trust?' In New South Wales, Morrison recruited political allies including Scott Briggs, Sasha Grebe and Hollie Hughes to work with him on the campaign. With the future of the Howard government at stake, the team worked sixteen to eighteen hours a day, fuelled by deliveries from Big Boy Thai. Night after night,

OPPORTUNITIES EITHER SIDE OF THE DITCH

Morrison would eat a massaman curry at his desk, only seeing wife Jenny when she popped into the campaign headquarters to deliver cakes and catch a rare moment with her husband.

As with all such campaigns, MPs in marginal seats and new candidates value ministerial visits in their electorates, while time-poor ministers often loathe these events, especially when staring defeat in the face. One of Howard's senior Cabinet ministers refused to help out in a marginal NSW seat despite intense lobbying from party officials and colleagues. Frustrated by the minister's recalcitrance, a more junior member of the NSW campaign team pushed and pushed, despite the minister repeatedly telling the staffer that he was simply too busy to make it to the photo opportunity. Finally, angered by the minister's defiance, the young campaign staffer exploded, telling their senior colleague in no uncertain terms that if he wished to remain in Cabinet after the election, 'he'd better get his arse to the seats'. Word of this exchange filtered back to Morrison, who absorbed the Cabinet minister's wrath and privately praised his campaign team. 'He always backed us up. He just knew what needed to be done. He didn't want sycophants around him,' says one former colleague.

But Morrison didn't have everything his way. Buoyed by research and focus groups suggesting voters were scared that interest rates would rise under Labor, the Coalition aggressively pursued a campaign linking previous Labor administrations with record high interest rates. Morrison instructed NSW MPs and candidates to relentlessly reinforce

87

this perception. But there was pushback from those who felt that not only was the claim false, it would create a headache for the government should the Coalition win and interest rates rise. A number of MPs who refused to campaign on the interest rates platform believe they were denied resources from the NSW branch that were instead sent to more malleable candidates.

On election day, 9 October 2004, John Howard shocked himself and the nation when he strengthened his grip on government, smashing Mark Latham. In New South Wales, there was a 2 per cent swing to the Liberals, an improvement on the party's strong showing in 2001. A day after the election, a cocky Morrison described it as an 'historic high watermark'. He asserted that: 'As far as Labor is concerned, this was a state they had to make inroads into and they were just unable to.' Morrison was clearly very pleased with the result, especially in Wentworth where Turnbull romped it in with 43 per cent of the primary vote; Peter King received just 18 per cent of that vote. Against the odds, the Liberals also picked up the seat of Greenway. However, voters in Parramatta punished Ross Cameron for his confessed adultery and he lost his seat.

The win in Greenway, which had been dominated by the Labor Party for two decades, represented John Howard's gentle takeover of suburban Australia. The theme arose again in December 2004, weeks before Howard notched up enough time at The Lodge – or in his case Kirribilli House – to be crowned Australia's second-longest-serving prime minister, when Scott Morrison had an idea. He told Howard he wanted to hold the NSW Liberal Party's state council at the Blacktown Workers Club. 'He [Howard] thought it was delightful,' says Morrison. Howard, like Morrison, wanted voters to see the Liberals as the party of opportunity, not of privilege, wealth and the big end of town, and where better to demonstrate that than in working-class western Sydney.

Addressing the Liberal faithful at the Blacktown Workers Club, Howard said:

> [The Liberal Party] seeks membership and support from every section of the Australian community … It doesn't matter where you were born, it doesn't matter who your father was or what he did. What matters is the contribution that you make to your society. And it doesn't matter what your name is, or where your ancestors may have come from — they may have been born here or they may have been born in Italy or Indochina or the Middle East, it matters not. What matters is the contribution that you are willing to make to this country.

Parallels can be drawn between that speech and the victory speech given by Scott Morrison in 2019. Howard was speaking to his battlers, Morrison to his quiet Australians:

> This is the best country in the world in which to live. It is those Australians that we have been working for … it has been those Australians who have worked hard every day, they have their

dreams, they have their aspirations. To get a job, to get an apprenticeship, to start a business, to meet someone amazing. To start a family, to buy a home, to work hard and provide the best you can for your kids. To save your retirement and to ensure that when you're in your retirement, that you can enjoy it because you've worked hard for it. These are the quiet Australians who have won a great victory tonight.

Chapter Four

What the Bloody Hell Happened?

After his October 2004 federal election victory, John Howard made few changes for his fourth-term bench. He promoted two new junior ministers and seven new parliamentary secretaries but otherwise kept his Cabinet largely intact. One of the winners in the mini ministerial reshuffle was Fran Bailey, who held the marginal seat of McEwen in Victoria. Bailey knew a thing or two about political disappointment: a decade earlier, her political career had seemingly expired when her seat fell victim to John Hewson's failed push for a GST, but she was re-elected in

1996 and had made her way back into the ministry. It was her second promotion in six months, having been elevated to employment services minister in 2003 – now she was in charge of small business and tourism.

It's somewhat refreshing for politicians to admit weakness, but it's not always wise. Having run her own farm and retail enterprise, Bailey knew a lot about small business, but tourism – especially international tourism – was relatively new to her. She publicly confirmed this within days of her appointment, telling the *Gold Coast Bulletin* she had 'no experience' with tourism at the national level. Bailey's uncertainty about her new role was matched by tourism industry suspicion concerning their new minister. Normally, ministerial appointments are met with an outpouring of goodwill by industry groups and peak bodies excited by the prospect of having a new minister in their corner. This was not the case with Bailey. Gold Coast Combined Chamber of Commerce chairman John Witheriff delivered the ultimate insult by asking, 'Who is she? I haven't heard of her' when his local newspaper called for a reaction. It was a bad start for Fran Bailey.

Meanwhile, after serving for four years as state director of the NSW Liberal Party, Morrison was looking for a chance to return to the tourism sector. Under his watch, the Liberal Party had increased its hold on federal seats in New South Wales to a record-high number and he'd helped stabilise the state party after years of bitter factional brawls. As Howard had told him, if he did a good job, the next job would look after itself. It was time for a new challenge. Fortunately, a rather timely appointment was on the horizon.

In late 2003, the Howard government announced that four existing tourism organisations – including Australia's global tourism body, the Australian Tourism Commission (ATC), and its local body, See Australia – would be merged to form Tourism Australia. And following a three-month hunt, Scott Morrison was offered the $320,000 per year role as managing director of the federally funded body – he replaced Ken Boundy, who had served as managing director of the ATC before the merger. In his new role, Morrison would report to the Tourism Australia board chairman (and former deputy prime minister) Tim Fischer and to the new Minister for Small Business and Tourism, Fran Bailey.

Morrison had his work cut out for him. At the time of his appointment, monthly tourism data showed that the number of foreign tourists arriving in Australia was lower than the number of Australians heading overseas. It was the third time in five months that the outflow of tourists trumped the inflow, a situation that had not happened for over a decade. Australia needed a bold plan to lure the tourists back.

As managing director, Morrison technically sat on the board under the chairmanship of Fischer; the other board members included Andrew Burnes, the owner of what is now the Helloworld travel company, and Tony Clark, a former NSW boss of KPMG. Bailey had no say in Morrison's appointment, nor had she had much to do with him in his previous NSW Liberal state director role – she was a Victorian after all. But a few weeks after Bailey had been sworn in as the minister for tourism, Clark and Fischer asked to meet her for lunch at Old Parliament House. Bailey assumed the lunch would be a somewhat bland meet-and-greet, but those familiar with the meeting say the board chair and deputy chair came to Canberra for one reason only: to warn Bailey about Morrison, who was already proving difficult.

The first meeting between Morrison and Bailey, which took place at the Sydney headquarters of Tourism Australia, apparently went smoothly enough: Morrison talked a lot and Bailey listened. But it didn't take long for things to sour. Morrison was a marketing man and wanted to be the face of tourism in Australia. After stints at the TTF, TCA and NZTB, Morrison knew the tourism industry and its characters intimately and didn't seem interested in kowtowing to the minister. Within months of that initial introduction, Bailey privately began to criticise Morrison for trying to steal the limelight, including by issuing press releases without approval from her office. 'There was a clash of personalities from the start,' one Howard government staffer says, adding that Morrison 'just had a strong self-belief in what he was doing, and he wasn't going to let the minister stop him'. To make matters worse, at the Cabinet level, tourism was overseen by industry minister Ian Macfarlane: Bailey and Macfarlane loathed one another, whereas Morrison and Macfarlane got along well.

Those familiar with the stoush believe Bailey wanted more transparency in and influence over Tourism Australia, while Morrison did everything he could to avoid dealing with his minister, resulting in accusations that he was bypassing her office on key decisions.

* * *

One of the few things that Morrison and Bailey agreed on was the need to attract more tourists to Australia. Ultimately, achieving this would make them both look good. Within six months of Morrison taking on his new job, the Tourism Australia board kicked off the search for a new ad agency to help lure international travellers. Selling Australia to a global market is an ad agency's dream and many leading advertisers bid for the work. Morrison had already worked with international agency M&C Saatchi, which had engineered the successful '100% Pure New Zealand' campaign, and he seemed keen to recruit the agency to market Australia to the world.

Inside advertising circles, rival agencies were critical of the tender process, complaining that the criteria were skewed towards an individual agency to deliver a predetermined result. 'The advertising industry was up in arms,' one tourism insider recalls. 'There was absolutely no doubt he [Morrison] wanted Saatchi to make the ad.' Tourism Australia did little to counter this narrative when it refused to reveal how many agencies had tendered for the work, nor would it divulge which companies had made the shortlist.

This got back to Bailey, who demanded to know what was going on, not least because any contract worth more than $5 million required ministerial approval. 'I was the one that had to sign off on $180 million worth of funding,' Bailey says. 'Scott is unrelenting in pursuing his agenda.'

Anticipating scrutiny, Tourism Australia called in auditors from KPMG to review the tender process for the multimillion-dollar account. Government sources who worked alongside Bailey at this time believe that her primary concern was whether the process was in line with the federal government's procurement guidelines which, if breached, could lead to a minister being sacked. As it turned out, she was right to be concerned. Auditors would later find that documents submitted by Tourism Australia to assess the ad agencies were not comprehensive and the process lacked transparency. Former government staff report that Bailey became increasingly suspicious that she was being bypassed by the board and she directed the blame at Scott Morrison.

Bailey was reluctant to release such a large amount of money without more information and direction from the ad agency. She was eventually persuaded to sign off on the first tranche of funding for an advertising campaign after being told Australia was at risk of missing out on lucrative advertising space in target markets if she delayed the process any longer. However, she says that she still wanted more information:

It was my signature that was going to go on an amount of
$180 million and I had to be satisfied that there had been full
probity. This was an industry that was contributing so much to our
national economy, [so] I had to move forward with the first tranche
of the ad otherwise we would have missed out ... but I also had to
protect the government.

As the relationship between managing director and minister deteriorated further, Morrison's team at Tourism Australia and Bailey's ministerial staff were forced to act as intermediaries between the pair. 'Scott was doing what he was doing and thought he was doing it very well, and the last thing he needed was a minister standing in his way,' says one Liberal Party staffer. 'Equally, Fran had worked hard, she had been a backbencher in a marginal seat and she was now the minister, and she wanted to be in control. It just wasn't going to work.'

Board members became instrumental in ensuring there was some form of collaboration and consultation between the feuding pair. Tony Clark would liaise with Bailey's office and deliver messages back to Morrison. Clark was a close friend of John Howard — they regularly played golf together when Howard's schedule allowed it — so it's difficult to imagine Howard wasn't kept well informed about the situation.

* * *

In February 2006, after spending millions of dollars on market research, Tourism Australia finally unveiled its big new international advertising effort. The campaign, which asked the world 'So where the bloody hell are you?', was meant to entice would-be tourists in key markets, including the United States, the United Kingdom, Germany, Japan, China, South Korea and New Zealand, to visit Australia. It was the culmination of many months of work by marketers and the Tourism Australia board, especially Morrison, who had reviewed every detail of the campaign.

It has been misreported that Morrison arranged a private viewing for Howard in his office. In reality, Bailey and Fischer went to see the prime minister in Sydney to show him the final product. There were twelve different versions of the commercial, but the one in which the smiling bikini-clad model Lara Bingle voiced the tagline was considered a standout. Bailey was rightly nervous during the screening: a lot of money had been poured into the campaign and its catchphrase was expected to grate on some. But after seeing the ad with Bingle the first time, Howard is said to have turned to Bailey and smiled approvingly, saying: 'She's a very nice young woman, isn't she, Fran?'

The commercial represented a huge shift away from previous tourism campaigns featuring Aussie celebrities like Paul Hogan. Instead, it included so-called 'everyday Aussies' such as Riley the Bronte surfer, Fred the Broken Hill farmer, Peter the Victorian golfer and Newcastle University student

Kelli. But viewers weren't really meant to remember the ad's characters. The focus of the commercial was the final line: 'So where the bloody hell are you?'

Tourism Australia had even anticipated criticism of use of the word 'bloody' to attract tourists as a little crass, preparing a pamphlet for the ad's launch to defend its decision. 'Bloody' was described as an Australian adjective that had appeared in legendary Australian publication *The Bulletin* as far back as 1894 – coincidentally, around the same time Dame Mary Gilmore's by-line first appeared in its pages. Ahead of the launch, the tourism minister also was briefed on issues that could potentially arise from the colourful language used in the commercial. Bailey knew what to say: 'It's the great Australian adjective. It's part of our language. This is presenting Australia as we are – we're plain-speaking, we're friendly ... If it's good enough for Harry Potter at the movies, it's good enough for us. My kids use the word.'

Within days of its launch, the campaign was making headlines globally – it was proving somewhat controversial but it was a marketer's dream. John Howard weighed in to support the commercial, saying it reflected the humour of Australians: 'I think the style of the advertisement is anything but offensive. It is in context and I think it's a very effective ad.'

But not everyone agreed. Within days of the ad's release, Tourism Australia was accused of both pandering to crude stereotypes and offending foreign guests. Advertising standards bodies in Asia requested changes to the ad so as not to offend locals. Subtitled translations of the slogan were altered to reflect 'cultural differences'. In the United States, the commercial escaped modification but it still caused a stir, with the American Family Association objecting to the use of the word 'hell'. Marketing gurus will tell you that there's no such thing as bad publicity, but this was a fine line. Tourism Australia, meanwhile, insisted it was all part the plan. Australia was receiving unparalleled media attention and the heat was apparently worth it. Morrison himself doubled down on the approach, spinning the slogan as a 'uniquely Australian invitation'.

Just as he had done as NSW Liberal state director, Morrison put his faith in the data that had been collected over months and months by both Tourism Australia and M&C Saatchi. The message had even been tested in key markets to gauge the reactions of the targeted travellers. Tourism Australia argued it wasn't going after busloads of baby boomers but rather was targeting a different type of international guest, known as 'experience seekers'. According to the research, experience seekers made up between 30 and 50 per cent of all potential long-haul travellers from Australia's key tourism markets. These visitors were considered 'opinion leaders', an early term for 'influencers', meaning they could impact the behaviour of other tourists. Instead of changing its messaging in different markets, Tourism Australia wanted to create a catch-all commercial aimed solely at the demographic it was trying to attract to Australia.

The ad agency also claimed the campaign was based on the latest marketing buzzword: pyschographics. In the eyes of the marketers, the target travellers might come from different cultural backgrounds but they shared the same qualities, or so the science suggested. Marketing experts concurred that the tourists who visited Australia were usually well-travelled types chasing unique experiences to check off their bucket lists. These people wanted to actively participate in their holidays, not just gaze out from a viewing platform. Importantly, they wanted an authentic exploit they could later brag about to family and friends. The data showed these tourists were open-minded, affluent and educated. They weren't going to be offended by some straight-talking Aussies – on the contrary, that was the very experience they craved. 'This is not a cultural essay but a carefully crafted and well-researched campaign designed to encourage international travellers to get Australia off their wish list and into their travel itinerary,' Morrison said at the time.

Despite the initial controversy, the hype began to work. Within days, the campaign had made headlines around the world, leading would-be travellers to hunt it down online, especially in the markets where it was banned. In the month from the ad's launch, more than 100,000 hits were recorded on a dedicated website set up for the campaign. The commercial was also downloaded in 80 per cent of the world's 191 nations at the time.

But within weeks of its release, the taxpayer-funded 'So where the bloody hell are you?' campaign hit a major roadblock. Fran Bailey's plane had just landed at Melbourne Airport when she received a phone call from John Howard's chief-of-staff, Arthur Sinodinos. Britain's advertising regulator, the Broadcast Advertising Clearance Centre (BACC), had followed Asian regulators and banned the ad from free-to-air television. The potty-mouthed Poms had ruled that the world 'bloody' was only acceptable in a clinical setting, such as in promoting a treatment for injuries sustained from a wayward hedge clipper. The sticking point was section 6.1 of the advertising code, which stated that such words could cause serious and widespread offence. The ad was duly struck out. Tourism Australia was only permitted to show a doctored version of the ad in cinemas and in print, and they would have to direct tourists online to see the full, uncensored version.

Publicly, Bailey was furious with the ruling, pointing out the inconsistency given the United Kingdom was the home of gauche and smutty TV shows like *The Benny Hill Show* and *Little Britain*. 'How anyone can take offence at a beautiful girl in a bikini on a sunny beach inviting them to visit Down Under is a mystery to me,' she said. 'The regulator is out of touch with British opinion. Based on our research and the initial feedback, the British are loving our cheeky sense of humour.' But privately, Bailey was starting to question the research of Morrison and his team. When she demanded to know whether anyone at Tourism Australia had checked the British advertising code before commissioning the campaign, it soon became apparent that no-one had bothered. 'It was really serious,' says another former Howard government minister about the controversy. 'It could have torpedoed the entire campaign.'

At Tourism Australia's Sydney headquarters, Morrison and the board tried to convince minister Bailey that the censor's decision was not entirely unexpected. He had effectively hired the firm responsible, he had seen the data, he believed the research, and he wanted to be the one to go to the United Kingdom and save the day. So he packed his bags and booked a flight. At the same time, the Howard government was plotting its own rescue mission: an Aussie delegation, led by Bailey, would fly to England and talk some common sense into the stuck-up Poms. Bailey quickly called former British high commissioner Sir Alastair Goodlad to help arrange a series of meetings, and on 10 March she flew to London to push Australia's case, shadowed by the ad's star, Lara Bingle.

Morrison had been blindsided. He made his way to London but was excluded from every meeting. Bailey told Howard's office that there was no way that Morrison could be involved in any confabs because 'he'd stuffed it up', according to government staff from that time.

Bailey's trip was heavily covered by the British media, which was highly critical of the BACC's ban, and more generally the organisation's broad powers to censor TV commercials. In London, Bailey met with Sir Gordon Borrie, chairman of the Advertising Standards Authority, and James

Purnell, the UK Minister for Creative Industries and Tourism, to seek advice. Bailey also met with Baron Saatchi, who'd founded the firm responsible for the ad alongside his brother Charles. The mogul siblings met with Bailey one lunchtime and Charles asked the Australian minister to stick around for lunch as his wife had prepared some food – Bailey didn't realise it at the time but Charles's then wife was celebrity cook Nigella Lawson. Inside M&C Saatchi's London office, meanwhile, staff uncovered a range of commercials that also had used the apparently offensive word 'bloody' to sell their wares – beer company Fosters and car manufacturer Toyota had both used the word in advertising campaigns in the 1980s. Staff at Australia House, home to the High Commission of Australia, tracked down the twenty-year-old commercials to help Bailey build her argument. All Morrison could do was watch from the sidelines.

At the BACC, Bailey then met with Andrew Barnes, chairman of the centre's copy committee, and a sales and marketing manager with Channel 4. She learned that a number of the commercial's reviewers had recommended striking it out based solely on the script rather than on the full commercial. Bailey, who had been documenting her trip in a diary for the Australia media, summarised what happened next like a lawyer summing up her case:

I then presented what I considered were three powerful arguments to Andrew. Two commercials using the word 'bloody' had previously

run on British television. Extensive research costing more than
$1 million conducted in the UK indicated that our ad was not seen
as offensive by UK consumers. The timing and context of the ad
could not cause serious and widespread offence.

Bailey then requested that the BACC review its finding and she returned to Australia confident that the Brits would change their minds. While the decision hadn't yet been overturned, Bailey felt her trip had been a success, with the rescue mission given the sort of attention and promotion money just can't buy. Jet lagged from the long flight, Bailey was asleep at home when, shortly after midnight, she was woken by her phone ringing. It was her chief of staff, Dan Tehan, who passed on the news that Britain's advertising regulator had reversed its decision.

Within days, Bailey had detailed every minute of her trip in a piece for *The Australian* under the headline 'Bloody hell, here's how we did it!', which included the following from a section titled 'Fran Bailey's five-step lobbying campaign to save Australia $180 million':

I'm convinced that we were successful in reversing the decision
because the attempted censoring was unfair and I was passionate and
persistent ...

Undoubtedly, the trip to London was worthwhile because it
demonstrated ... that I took the situation very seriously ...

The words that stick in mind came from Andrew Barnes, who
admitted to being surprised and impressed with the way I put my

case: '*I couldn't believe that an Australian minister of the Crown
had hopped on a plane and travelled 22,000 kilometres to see me
about these tourism advertisements.*' *I wouldn't have achieved the
same result if I'd sat at my desk in Canberra and sent emails.*

* * *

Several former Tourism Australia staffers pinpoint the London
trip as the tipping point in the already tense relationship
between Morrison and Bailey. Months earlier, at the 'So
where the bloody hell are you?' campaign launch, Bailey had
been unhappy with the role she had been allocated and angry
at Morrison for being front-and-centre. Now she had been
the leading lady in a David–and–Goliath battle that had pitted
the Aussies against the Brits.

One close associate of Morrison's muses:

*He had immersed himself in the process more than Fran [Bailey].
He had analysed the data on every bit of research they did on that
advertisement. He knew everyone in the industry. He would have
convinced the bureaucrats, talked to the staff, written the speech
ready to go. He would have known nine thousand times more things
about the subject than she did and been very confident that he had
covered every base.*

But this was politics. Morrison wasn't the minister but
answered to the board, which in turn answered to the minister.

The accolades for rescuing the expensive advertisement and reviving the campaign were saved for Bailey.

And things were about to get worse. As part of a review into federal administration, the Howard government was considering whether Tourism Australia, with its $140-million-a-year budget, should be handed over to the public service. If that were to occur, the board effectively would be scrapped in favour of a government advisory panel that would be more likely to involve the tourism minister. Morrison of course vehemently opposed any plan to put bureaucrats in charge of the tourism market.

Initially, the Tourism Australia board had been very supportive of Morrison and had even done its best to smooth tensions between his office and the minister's. But board members increasingly became annoyed when they learned what Morrison was doing by reading about it in a newspaper. On one occasion, Morrison dreamed up a campaign to encourage Australian workers to use $11 billion worth of stockpiled annual leave. He had commissioned research which found that 60 per cent of full-time workers did not use their full leave entitlements and that one-third worked at least a year straight before taking it. Tourism Australia had then coined the slogan 'No Leave, No Life' as a way of incentivising working Australians to take some of their collective 70 million annual leave days by helping them find holiday ideas and destinations. It was straight out of the Morrison playbook – he used the data to get broad coverage of the issue in TV and print media, just as he had gained attention by weighing all the duplicate planning laws in the early 1990s. Morrison argued that Australia's economy would be $2 billion better off if workers took holidays: 'Annual leave stockpiling has critical ramifications, for businesses, individuals and the economy.' It got a great run in newspapers and on television news across the country.

But again, Bailey and some board members had been kept in the dark and were gobsmacked when they read about it in the media. To complicate matters, the government was in the midst of trying to negotiate its contentious Work Choices bill, a set of controversial industrial relation reforms that limited the work rights, protections and bargaining power of millions for Australians. Bailey and some board members felt that the new Tourism Australia campaign had a threatening tone, that it looked as if the federal government was forcing workers to use up their precious leave entitlements.

Reflecting on this period, John Howard says he knew that the relationship between Bailey and Morrison had become unworkable: 'I was aware things were progressing as they did. The explanation for the dispute was a clash of personalities. They obviously didn't get along.'

After returning from the United Kingdom, Bailey had sought advice from the then secretary of the Department of the Prime Minister and Cabinet, Peter Shergold. The pair had a heated discussion about Morrison's future, but Bailey had essentially made up her mind: Morrison no longer had her backing or that of the board. In July 2006, Bailey met with Howard and convinced him the relationship had deteriorated to the point where Morrison had to go. 'I accepted the minister's advice and backed her,' says Howard.

That month, Morrison was at a Tourism Australia roadshow in regional Victoria when he got a phone call requesting he return to Sydney. Tim Fischer broke the news, sacking him just over halfway through his three-year contract. Those closest to Morrison at the time believe he didn't see it coming. 'He would have thought he was safe and should be running the place,' one of his friends quips. 'He really didn't see it, and he was gutted.'

Morrison's departure was formalised at a board meeting in August 2006. Tourism Australia issued a statement saying Morrison had 'agreed to depart' but it was clear he had been fired. And while the board praised his service, Bailey's silence was deafening.

* * *

In 2008, the auditor-general released a scathing report of the way in which Tourism Australia had handled major contracts during the period when Scott Morrison was managing director. In 2005–06, Tourism Australia's three major contracts consumed approximately 35 per cent of the organisation's annual budget of $167.8 million. Auditors found that information was kept from the board, procurement guidelines were breached, and private companies were engaged before all the paperwork was signed and without appropriate value-for-money assessments. They also criticised Tourism Australia for not including performance indicators in its contracts, meaning it was difficult to assess whether or not the services provided under these contracts achieved their objectives.

In their final report, the auditors also said a number of industry stakeholders had expressed the view that there was a perceived conflict of interest concerning board members when dealing with contracts and that this was a 'major risk to Tourism Australia's reputation'. The report went on to make the following recommendation:

It is therefore important, particularly in the competitive tourism industry, that the decisions of the Board are transparent and that any perceived or actual conflicts are being (and are seen to be) appropriately addressed. The Board did not adhere to the procedures outlined in its Charter for managing potential conflicts of interest and revised the Charter to reflect its practices rather than procedures being changed to meet the Charter's requirements.

The auditors were also critical of Tourism Australia's decision to allow work to commence before contracts were in place – specifically, it found that the organisation had asked a 'preferred tender' to begin work before the contracts were executed in October 2005. To mitigate the risk, Tourism

Australia refused to pay invoices until the contracts were signed, even though it had requested that services commence. But according to the auditors, this was an ineffective protection method for Australian taxpayers because simply requesting a service created an obligation, whether contracts were executed or not.

In late 2018, after Scott Morrison had become prime minister, Tim Fischer broke his silence on the dramatic events that had led to the former managing director's departure. Now free of the Tourism Australia chairmanship, Fischer said in an *Australian Financial Review* piece that he believed Morrison deserved 'full credit' for the 'So where the bloody hell are you?' campaign and was 'wrongly, perhaps' removed from his role. 'It took some courage to run that campaign and he saw it through,' Fischer said. 'They were electrifying times at Tourism Australia with a strong minister and a strong CEO.' Indeed, it's clear from interviews with board members and government and tourism staff conducted for this book that the board, while unhappy with Morrison's tactics and attitude, believed him to be an effective managing director. In that same *Australian Financial Review* article, however, Fran Bailey took a not-so-veiled swipe at Morrison and reiterated that the decision to move him on had been backed by the board:

> There's been a bit of mystery surrounding it over the years, but all I'll say is sometimes things work out in an organisation, and sometimes they don't. In this case, Scott Morrison didn't work out.

I'm sure he's learned how to work with people better these days. His career has certainly had a few twists and turns.

Bailey was right. Morrison, who was yet to turn forty, had had early exits from his role in New Zealand, John Brown's task force and now his lucrative job at Tourism Australia.

Despite the criticisms levelled at Morrison, there was sympathy for him within the Liberal Party. It wasn't the only clash Bailey had had in Canberra – her office had a high turnover of staff, and many of her colleagues, even those who liked her, used the term 'prickly' to describe her personality.

The then member for Cook, Bruce Baird, was particularly disappointed with the way Morrison had been forced out of Tourism Australia. 'I thought it was particularly rough,' Baird recalls. 'I rang him and said, "I am really sorry that happened. It's inexcusable".' Baird also told Morrison that he was reconsidering his own future in Canberra, something very few people knew at the time.

Chapter Five

A Miracle Child

In late 2006, Scott and Jenny took a trip to the Blue Mountains where they had recently purchased a cottage in Blackheath. But although the pair were meant to be having a break in one of Australia's most beautiful natural landscapes, Jenny felt unusually agitated. She finally popped out to the shops and purchased a pregnancy test. For more than a decade the Morrisons had repeatedly tried and failed to conceive a child, with each new pregnancy test ending in despondency. Jenny didn't expect to get a positive result this time, but it was worth a try on the remote chance it was the cause of her discomfort. The result? Double lines. After years and years of bitter disappointment, Scott and Jenny were going to have a child.

Shortly after her wedding in 1990, Jenny had stopped taking contraception, hoping to fall pregnant. She and Scott were both in their early twenties, a youthful age being an advantage for couples hoping to conceive. But it didn't happen. Initially the couple thought their timing must be out and for months and months they tried to conceive naturally with almost military scheduling. Still nothing.

All around her, Jenny's friends and family members were falling pregnant. 'There are babies everywhere,' Jenny later observed. Friends of the Morrisons say they felt guilty when they fell pregnant, and yet Scott and Jenny were always the first to congratulate and support them when their babies were born.

Few who haven't personally experienced it can truly understand the trauma of infertility – the hope, anxiety and grief. Those who have lived this battle say it changes how you see yourself in the world. Scott Morrison describes the desire to be a parent as one of the most 'positive, life-affirming instincts we have as human beings', and it is a desire that doesn't simply disappear when doctors tell you that it will be difficult to fulfil.

In 1993, Scott and Jenny sought help to have a baby, eventually embarking on in-vitro fertilisation (IVF). Jenny has since described parenthood as the Holy Grail – to her, it meant everything, and with each unsuccessful attempt to fall pregnant, her desire to become a mother only intensified. In the early years of the infertility battle, Scott threw himself into his work as a way of distracting himself following each unsuccessful round of IVF. Jenny worked too, first in a childcare centre, then in retail, but nothing could stem her desire to have children of her own. At one point her well-meaning husband even purchased a cat, hoping it would help Jenny cope with the invasive and mentally gruelling trial she was going through. Scott would tell his wife, 'You are enough' and 'We don't need the children to be happy'. But inside he was hurting. Friends of the couple describe Jenny as a 'natural born mother' which made it all the more difficult to watch the Morrisons' battle infertility. 'She has a caring personality, she is a beautiful person,' one friend says.

In 2009, Scott Morrison wrote about he and Jenny's infertility struggle for the parenting website *Essential Baby*:

> *The feeling of loss at every failed attempt is indescribable. As others, removed from the emotional hell, rationalise the failure as 'embryos failing to take', as parents we grieve the loss of children. We console ourselves with the thought that one day, we'll be reunited with our unborn beyond this life … For families going through this dark chapter of their lives, it's all-consuming – spiritually, emotionally, physically and financially. You question everything: God, each other, your priorities, your future – nothing escapes. Along this road, you will find the wreckage of shattered lives, marriages and families. These are the risks we take.*

Fertility doctors observe the dramatic impact IVF can have on even the strongest relationship. It glues some couples together for life, while other couples succumb to the pressure and their relationships break down. This is backed up by research. A Danish study of more than 47,000 couples struggling to have children found that those who don't fall pregnant after treatment are three times more likely to divorce or otherwise end their relationship. In a separate study conducted in 2009, 37 per cent of women reported that IVF had had a positive impact on their marriage and brought them closer together.

The Morrisons were only too aware of the stress that the effort to fall pregnant can place on a relationship. Jenny has said that at times she would be so overcome by grief or anger that she would lash out. In 2015, during an appearance on the television program *Kitchen Cabinet*, Morrison said:

> *A lot of things get tested when you go through those sorts of experiences. It brought us closer together but for many couples it finishes them off, it drives them apart. That is no reflection on them, it's just one of life's bitter hands.*

During the Morrisons' fourteen-year infertility battle, family and friends would regale them with stories of couples who finally had been blessed with children after decades of trying. Scott Morrison has said, 'That's the worst thing you can hear when you are in that situation, because … it might not work out. The hardest thing is coming to terms with that possibility.'

Everything in Jenny's life during those years of trying to fall pregnant was framed by her desire to become a mum. 'Sometimes you can get quite depressed and people around you are well meaning but they don't know what to say. Unless you have been in it yourself you just cannot understand what they are going through,' she recalled in 2019.

Scott and Jenny only shared their very private battle with those closest to them. In her late twenties, having failed to fall pregnant after yet another round of IVF, Jenny, not knowing how to tell her friends, sat down and wrote them an email, admitting to her close-knit group that parenthood might not be her path.

After the Morrisons had halted their efforts to have a baby, friends began to act differently around the couple. One close friend says:

> *You almost have a sense of guilt that we could have children. They were always wonderfully warm with our kids. Never once would you have felt that they were anything other than happy for us, but we still felt a deep sense of guilt. It made us think about how you speak about our kids around them. You wanted to talk about the joys of having kids but we were also cognisant of the fact they probably weren't going to have kids because they had been through such an ordeal.*

When Jenny was thirty-two, a doctor suggested she give up and think about adopting. Yet Jenny still longed for a baby of her own – her close friends sensed this longing and encouraged her to get a second opinion. Jenny went to see a new specialist and subsequently was diagnosed with complex endometriosis, a condition that causes tissue similar to the lining of the womb to spread across other parts of the body, including the reproductive organs, bowel and bladder. It can be incredibly painful and is a common cause of infertility in women. More than 11 per cent of Australian women suffer from endometriosis at some point in their lives, but until recently it was rarely talked about.

Scott and Jenny put their faith in medical experts, including fertility and reproductive specialist Dr Anne Clark and eventually Professor Alan Lam, a leading expert in the endoscopic treatment of complex endometriosis. Jenny underwent a five-hour surgery to remove the endometrial tissue that had built up, in the course of which doctors discovered the tissue had spread all the way to her liver.

In 2006, following Jenny's surgery, she and Scott took that memorable trip to the Blue Mountains. Taking a pregnancy test had become somewhat of a chore over the years, but not this time. Jenny told her husband that a planned trip to Rwanda the following January would need to be postponed: she was expecting a child.

Although this was fantastic news, as far as pure timing went, it couldn't have been worse. Her husband had just been sacked from his $320,000-a-year position as managing director of Tourism Australia, and with a federal election due within a year, Morrison had his eye on a seat in the Australian Parliament. But Jenny had wanted to be a mum for well over a decade and nothing could curb her joy. She has described it as 'ironic' that after years of living a more normal life, her husband would embark on a political career, taking him away from the family home, right at the time she finally fell pregnant naturally: 'It was just the most bizarre sort of set of circumstances. I've just had to roll with that and deal with it.'

In the weeks leading up to the birth of their first child, Scott Morrison in fact would (initially) lose a very public preselection in the seat of Cook in Sydney's southern suburbs, despite the best efforts of his wife, who stuffed envelopes during the campaign. The loss hurt the ambitious Morrison. But the birth of Abbey Rose Morrison on 7 July 2007 – the seventh day of the seventh month of the seventh year of the new millennium – felt like a divine miracle. He has said that being blessed with a baby reminded him of 'who's in charge'. He reiterated this theme when addressing parliament following the birth of his second daughter, Lily, in 2009: 'That tells me that God has a very good sense of humour in reminding us of his faith in us, and his faith being expressed through these two children is remarkable.'

Arthur Ilias, a close friend of the couple, remembers that he was in Greece when he found out Scott and Jenny had welcomed their first healthy baby girl: 'I know exactly where I was ... that's how special it was. I couldn't tell you that for other friends.'

An MP's inaugural address to parliament is an important occasion. Convention derived from the British Parliament dictates that maiden speeches – or first speeches, as they are increasingly referred to – are heard without interjection or interruption. It's a chance for new members to outline their hopes and aspirations for the role, and to reflect on their life, their achievements and the character of the community they represent. It's also a deeply personal moment when new politicians invite their families, friends and other supporters into the chamber and thank them for their help. On 14 February 2008, Scott Morrison's parents and wife made the trip to Canberra to hear him speak in the House of Representatives for the first time.

The address followed the normal Liberal narrative with Morrison describing his seat, detailing his passion for business-friendly policies and pitching economic reforms. But he also showed a rare vulnerability when he outlined the struggle Jenny had faced trying to have a baby:

To my wife, Jenny, on Valentine's Day: words are not enough. She has loved and supported me in all things and made countless sacrifices, consistent with her generous, selfless and caring nature. However, above all, I thank her for her determination to never give up hope for us to have a child. After fourteen years of bitter disappointments, God remembered her faithfulness and blessed us with our miracle child, Abbey Rose … to whom I dedicate this speech today in the hope of an even better future for her and her generation.

* * *

With two young girls at home and her husband often in Canberra or interstate for work, Jenny Morrison frequently would find herself alone. She recalled sitting on her doorstep on the Thursday nights after parliament had adjourned, holding a baby and waiting for him to arrive:

> *It was hard. It was really, really hard. I can't downplay it ... I don't know what I was wishing for, really. Because he would be off doing 100 things over the weekend, Friday, Saturday and Sunday. Then he'd go again on Sunday night ... It's tiring because there's no-one else to hand the children over to when you just need a little break, and that can play havoc on your mind as well.*

Soon Jenny found herself sitting in front of her GP asking for help. The appointment was meant to be focused on an unusual freckle on one of her legs, but she discovered she was suffering from depression: 'I found myself at the doctor's going, "I'm trying to do everything and I just can't seem to do it all".' Jenny saw a psychologist and leaned on her friends and family, who helped manage her perinatal anxiety and depression. She recently said: 'I learned that it is so important to reach out for help, say yes when that help is offered and to talk to others.'

Politics is hard on marriages. Of the twenty or so ministers Scott Morrison has served alongside in his prime ministerial Cabinets, about one-third have been divorced. Many of

Morrison's closest colleagues and confidants point to his wife Jenny as playing a pivotal role in his rise. 'Jenny does a wonderful job in keeping it all together,' one close friend of the couple says. 'It's not an easy task to be a politician's wife, let alone a prime minister's wife, but she managed it well.'

Arthur and Ingrid Ilias knew the Morrisons as a young couple in the late 1980s. The four friends would meet up for a drink in Bondi or Coogee, but politics was never discussed. To Arthur Ilias, Morrison hasn't changed, remaining an 'average, normal, bloke'. 'What I see on television is quite authentic. That is the person that he is,' says Ilias.

Other friends observe that Morrison has managed to stay grounded after taking on the prime ministership, with both Scott and Jenny staying close to all of their non-political friends. They speak of the Morrisons joining Zoom drinks during the COVID-19 lockdown from Kirribilli House or The Lodge, and describe how they still invite friends over for dinner, although it's always at short notice. 'You might get a text mid-morning on a Saturday asking us over for dinner that night. It's never planned two or three weeks out, but we have adapted,' one friend says. 'But when we catch up, he drops his guard, he has a drink and he can relax.' At these catch-ups, Morrison regularly embraces the role of DJ, playing his favourite compilations on the music-streaming service Spotify. Friends say his music tastes are firmly stuck in the 1980s, and he will challenge dinner guests to name a song title, artist and album over a few drinks.

As a family, the Morrisons chose to live in Kirribilli House, the PM's residence in Sydney, over The Lodge in Canberra, in an effort to keep life as normal as possible for their two young daughters. Abbey and Lily were at primary school in 2018 when their father became prime minister. Initially they were somewhat disappointed that they had to move from their home in Port Hacking, in Sydney's southern suburbs, to Kirribilli on the north shore of Sydney Harbour, because the property didn't have a pool. To help settle his daughters, Scott Morrison asked his new next-door neighbours at 109 Kirribilli Ave – also known as Admiralty House and the official Sydney residence of the governor-general – whether Abbey and Lily would be able to pop over on occasion for a swim. A deal was soon struck.

Scott Morrison entered politics the year his first daughter was born – both girls have grown up with their father spending weeks away in Canberra and abroad. Friends say Morrison makes the most of his time at home by taking a hands-on approach to parenting. In 2020 he built a cubbyhouse with Lily in their Kirribilli backyard. 'The greatest blessing as a dad is spending time with my girls. Just being in each other's company is wonderful,' he said at the time. 'It's hard to find that time, especially given the demands of dealing with the COVID-19 pandemic and recession.'

Chapter Six

Cooked

Ask any politician about the preselection process and most will describe it as 'bruising'. The mid-2007 battle for the seat of Cook in Sydney's south would go down as one of the most acrimonious Liberal preselections in history.

Six months earlier, over the 2006 Christmas break, Judy Baird, the wife of incumbent Cook MP Bruce Baird, recruited the couple's children, including Mike Baird – who in 2014 would become the premier of NSW – to convince Bruce to walk away from politics for good. Baird had been in federal parliament for almost a decade, prior to which he was a member of the NSW Parliament from 1984 to 1995, serving as a minister in the transport, Sydney Olympics bid, and tourism and roads portfolios. The family's pestering worked and Bruce decided to stand down before the 2007 federal election.

When Bruce told his wife about his decision, she gently suggested he call Scott Morrison to let him know the Liberal Party would be in the hunt for a candidate for the seat of Cook. Bruce had worked with Morrison at the TCA – he had been a mentor to Morrison and was responsible for him joining the Liberal Party in 1995. Judy also had taken a liking to Morrison and could think of no better candidate to replace her husband.

His family's badgering wasn't the only motivation for Baird's retirement. Towards the end of 2006, while he was in New York for the coveted three-month secondment at the United Nations (UN) offered to two federal MPs each year, he received a phone call from a journalist asking him whether he knew about a jump in members in one of the twelve Liberal branches within his electorate. It seemed that in his absence, a membership drive had resulted in 432 new members joining the party, meaning they were eligible to vote in a preselection. Baird realised branch stacking was taking place, meaning he might be in for a fight to remain the Liberal Party candidate for his seat. He was already weighing up his future and news of the branch stacking was the final straw – Baird was confident he could withstand a challenge, but it was time to move on.

The Cronulla-based seat of Cook has been in Liberal hands since 1975 and is a glittering prize for any would-be prime minister. As the previous NSW Liberal state director, Scott Morrison was considered an early frontrunner in the preselection race, particularly as he had the blessing of Bruce and Judy Baird. Judy was a woman of strong Christian faith and, according to Bruce, she believed that Morrison was meant to take that seat. 'It's a God thing,' she would tell her family. Years later, when Morrison's name was mentioned as a potential candidate in the final days of the Turnbull government, she predicted he would again win. In politics, never underestimate the influence wielded by a politically engaged spouse.

Barrister Mark Speakman, who in early 2017 became the NSW attorney-general, was also considered a chance to take over the safe Liberal seat. Speakman's résumé spoke for itself; he had attended the University of Sydney and Cambridge before embarking on a successful legal career as a partner at law firm Blake Dawson Waldron. A darling of the moderates, Speakman also wielded influence over the Cook branches and had been instrumental in controlling the seat a decade earlier when the incumbent Stephen Mutch lost preselection to Bruce Baird.

Then there was Michael Towke, a Lebanese Christian who had previously been a member of the Labor Party. He was the preferred candidate of the right, who had been linked to a vigorous recruitment drive in the Miranda branch. Baird had met Towke in 2006 at a Liberal Party barbecue. Towke's then girlfriend lived in nearby Sylvania Waters and he had become president of the Miranda branch. Baird described him as 'a really nice guy. He even let me know he wanted to build up the branch.'

With the Howard government's term due to expire in November 2007, the preselectors of Cook were first due to meet in June to select a Liberal to replace Bruce Baird on the ballot paper. John Howard's time as prime minister was coming to an end and the Coalition was trailing Labor in the polls, so a messy preselection battle was the last thing Howard needed. The new member for Cook would be decided by a vote involving local branch members and delegates drawn from the party's state council and executive.

The drama in Cook kicked off weeks before the scheduled ballot when Towke challenged what he said were two clear breaches of Liberal Party rules and demanded that, due to technical irregularities, fifteen preselectors from two sub-branches be ruled ineligible to vote. There were concerns that one branch had conducted a ballot by a show of hands when it should have been held in secret, while another branch had held a meeting in a suburb just outside its boundaries. It's the sort of nonsense that keeps political types up at night, but rules are rules. The Liberal Party initially ruled against Towke, but he won on appeal.

The decision angered the remaining candidates, including David Coleman, a magazine publishing executive and future minister in the Morrison government, who kicked off a courtroom battle on the eve of the preselection. An injunction was granted in the Supreme Court to halt the vote, which was due to be held at 9 am the following morning. Coleman was worried that, with eight candidates running in Cook and a total of 160 preselectors, ruling fifteen of them as ineligible could swing the result. Optus executive Paul Fletcher, another preselection candidate (and future Morrison government minister), joined Coleman in his court action. The preselection was rescheduled for 14 July.

* * *

While Scott Morrison was considered a leading contender for preselection in Cook, enjoying the backing of both prime minister Howard and sitting MP Baird, he didn't have the approval of a formal faction. And he had made a number of enemies during his stint as state director from 2000 to 2004. As one of his Liberal colleagues puts it, when 'you have told a lot of people "no" over the years and you have upset a lot of presidents and secretaries of branches, you tend to carry a lot of baggage'. The right was especially suspicious of Morrison. As state director, he'd had the final say in approving memberships during a mammoth recruitment drive in the seat of Wentworth. The left's candidate Malcolm Turnbull had emerged victorious and the right held Morrison at least partially responsible.

Morrison's controversial stint as managing director of Tourism Australia and his spat with federal tourism minister Fran Bailey was also used against him. According to leading figures in the NSW right, Bailey contacted state MPs in the lead-up to the vote and urged them to prevent Morrison from being preselected.

The upshot was that while Morrison had high-profile support, his closest allies warned him that without the backing of a faction he would struggle to make it over the line. One of Morrison's backers, who was loosely aligned with the right, remembers offering Morrison some words of advice ahead of the rescheduled vote: 'I told him I can only get him eight votes in the first round.' And that's exactly what happened. Despite heavy hitters like Howard and Baird being in his corner, Morrison polled just eight votes and was eliminated in the first round. His enemies say he immediately left the room, visibly upset by the result. Towke went on to defeat Paul Fletcher in the final round by eighty-two votes to seventy – Fletcher appeared to have been too moderate for the preselectors, giving Towke the upper hand.

Morrison had even received a letter of support from John Howard, but still his bid failed. As one member of the NSW Liberal Party state executive quipped, 'historically people that have letters from Howard have very rarely won. Liberal Party preselectors don't like being told what to do, and whilst everyone has the uppermost respect for John Howard, they are going to make up their own minds.' Perhaps Labor's Anthony Albanese said it best when, speaking days after the ballot, he suggested Morrison had more references than he had votes that day.

Howard now distanced himself from the messy battle for Cook, claiming he played 'absolutely no part' in the ballot. He may have wanted Scott Morrison to join him on the Treasury bench, but he was given little choice but to back Towke after the win. In the wake of the result, Howard said: 'I spoke to him [Towke] last night to congratulate him. I think he's an excellent candidate, he's a successful small businessman. We always like those people in the Liberal Party.'

A key reason why the vote was so unpleasant was that the candidates, including Towke and Morrison, were targeted by internal rivals with explosive and damaging allegations. That said, it's not unusual to see preselection candidates subjected to anonymous documents, known as 'shit sheets', which are routinely provided to journalists and preselectors in order to influence a result.

In the lead-up to that first vote, it was alleged that Morrison had threatened to sue the Commonwealth over the terms of his payout, believed to be more than $300,000, after his contract at Tourism Australia was cut short. That came alongside allegations that the independent Remuneration Tribunal, which determines salaries for all MPs and parliamentary office-holders, believed Morrison had been overpaid – tribunal president John Conde was said to have told Tourism Australia chairman Tim Fischer that Morrison's payout should have been below $120,000. Another shit sheet doing the rounds at the time, allegedly prepared by a 'high-level Tourism Australia figure', accused Morrison of cultivating an 'intimidating, aggressive and argumentative style'.

Towke faced his own damaging claims. Liberal Party heavyweights who opposed his candidacy routinely hit the phones to challenge whether Towke was a training officer in the Army Reserve, as he had said he was. There also were questions over who had paid for the party memberships of some of those recently recruited into the Miranda branch. And then there was the unexpected phone call taken by ALP powerbroker Sam Dastyari at NSW Labor's Sussex Street headquarters. Dastyari confirms he was contacted by an influential Liberal who supported Scott Morrison and wanted Labor's help in collecting dirt on Towke, specifically on his links to the ALP. 'We were asked to do a job on him for the wet Libs backing Morrison,' Dastyari says. 'They asked us for his Labor Party membership details to blow up Towke. So we compiled a dirt file on the guy and leaked it to them … it ended up in the media.'

Out in the open, the members and supporters of the major parties line up against each other like soldiers preparing for war. Behind closed doors, however, politicians and their backers play a different game. Internal enemies can be viewed as more of a threat than rivals from the other party – often they are seen as greater obstacles on the pathway to success. But even Dastyari, who is no stranger to the nastiness of factional politics, thought this request was unusual. Still, he agreed to it for the simple reason that it was an election year and he assumed the leak would create chaos and ultimately hurt the Liberal Party. 'It was very rare and weird,' he says.

* * *

The power in preselections comes from sheer numbers, but fast recruitment is often met with suspicion. One person's gun recruiter is another person's branch stacker. In fact, rumours of branch stacking by Towke had swirled for months after the NSW Liberal Party was allegedly provided with claims by two members that they had had their membership fees reimbursed by Towke. It had been impossible to prove the allegation before the first ballot, as it was essentially one side's word against the other's. But after his unexpected win, Towke faced further allegations of branch stacking as stories from more members claiming their fees had been paid on their behalf appeared in newspapers, though there was no formal finding made. Then came stories about how Towke had allegedly misled preselectors on his nomination form over whether he had graduated from university and exactly when he had been a member of the Labor Party, the latter backed up by evidence provided by Dastyari.

Going into the vote, to defuse some of the controversy, Towke had produced references from a former president of the local St Vincent de Paul Society and from Liberal NSW Senator Concetta Fierravanti-Wells. He had a Bachelor of Arts from the University of Sydney and had won the

Alan Davis Memorial Prize, the university's top award for sociology. He was a practising Catholic, had a Master of Business Administration and had served in the Army Reserve. He also had volunteered at St Vinnies since the age of fifteen. But his impressive résumé and convincing preselection win did little to stop the torrent of damaging attacks. Six days after the vote, the party's NSW state director Graham Jaeschke put Towke's endorsement on hold as more damaging claims were aired in the media. The state executive remained split on whether or not to tick off the appointment.

By late July, Howard's initial public support had begun to waiver. 'If there is evidence in relation to memberships having been paid, he shouldn't [be endorsed] because that is a clear breach of the party's rules,' Howard said at the time. Privately, it is understood that John Howard was determined to overturn Towke's preselection as it was proving to be a constant distraction in an election year. And so, with Howard looking indecisive, the state executive narrowly voted in favour of dumping Towke, ruling that he had misled the party about his past. A second ballot was scheduled for late August. In a surprising move, the moderate candidates Mark Speakman, David Coleman and Paul Fletcher – who had faced Towke in the final round – dropped out of the running, delivering a moderate block of votes to local businessman Peter Tynan, while the right now had to find a new candidate to support in the race for the prized seat.

Ahead of the new vote, Morrison met with right powerbrokers David Clarke and Concetta Fierravanti-Wells. Both had backed Towke in the first ballot and Morrison now needed their support if he wanted to win the second. According to those familiar with the meeting, Morrison made a number of concessions about staffing and did his best to convince his potential backers that he was not beholden to the moderates, as he had been framed. In this, he was successful. One senior NSW right figure describes the choice to back Morrison as 'the path of least resistance', adding: 'Howard was backing him ... there was clearly a push for Morrison. A deal was struck and so we moved our support behind Scott.'

While the second ballot lacked the nasty tactics and damaging leaks of the first preselection vote, Tynan's opponents seized on a book he had co-authored in 2004 called *Imagining Australia: Ideas for Our Future*, which supported an inheritance tax and a public holiday to honour Eddie Mabo, and called for the Eureka Stockade flag to be adopted as Australia's national flag. Meanwhile, the NSW executive rushed to approve the fewer than forty-five preselectors who would override the 160 members who voted in the first ballot. On 23 August 2007, Morrison won the Cook preselection ballot by twenty-six votes to Tynan's fourteen; there was one informal vote and the rest went to a third nominee, Bruce Morrow.

With his preselection overturned and his political credibility destroyed by the wave of damaging stories, Towke started defamation proceedings against Nationwide News Pty Ltd, which publishes the *Daily Telegraph*. He claimed that the many damaging articles aired by the newspaper had destroyed his political career and inflicted immense stress on his family. Shortly before the matter was due in court, Towke reached an out-of-court settlement with Nationwide News. With his name cleared, his backers hoped he would get another chance to run for a seat, perhaps in the NSW Parliament. In pursuit of this goal, Towke briefly worked for Senator Fierravanti-Wells, but he was scarred by the preselection experience and eventually returned to the private sector.

* * *

Seven weeks later, John Howard called a federal election.

If the battle for the seat of Cook was messy, the 2007 federal election was chaotic. On 24 November, prime minister John Howard was decisively defeated by Labor's Kevin Rudd in a win that surpassed all of the Opposition's expectations. In total, the Coalition lost twenty-two seats, including Howard's own seat of Bennelong. While a redrawing of the electoral boundary had made his seat less safe, it nonetheless was an embarrassing blow for Howard, who had represented the division for thirty-three years. It also was the first time since 1929 that an Australian prime minister had lost their own seat. It seemed that, right across the country, Howard's 'battlers' – a voting bloc the Coalition had long relied on for support – had turned against the conservative government. The Liberals spun the loss as inevitable given Howard had been in power for nearly twelve years, but it was still devastating to the party. Australians had shown they were ready for change and were willing to give Labor's Rudd a chance.

Rudd had been elected leader of the Labor Party in December 2006 and the gloss hadn't yet worn off. Pitched against Howard, Rudd seemed youthful but at the same time not a risky choice. He offered new policies, such as bringing combat troops home from Iraq in a phased withdrawal and ratifying the Kyoto Protocol, but he also was a self-described economic conservative. The books were balanced. As Christopher Pyne put it, voters believed they could 'change the government, get a fresh face at the top, without changing the country'.

The loss hurt: John Howard had been the second–longest-serving prime minister in Australia after Menzies, a Liberal legend; along the way, he had won four elections. Liberal MPs were devastated. But in the seat of Cook, while Scott Morrison lost significant ground to Labor's Mark Buttigieg, who halved Baird's margin, a win was still a win – Morrison was on his way to Canberra.

Morrison hadn't spent much time in Cook prior to his victory there; up until his preselection, he was still living in Bronte. After renting for a few years, the Morrisons purchased a three-bedroom, two-bathroom house in Port Hacking for $920,000 in 2009. Port Hacking, in the Sutherland Shire, sits on the north shore of the Port Hacking estuary, close to the Royal National Park and about 30 kilometres south of Sydney's CBD.

The federal seat of Cook was named after Lieutenant (later Captain) James Cook, who in 1770 landed at Kurnell, which is part of the electorate. Most of the voters in Cook live on the peninsula squeezed between the Georges River and Port Hacking, taking in the suburbs of Cronulla, Caringbah, Miranda, Sylvania and Gymea. According to the 2016 census, just 23 per cent of Sutherland Shire residents are foreign-born, compared with an Australia-wide average that sits above 30 per cent. Most are married, Christian and overwhelmingly speak English at home.

Morrison has since made 'The Shire', as it is known, part of his persona. Its working-class-done-good vibe is central to his political philosophy. He believes Australians are aspirational and lack pretension: they want to work hard, buy a house and have a family; they love sport and are proud to be Australian. Morrison is proudly and loudly suburban. Since moving to The Shire, he has even embraced the Cronulla Sharks, attending as many games as he can, many of them at the team's home ground, Shark Park. Until he became the Member for Cook, Morrison actually preferred rugby union; while living in Wellington in the late 1990s, he even described New Zealand as a 'bit of a nirvana' because in Sydney, union usually takes second place to league. Insiders from his beloved Cronulla Sharks confirmed that Morrison wasn't spotted at games until after he won preselection. Bruce Baird also confirms he never saw his predecessor at the footy while he held the seat, adding: 'I was exactly the same. And after I was no longer the member, I never went to another match again.'

While Morrison has been called out as being overly eager to convince others that he is a Shire man through and through, he cannot be faulted for the way he has embraced his electorate. The Shire reminds him of his carefree life in Bronte when he was a child. Shortly after he was elected, Morrison moved his family to The Shire, into a new house he and Jenny had decided to rent in the electorate – he'd driven past some kids playing rugby on the nature strip and realised he'd found his home. 'I have always been most at home in suburbia,' Morrison says. 'That's why I like The Shire so much … It's classic suburbia.'

Personal friends and neighbours of Scott Morrison defend his pumped-up suburban persona. They describe Scott and Jenny as a down-to-earth couple who could regularly be spotted on the front deck of their modest Shire home. Bruce Baird, who understood the electorate, believes it perfectly reflected Morrison: 'Morrison fitted in well to The Shire, which is your average middle-class seat with some degree of conservatism. They are genuine, down-to-earth folk with not a whole lot of pretension.'

However, colleagues from Canberra roll their eyes when asked about the daggy dad persona. 'It's completely exaggerated,' says one long-serving Liberal Cabinet minister. 'He's actually a highly political person and he plays all the political games.' This perception goes against Morrison's portrayal of himself as the anti-politician, the man who regularly rejects his habitat by attacking the so-called 'Canberra bubble'. He relied heavily on the bubble-branding as a senior minister – and still does so now as prime minister – in an attempt to gain favour with everyday voters who increasingly feel alienated by the goings-on in Canberra. As a political tactic it works, in the same way as Donald Trump's promise to 'drain the swamp' in Washington, DC.

A relentless pursuit of power, as Scott Morrison showed in his fight for the seat of Cook, is needed by any politician who wants to make their mark in the Australian Parliament. One Liberal MP says, 'I've met ruthless people in political life and he [Morrison] is the most ruthless.'

Chapter Seven

Faith is Personal

Acclaimed Australian photographer Ken Duncan patiently waited for two hours in sub-zero temperatures in Finland to capture the image he wanted of an eagle. The photo, which he titled 'Soaring Majesty', shows the huge bird, wings spread, coming in to land with a look of intense determination in its eyes. The incredible image hangs on the wall of Duncan's Erina Heights gallery, in the marginal NSW electorate of Dobell.

A few weeks out from the 2019 election, and lagging in the polls, Scott Morrison was searching for a sign from God. As he revealed to the 2021 national conference of Australian Christian Churches (ACC), Australia's largest Pentecostal church network:

I was saying to myself, 'You know Lord, where are you, where are you? I'd like a reminder if that's OK.' I didn't know it was supposed to be Ken's gallery ... and there right in front of me was the biggest picture of a soaring eagle that I could imagine and of course the verse hit me.

Morrison had popped into the gallery for a coffee with Liberal MP Lucy Wicks, a factional ally and fellow Christian, when he'd glimpsed the framed image. He said the limited-edition photo, priced at around $1900, reminded him of a verse from Isaiah 40:31:

The message I got that day was, 'Scott, you've got to run to not grow weary, you've got to walk to not grow faint, you've got to spread your wings like an eagle to soar like an eagle.'

Morrison's revelation about this apparent sign from God was met with scepticism and the obvious rebuttal that God, should he exist, is probably not into party politics. But to understand Morrison's faith, it's important to realise that the prime minister and many of his supporters truly believe God is on his side.

* * *

The Shire was where Scott Morrison found his Pentecostalism. He was raised according to the Presbyterian–Uniting Church faith, attending Sunday school at the local gospel chapel each week. His mother Marion ran the local Girls' Brigade unit, while his father John ran the Boys' Brigade. Aged eighteen, he followed his soon-to-be-wife Jenny and his brother Alan to the Christian Brethren Assemblies, which is not to be confused with the Exclusive Brethren, a very restrictive breakaway group. The Christian Brethren movement, also known as the Open Brethren, started in the 1820s as part of the Assembly Movement, following a split with the Church of England. The assemblies tend to be a grouping of Christian churches rather than an organised denomination. Each congregation is independent but usually they all share a strong commitment to evangelism. In Morrison's case, there wasn't a higher being drawing him to the Christian Brethren Assemblies. It was about love. 'It was where Jenny went,' he says. 'We have always been Protestant but never particularly denominational.'

Their shared faith brought them together and ultimately kept them together during their fourteen-year battle with infertility, which was the ultimate test of that faith. Morrison believes deeply that those years of disappointment were part of God's plan, hence his reference to 'our miracle child' in his maiden speech to parliament. It was in that speech that Morrison also revealed how his deep Christian faith had influenced his world view and would shape him as a politician:

My personal faith in Jesus Christ is not a political agenda.
As [Abraham] Lincoln said, our task is not to claim whether

God is on our side but to pray earnestly that we are on His.
For me, faith is personal, but the implications are social –
as personal and social responsibility are at the heart of the
Christian message. In recent times it has become fashionable
to negatively stereotype those who profess their Christian faith
in public life as 'extreme' and to suggest that such faith has
no place in the political debate of this country. This presents a
significant challenge for those of us ... who seek to follow the
example of [abolitionist] William Wilberforce or [Nobel Peace
Prize winner] Desmond Tutu, to name just two. These leaders
stood for the immutable truths and principles of the Christian
faith ...

From my faith, I derive the values of loving kindness,
justice and righteousness, to act with compassion and kindness,
acknowledging our common humanity and to consider the welfare
of others; to fight for a fair go for everyone to fulfil their human
potential and to remove whatever unjust obstacles stand in their
way, including diminishing their personal responsibility for their
own wellbeing; and to do what is right, to respect the rule of law,
the sanctity of human life and the moral integrity of marriage
and the family. We must recognise an unchanging and absolute
standard of what is good and what is evil.

Desmond Tutu put it this way: '... we expect Christians ...
to be those who stand up for the truth, to stand up for justice,
to stand on the side of the poor and the hungry, the homeless
and the naked, and when that happens, then Christians will be
trustworthy believable witnesses'.

In that maiden address, Morrison also thanked Brian Houston, the founder of the Hillsong Church empire and one of the world's most powerful pastors, as well as a close friend, for his 'great assistance', describing him as a mentor. A decade later, in 2018, Brian Houston would be the subject of a police investigation over his handling of the sex crimes allegedly committed by his father, Frank Houston, a Pentecostal Christian pastor in the Assemblies of God churches in New Zealand and Australia. Frank Houston, who died in 2004, is considered the father of Pentecostalism in Sydney.

Brian Houston was the president of the Australian Christian Churches in the late 1990s when a man in his mid-thirties came forward to reveal that Frank Houston had abused him about thirty years earlier. Brian Houston didn't report the accusation at the time. Instead, he is suspected of helping his father to quietly leave the church. In October 2014, he told the Royal Commission into Institutional Responses to Child Sexual Abuse:

> *Rightly or wrongly I genuinely believed that I would be pre-empting the victim if I were just to call the police. If he decides to go to the police, he can, or if anyone else decides to go to the police, they can. If this complaint was about someone who was under eighteen then and there, I am absolutely certain we would have reported it to the police. We would have made sure that's where it went.*

The royal commission, in its findings, criticised Houston and other church executives for not going to the police:

> *We are satisfied that, in 1999 and 2000, Pastor Brian Houston and the national executive of the Assemblies of God in Australia did not refer the allegations of child sexual abuse against Mr Frank Houston to the police. We consider that a conflict of interest first arose when Pastor Brian Houston decided to respond to the allegations by confronting his father while simultaneously maintaining his roles as national president (of the Assemblies of God in Australia) and senior pastor. The commissioners express the view that the NSW executive failed to appoint a contact person for the complainant, interview the complainant, have the state or national executive interview the alleged perpetrator, or record any of the steps it took.*

In 2018, NSW Police announced an investigation into Brian Houston. A year later, Scott Morrison requested that his friend be placed on the guest list for a glamorous state dinner at the White House with then US president Donald Trump. The *Wall Street Journal* broke the story after Morrison had arrived in the United States, revealing that the White House had rejected the Australian PM's request during the planning of the dinner. At the time, Morrison dismissed the report as 'gossip', but he later admitted during an interview on Sydney radio station 2GB that he had in fact asked that Brian Houston attend the lavish dinner in the Rose Garden, in the company of golfer Greg Norman and business leaders Kerry Stokes, Gina Rinehart, Andrew Forrest, Anthony Pratt and Lachlan Murdoch. 'On that occasion, we put forward a number of names – that included Brian – but not everybody whose name was put forward was invited,' said Morrison.

* * *

While Morrison acknowledges that his faith is an integral part of his life, he insists the Bible is not a policy handbook. This hasn't stopped critics from questioning the impact his religious beliefs have on his leadership. Non-believers seem somewhat spooked by Morrison's overt Christianity, leading them to forcefully defend the separation of church and state. That protection should be guaranteed, the argument goes, and so too Morrison's right to bring his belief system to the decision-making process – after all, it is so deeply embedded in him that it would be wrong to think that he or any other politician of faith should deny something so important to themselves. But politicians of faith like Scott Morrison also have a responsibility to represent all those they serve, regardless of their beliefs.

When Morrison asks himself what values he derives from his faith, he turns to a passage in the Book of Jeremiah, 9:24: 'I am the Lord who exercises loving kindness, justice and righteousness on earth; for I delight in these things, declares the Lord.' Yet his strongest critics argue that his hardline

THE ACCIDENTAL PRIME MINISTER

stance on asylum seekers during his time as immigration minister and his attitude towards the welfare-dependent run counter to this verse and his belief in justice for all. They fear he is simply able to separate his personal faith from his politics.

During the debate to legalise same-sex marriage in December 2017, Morrison was one of ten MPs – the others included former prime minister Tony Abbott, Stuart Robert, Michael Sukkar, Kevin Andrews and George Christensen – to abstain from the vote in parliament. That was despite his electorate of Cook voting in favour of same-sex marriage by a margin of 55 per cent to 45 per cent. He also mounted a conservative rearguard action to lobby for greater protection of religious freedom in the marriage bill. Speaking on the bill in parliament, he said:

> We may be a secular state, but we are not a godless people to whom faith, belief and religion are not important. Quite the contrary: it is deeply central to the lives of millions of Australians. In my own church, we refer to Australia as 'the great south land of the Holy Spirit'. Whether you raise your hands, bow to your knees, face the Holy City, light incense, light a candle or light the menorah, faith matters in this country – and we cannot allow its grace and peace to be diminished, muffled or again driven from the public square. Separation of church and state does not mean the inoculation of the influence of faith on the state. The state shouldn't run the church and the church shouldn't run the state. In fact, the separation of

church and state was set up to protect the church from the state, not the other way around – to protect religious freedoms.

* * *

Morrison is not Australia's first Christian prime minister, although he is perhaps one of the most overtly so. Kevin Rudd convened a club of Christian MPs and senators within the Labor Party and regularly staged press conferences outside his church. Tony Abbott studied for the Catholic priesthood before entering politics. And Malcolm Turnbull converted to the faith of his wife's family, Roman Catholicism, but he always maintained that his religious views were 'off limits' to the public.

When in Canberra, while colleagues flocked to watering holes like the Public Bar in Manuka, Morrison would meet with fellow Coalition worshippers – including Alex Hawke, Steve Irons and Stuart Robert, who Morrison refers to as 'Brother Stewie' – on Tuesday nights at Parliament House. Together they would pray, a pairing which ultimately transformed into a powerful political partnership.

Over his time in Canberra, the prime minister's beliefs have connected him with other people of faith, including Julian Leeser, the Jewish MP for the northern Sydney seat of Berowra, and fellow Christians Andrew Hastie and Amanda Stoker. It's an alliance more than a faction, but the common bond is undeniable.

Morrison is also Australia's first Pentecostal prime minister. This has attracted suspicion from those who aren't used to the bright lights, live music and packed auditoriums that characterise Pentecostalism. Shortly before he won the Cook preselection, Morrison met Michael Murphy, the lead pastor at Shirelive in Sutherland, which later became Horizons Church. Murphy has said that while the church is theologically conservative, it changed its methods to attract a new generation of worshippers, culminating in a much broader demographic than your regular stone church. Asked to describe what goes on behind the sanctuary's big white walls, Murphy has referred to 'a contemporary spirit-filled church but with an age-old message ... it wouldn't be that different to an alive Baptist church or something like that'.

Pentecostal churches have replaced archaic hymns and organ accompaniment with more emotional modern songs performed with more contemporary instruments. The objective of any sermon is to move the congregation, not just teach the word of the Lord. And at a time when attendance at more traditional churches is in decline, Pentecostalism is on the rise. According to the Australian Bureau of Statistics (ABS), the number of Pentecostal church members jumped by almost 20 per cent between 2006 and 2016. Researchers believe that while Pentecostals tend to support conservative parties on social issues like same-sex marriage and abortion, they also are often concerned about environmental issues and asylum seekers.

This large voting bloc also tends to live in marginal electorates in New South Wales and Queensland – eight of Australia's twenty-one most Pentecostal-oriented electorates are marginal seats that help decide elections. The knife-edge seats of Cowan and Pearce in Western Australia are home to thousands of Pentecostal Christians. In Queensland, seats like Forde, Dickson, Petrie and Herbert, which Labor chases at every election, are home to growing numbers of evangelical worshippers.

Morrison's decision to join a rapidly growing denomination has been met with cynicism by many of his colleagues. Few deny his deep personal faith, but some are wary of how he has used his faith to establish political allegiances and potentially court votes. As a university student, Morrison revealed through his academic writing a belief that church congregations could be powerful communities for change. He also showed an early interest in spreading the word of the Lord to non-believers. At university, his honours thesis argued that the Christian Brethren Assemblies, where Morrison worshipped at university, could grow its congregation by holding more 'bridge-building' activities in the community. He lauded the work of influential Christian writer Jim Petersen, who advises Christians on working with non-believers and how to sell God's messaging in a non-threatening manner.

Morrison is far from the only politician who has used his connections, knowledge and networks – whether they involve church, sport, business or the union movement – to help his career. And it's hard to imagine that he did not see the powerful potential of the church as a solid foundation on which to build support.

* * *

During the 2019 federal election campaign, Ashley Evans, a Pentecostal pastor from South Australia's Influencers Church and the son of former South Australian upper house MP Andrew Evans, sent the following email to his parishioners, warning them against voting for Labor or the Greens:

> *A vote for Labor and the Greens and anyone who represents anti-Christian rhetoric, policy positions or beliefs … will undermine our nation, will cripple church schools' ability to teach faith in the way they do today, and threaten to silence Christians from sharing their faith with others. The next steps after this will be to deem the Bible as hate speech.*

It's difficult to measure the impact of such a letter, but there is little doubt that the images of Scott Morrison recorded by television crews at Easter that year, with his eyes closed and hands raised, publicly praying, spoke to worshippers across Australia who had increasingly felt under attack. It's a widely held belief among Liberal and Labor strategists that Morrison's strong faith worked in his favour in the election campaign, as it gave religious communities confidence he was on their side.

At first, Labor couldn't believe its luck when those images of Morrison were broadcast. 'We were stunned and initially thought it would play badly,' says one Labor insider. The ALP denies that there was ever a deliberate strategy to use Morrison's faith against him. Instead, they simply believed Australians would feel uncomfortable with such an overt display of faith, which is unusual in Australian politics. Labor leader Bill Shorten also went to a service that weekend, but he chose a more traditional Anglican church in Brisbane, attending with his wife, Chloe, his children and his mother-in-law, Quentin Bryce.

While Labor didn't directly attack Morrison at the time, many left-leaning supporters did. On social media, progressive trolls likened his hand waving and worshipping to a Hitler salute. But the attacks merely emphasised the need for Morrison's promised laws to further protect religious freedom in Australia; they allowed him to turn a potential negative into days of positive coverage. 'It's disgusting. These grubs are gutless, and they're keyboard warriors in their mother's basement trying to make heroes of themselves. But the great Australian people are much bigger than them,' he said at the time.

Weeks later, a social media post by football cross-code star Israel Folau became a major election test for campaigners given its ability to divide opinion between those that champion religious freedom versus hate speech. Folau faced being sacked by Rugby Australia for a code of conduct breach after posting a message on Instagram that said hell awaited 'drunks, homosexuals, adulterers'. During a press conference, Morrison was asked, as a passionate Christian and devoted rugby fan, to comment on the Folau case. He was asked directly whether he agreed with Folau that gay people would go to hell unless they repented. Morrison tried to deflect the question and failed to condemn the rugby star's comments.

At Labor's campaign headquarters, strategists agreed that Shorten should be ready to denounce Folau and also criticise the prime minister for his wishy-washy response, but only if asked. Instead, Shorten went on the offensive. On 14 May, during a doorstop interview in Burnie, Tasmania, Shorten made the following comment in response to a question about whether he agreed with former Labor PM Paul Keating's attack on home affairs minister Peter Dutton, whom Keating had described as the 'meanest' politician he had encountered:

> *The meanest commentary I've seen in the election is actually the propositions that are being advanced that gay people are going to go to hell. I can't believe the prime minister has not immediately said that gay people will not go to hell. I think if you want to be prime minister of Australia you've got to be prime minister for all people ... The nation's got to stop eating itself in this sort of madness of division and toxicity.*

Shorten's staff could see how it would play out. They knew that his call to rid Australia of disunity would be turned into an attack on Morrison's religion. As one former staffers says, 'Bill walked straight into it.'

Sure enough, the day after the doorstop, conservative newspapers led with headlines such as 'Shorten ignites unholy war by targeting Morrison's religion'. forcing the Opposition leader to retreat. It gave Morrison time to provide a more nuanced answer. Also speaking from Tasmania, he declared that he did not believe gay people went to hell. 'These are issues about religion, and I don't want to see those controversial topics brought into the political debate. I don't see how that helps anybody,' he said. Morrison used the controversy as a pitch to promise greater religious protections for Australians, and it worked. The electorates that would go on to turn their backs on Labor in the 2019 poll overwhelmingly had more people of faith than the national average.

* * *

Morrison understands the power of the Pentecostal vote better than most. Under Morrison's watch in 2002, while he was state director of the NSW Liberal Party, John Howard opened the Hillsong Church's 3500-seat auditorium in Sydney's north-west. Morrison also had played a key role in recruiting Hillsong parishioner Louise Markus to successfully contest the western Sydney seat of Greenway in 2004.

Pentecostalists are often called 'happy clappers', a term which refers to the enthusiastic style of worship embraced by the church. It's a label that Morrison has described as 'a bit dated', adding: 'These churches are incredibly mainstream and I think most people who have had anything to do with them understand [that] and often people attack what they don't understand or don't feel comfortable with.'

Morrison, along with those closest to him who share his faith, believes his successes have all been part of God's plan. Hillsong Pastor Michael Murphy once told a congregation that he believed a future community leader or prime minister would be chosen from it. 'That wasn't necessarily prophetic but something that was informed by our theology that says, "serve God in the marketplace, in key leadership roles, in the arts, in sport or in the church like I have",' Murphy told Christian website *Eternity News*.

Judy Baird also believed God would bring Morrison success. In 2018, when Morrison announced that he would run for the leadership of the Liberal Party, Judy, who could no longer speak due to a degenerative neurological condition, managed to type out a message which said, 'Scott will win this, it's a God thing' – an echo of the comment she'd made when Morrison was contesting the seat of Cook in 2007. Morrison's Christian foot soldiers lobbied MPs on Morrison's behalf, but as a group they still relied on the power of prayer. In those final minutes before the party room vote, Morrison invited Stuart Robert to his ministerial office where together they prayed. This wasn't an attempt to court votes in the electorate but a deeply personal moment. In May 2019, the Pentecostal prime minister himself claimed that his election win had involved divine intervention.

The belief that worshippers are chosen by God to lead is a key tenet of Pentecostalism. This sits uncomfortably with those who see it as a declaration that God prefers one party or candidate over another, and argue that it goes against the separation of church and state. But even Morrison's Labor opponent Anthony Albanese is careful to not counter this claim too heavily. Albanese has repeatedly said he respects Morrison's faith, though he rejects the idea that God takes a political side. This is because he understands the power of faith communities as an electoral tool. But it seems many Christians interpreted Morrison's remarks differently, and saw them as describing a call to action rather than as a claim to have been chosen by God.

In April 2021, Morrison addressed the ACC national conference of Christians and again explained that, as prime minister, he had been called on to do God's work:

We are called, all of us, for a time and for a season, and God would have us use it wisely, and for each day I get up and I move ahead there is just one little thing that's in my head, and that is 'for such a time as this'.

Pentecostalism also encourages the benefits of praying in tongues, which is based on the idea that Satan can't understand what is being said. Morrison doesn't speak in tongues, but he, like many other Pentecostals, believes that there is evil in the world, and that it is the work of the Devil. Morrison also told the ACC national conference that he had very recently practised the laying on of hands, a Pentecostal tradition of healing and encouragement of faith. Referring to a visit to Kalbarri in Western Australia in the wake of Cyclone Seroja, Morrison said:

> *I've been in evacuation centres where people thought I was just giving someone a hug, and I was praying and putting my hands on people ... laying hands on them and praying in various situations.*

This practice is not uncommon in Christianity, but it is unusual for a prime minister to admit to doing so in secular Australia. And while seemingly well-intentioned, Morrison's admission came in the wake of some awkward forced handshakes with bushfire victims, for which he was roundly criticised.

While Morrison's personal faith so far has proven to be an electoral advantage for him, his advisers recognise that it also has the potential to be used against him. This is why the full transcript of his speech to the Australian Christian Churches national conference was never released on his website, unlike other addresses he has given at religious and secular events. It also explains why the prime minister spent months ducking and weaving when asked about whether or not he invited Hillsong preacher Brian Houston to the

White House. Consistent with his tactic of avoiding difficult questions, Morrison labelled the question as gossip in an effort to downplay its significance.

Cabinet colleagues, including the non-believers and twice-a-year Christians, report that Morrison never speaks about his faith at the Cabinet table or when discussing politics or policies. In fact, many Coalition MPs claim to find it difficult to reconcile the hardline politician with the man who holds a deep Christian faith. That's not to say Morrison doesn't understand the power of his faith as a political tool. He also uses it to build and maintain political alliances. The week that Morrison became prime minister, his Tuesday night prayer group had transformed itself into an influential voting bloc that ultimately helped him secure support for his ambition.

Chapter Eight

I Stopped These

While reflecting on the years that followed the Liberal Party's brutal 2007 federal election loss, Christopher Pyne described opposition as a 'special kind of hell' for the Liberal Party. He argued that while Labor is the party of the labour movement, Liberal MPs are far more suited to running the show than philosophising about it. As the apt saying goes, the worst day in government is still better than the best day in opposition.

On 24 November 2007, Australians decided they were ready for change after nearly a dozen years of Coalition leadership. Labor's Kevin Rudd was viewed as a safe pair of hands – voters felt they could get a younger, fresher leader without risking the prosperity of the nation. And so Labor campaigned off his popularity, running an entirely presidential-style campaign. The Coalition appeared to be in electoral strife, but Morrison, having just welcomed a baby daughter and having been elected to a safe Liberal seat, had much to be thankful for.

Before the last ballot had been counted, when it was already clear the Coalition had been defeated, the Liberal Party turned its attention to a replacement for John Howard, who had lost his seat of Bennelong on election night. The following day, Howard's deputy and long-serving treasurer, Peter Costello, stunned the political world when he announced that he wouldn't contest the Liberal Party leadership and instead would retire from parliament during the coming term. It was Malcolm Turnbull, freshly re-elected in the seat of Wentworth, who was the first to announce he'd stand as a potential leader. The now former defence minister Brendan Nelson, along with Tony Abbott, Alexander Downer and Joe Hockey then hit the phones to sound out colleagues about their own chances. But Downer, Hockey and Abbott soon pulled out of the race, leaving Turnbull and Nelson to fight it out for the top job.

On 29 November, weary Liberals met in Canberra to vote for a new leadership team. The ballot was held in the Opposition party room – most of those present that day had never taken a seat in that room before. Nelson narrowly won the ballot by forty-five votes to forty-two.

Morrison was new to Canberra and floating around without a faction. In his first preselection ballot he had lacked strong support from either the party's moderate or conservative wings, which saw him eliminated in the first round. His ultimate success in Cook was delivered by the right of the party, when the conservative bloc shifted its support behind him. Newly appointed Liberal leader Brendan Nelson had taken a similar path, initially viewed as left-leaning but transforming himself into a hero of the right.

Over the next ten months, Nelson struggled to land a blow on Rudd. His party room was split on contentious issues such as climate change and same-sex marriage, and Nelson found it difficult to navigate the factional rifts. Under mounting pressure, Nelson called an unscheduled meeting of the Liberal Party on 15 September 2008, at which he announced that he would open up the party leadership the following morning. He made his position clear: if re-elected to the role of Opposition leader, he would reshuffle his frontbench and take a tougher stance against Labor's emissions trading scheme (ETS), a mechanism to try to reduce the amount of carbon dioxide being released into the atmosphere. But he never got the chance to follow through on this commitment: he was defeated by Malcolm Turnbull by a margin of forty-five votes to forty-one.

In a frontbench reshuffle, Turnbull promoted Morrison, giving him the role of Shadow Minister for Housing and Local Government as a reward for his support. Morrison hadn't been in parliament long but he had worked closely with Turnbull during his four years as the state director of the NSW Liberal Party. He was one of four backbenchers promoted to the shadow ministry by Turnbull.

Liberal MPs in both the right and the more moderate factions of the party have often been fascinated by the Morrison–Turnbull relationship. It would be easy to assume that it was, like many political relationships, simply a convenient political alliance. As party leader and later as prime minister, Turnbull certainly relied on Morrison to help him resolve factional spats in New South Wales. But Liberal MPs report that it was more than that. There is a broad view that in a profession where trust and friendship are rare commodities, Turnbull and Morrison's relationship, at least in those early years, appeared to be genuine.

Once appointed, Turnbull also battled to be effective in opposition. Voters may say they want more bipartisanship in politics, but in reality, an effective Opposition needs to constantly criticise the party in power and provide policy alternatives to have any hope of returning to government. Yet Turnbull's natural inclination was to work with the Labor government to fix its policies rather than oppose them. In the face of significant disagreement from his party room, Turnbull, a moderate, had even given in-principle support to Labor's ETS. The conservatives were ropeable. In November 2009, Victorian Liberal MP Kevin Andrews called for a vote to spill the leadership. The motion was defeated, but Turnbull was wounded. One by one, members of the frontbench – Eric Abetz, Sophie Mirabella, Mitch Fifield, Brett Mason, Mathias Cormann – resigned from Cabinet.

According to Turnbull, Scott Morrison asked to meet with him on 27 November, whereupon Morrison withdrew his support. Turnbull suspected he had earlier briefed the media, as they arrived at Turnbull's Edgecliff electorate office ahead of Morrison. By the end of the day, Turnbull realised he had little choice but to agree to hold another leadership ballot the following week. On 1 December 2009, Tony Abbott was elected the new leader of the Liberal Party, defeating Turnbull by a single vote. Joe Hockey also contested the leadership but lost in the first round.

Many of Morrison's colleagues reflect on this leadership spill as a moment that shaped the way Morrison played later leadership contests. He was too young and inexperienced to be a serious contender or shift any votes, but he turned on the man who promoted him. He quietly observed the behaviour, backstabbing and naked ambition of his colleagues, which some believe had a significant impact on how he later plotted his own path.

* * *

Leadership ballots usually result in a ministerial reshuffle, meaning that votes can be traded for lucrative frontbench positions. Ambitious backbenchers and outer ministers make their pitch and spend days waiting by the phone for their leader to call and invite them to join the frontbench. It's a nerve-racking time as portfolios are carved up and the winners are appointed. Scott Morrison recalls that it was a Sunday afternoon when he got the call. He and Jenny were on their way to collect their daughters, who had spent a few days with their grandparents, when Tony Abbott's name flashed up on the dashboard display. Knowing what the call was about, Jenny, who was driving, turned to her husband and said, 'Anything but immigration.' Upon answering the call, Morrison listened as Tony Abbott invited him to join the Coalition frontbench as Shadow Minister for Immigration and Citizenship.

Jenny's reservations were well-founded. No matter who happens to be the immigration minister, no matter which side of politics they are from, it is considered one of the most challenging and vexed portfolios. The policies are rarely fair to everyone but rather are designed to serve the greater good. And there is rarely an electoral advantage in showing compassion. Morrison once described it as like walking on the edge of a razor blade: 'You make one little slip and there's a fair bit of damage.'

That year – 2009 – more than 2700 asylum seekers were intercepted trying to reach Australia on fifty-nine unauthorised vessels. Globally, the United Nations High Commissioner for Refugees reported almost no change in the number of people seeking asylum in the industrialised world, but the number of refugees seeking asylum in Australia had jumped by almost 30 per cent. Politically speaking, the Labor government appeared to have lost control of Australia's borders. The political tension around the growing number of asylum-seeker boats steadily grew, with public opinion divided on what to do with the boatloads of vulnerable people headed for Australia. To complicate matters, in October, seventy-eight asylum seekers who were picked up by the Australian Customs vessel MV *Oceanic Viking* had refused to disembark in Indonesia, resulting in a month-long stand-off. As far as portfolios go, immigration was proving itself to be high profile, emotionally taxing and lacking a clear solution.

In many ways, Morrison was perfectly suited to this post. He had always favoured pragmatism over ideology, meaning his own views and Christianity seemed not to impact his policy formation. And the so-called 'boats issue' became so politically toxic for Labor that he didn't need to contend with the Liberal 'wets' or more socially progressive members of the Coalition, who often spoke out under the Howard government against mandatory detention and offshore processing. Morrison saw his immigration role as one which required a political fix. He had been handed a policy area where Labor was struggling and he was determined to relentlessly hammer the government on its failings while searching for an alternative approach.

As the clock ticked into 2010, Labor stuck with its policy not to process asylum seekers onshore, instead sending them to Christmas Island, an Australian territory in the Indian Ocean located more than 2500 kilometres north-west of Perth. But the processing facility on the island originally had been designed to house just 400 people and was struggling to cope with the surge in boat people. In a federal election year, the recently elected Liberal leader Tony Abbott identified the political potential of the asylum-seeker issue. He was determined to depict Labor, and especially prime minister Rudd, as unfit to protect Australia's borders.

By April 2010, the refugee issue was dominating media headlines. The Christmas Island detention centre had exceeded its capacity, the boats continued to come, and the battlelines were drawn for a bitter election fight. For both humanitarian and national security reasons, Australians overwhelmingly wanted the boats to stop. Asylum seekers were dying at sea. Scott Morrison saw an opportunity to capitalise on the rising community anger and promised stronger border security measures should the Coalition be elected.

It was about this time that Morrison's social circle and factional allegiances in Canberra started to shift. Morrison had turned on Turnbull, whose support came from the moderate faction, but he was never truly trusted by the NSW right, where Senator Concetta Fierravanti-Wells powerfully controlled the numbers; she was – and remains – suspicious of Morrison following both the Wentworth and Cook preselection battles. Having loosely aligned himself with the moderate faction during his initial preselection battle and on his arrival in federal parliament, but exhibiting few characteristics of a social progressive, Morrison joined a new faction known at first as the conservative progressives. The group – which included Queensland MP Stuart Robert and NSW MP Alex Hawke – formed in the wake of Abbott's leadership victory. Unlike those who belonged to the more ideologically driven factions, its members were drawn together by their age, ambition and, in many cases, a genuinely held Christian faith. However, long-serving conservatives were suspicious of the new group, claiming its participants had firmly hitched their political coat-tails to Abbott's right agenda solely in the pursuit of power. 'They describe themselves as Centre Right, but they are nothing,' said one heavily factional NSW MP. 'Hawke and his little grouping are all about power. There is nothing ideological about them.' Morrison's language had also changed – he was now toeing the Abbott line, showing himself as being tough when it came to national security.

Throughout his career, Morrison has been drawn to power. As a young tourism industry lobbyist, he saw Bruce Baird, a moderate Liberal, as a powerful ally and jumped to his rival lobby group when he understood the opportunities Baird could offer. In New Zealand, he latched onto then tourism minister Murray McCully, going to war with the board in order to please the boss.

The so-called Morrison–Hawke faction was, at its core, driven by pragmatism and the pursuit of power. Over the years it would grow to include MPs with quite differing outlooks, such as Western Australian Steve Irons, NSW federal politicians like Hollie Hughes, Melissa McIntosh and Lucy Wicks, and even Jim Molan, whose support base also includes the hard right. More senior members of the Liberal Party have long been sceptical of this unorthodox grouping, whose members cross factional lines. One former Liberal MP who firmly identifies as a conservative says Morrison is 'the perfect expression of the Hawke faction', describing the collective as 'political sluts' – an unedifying term that refers to the faction members' ability to align themselves with different groupings. 'They are lacking any ideological or meaningful content,' continues the conservative MP. 'A politician has to have something they believe in beyond power, a reason for being.'

According to more heavily factionalised MPs, the members of this group share a certain ideological plasticity, meaning they adapt their views to their environment. Outside of political circles, this could perhaps be regarded as a better way of representing the large number of Australians who consider themselves somewhere in the middle of the political spectrum. In Canberra, however, this idea is met with caution.

* * *

Throughout 2010, Labor was in turmoil. Abbott and Morrison were proving themselves to be ruthless opponents when it came to immigration policy. Their hardline stance was rewarded, with voters backing them in almost every public opinion poll on the issue, and the asylum-seeker issue ate away at Kevin Rudd's prime ministership. Finally, in June, deputy prime minister Julia Gillard emailed Rudd with concerns about the government's performance, particularly its asylum-seeker policies. Gillard believed the issue was driving voters away from the government and that there was a growing perception Labor had lost control of the country's borders. Two days after her communique, Gillard was sworn in as Australia's first female prime minister, having successfully challenged Rudd – he had ruled himself out of the contest when it became clear he no longer had the numbers to remain leader.

Three weeks later, Gillard called an election for 21 August, bracing herself for a tough fight on climate change, public debt and, of course, the asylum-seeker issue. In an attempt to stem the numbers of those trying to reach Australia by boat, which had surged to more than 4000 in the previous twelve months, Gillard announced a plan to create a refugee-processing centre in East Timor to house people seeking asylum while their credentials were checked. By contrast, Tony Abbott pitched a much more uncompromising approach, pledging to turn back any boat intercepted on its way to Australia. The Coalition would also restore the so-called 'Pacific solution' established by John Howard, which would see new arrivals placed in detention centres in Pacific states that included Nauru and Papua New Guinea.

At the beginning of the election campaign, the polls predicted Gillard would win, albeit with a reduced majority. But Labor's efforts were hampered by Cabinet leaks designed to destroy Gillard's credibility and hurt her election chances. The most damaging leak, which occurred during the second week of the campaign, revealed that Gillard had argued against introducing a paid parental leave scheme and boosting the age pension. The Opposition also was relentless, constantly attacking Labor on climate change, asylum seekers and health care. Subsequently, on election day, Labor suffered a 2.6 per cent swing on the two-party preferred vote, putting it only slightly ahead of the Coalition on the national vote. And Kevin Rudd's home state of Queensland turned against Labor, with the Coalition picking up seven seats in the Sunshine State. The equation was that, to govern outright, Labor needed seventy-six seats out of the 150 in the House of Representatives.

After intense negotiations, Greens MP Adam Bandt and Tasmanian independent Andrew Wilkie locked in behind Labor, ending more than two weeks of political deadlock following the inconclusive election result. The ALP now needed the support of the last two independents – Rob Oakeshott in Lyne and Tony Windsor in New England – to form government. Oakeshott and Windsor both represented regional NSW seats and had been members of the National Party in the past; political pundits, politicians and even many voters assumed they'd side with the Coalition. But the two men surprised everyone when they threw their support behind Julia Gillard, allowing Labor to hold on to power.

The finely balanced federal parliament descended into chaos. Gillard was hammered for pushing ahead with an ETS, which the Coalition labelled a carbon tax, after vowing she wouldn't do so during the election campaign. Opposition leader Abbott aggressively hounded Labor over the asylum-seeker issue and the so-called carbon tax, synthesising two highly complex issues into the three-word slogans 'Stop the boats' and 'Axe the tax'. Then, on 15 December 2010, tragedy struck off the coast of Christmas Island when a rickety fishing boat carrying some ninety asylum seekers, mainly from Iraq and Iran, was pounded against the limestone cliffs of Flying Fish Cove and smashed apart by the raging sea. Forty-eight people aboard the boat were killed; forty-two were rescued. In this calamity, Morrison saw political opportunity, leading him to take a heartless misstep that nearly cost him his job.

* * *

Following the disaster off Christmas Island, the Gillard government agreed to fly seven survivors to Sydney to bury family members. Among them were two fathers who had lost infant children and whose wives were missing, feared drowned. They had dreamed of a better life in Australia, but now, all alone, they faced the unthinkable task of farewelling their loved ones.

This wasn't a lavish affair. The Immigration Department had paid for flights and one night's accommodation for the grieving relatives, who were under a constant police escort. Yet, feeling bulletproof on Sydney radio station 2GB, a trap he would fall into time and time again, Scott Morrison attacked the government for flying detainees from Christmas Island to attend the funerals. He claimed it raised security issues and showed the government doesn't understand the value of the taxpayer's money, saying:

If people wanted to attend the funeral service from Sydney, for example, who may have been relatives of those who wanted these funeral services, well, they could have held the service on Christmas Island and like any other Australian who would have wanted to go to the funeral of someone close to them, they would have paid for themselves to get on a plane and go there.

The comments exposed deep divisions within the Liberal Party, as moderates and some conservatives distanced themselves from the hardline approach taken by Morrison. The brawl spilled into the public realm when Joe Hockey, no friend of Scott Morrison's, rejected the accusation that the government had simply wasted taxpayers' money on the funerals of people who had died off Christmas Island:

I would never seek to deny a parent or a child from saying goodbye to their relative. No matter what the colour of your skin, no matter

what the nature of your faith, if your child has died or a father has
died, you want to be there for the ceremony to say goodbye, and I
totally understand the importance of this to those families. I think
we, as a compassionate nation, have an obligation to ensure that we
retain our humanity during what is a very difficult policy debate.

The criticism continued. Bruce Baird, whom Morrison regarded as one of his political mentors, said that the current Member for Cook lacked compassion: 'I am disappointed that my successor would take such an approach.' Victorian Liberal senator Judith Troeth said: 'These are babies who died in the direst of circumstances, and I would have thought that decent human compassion would want the burials to be in accordance with family wishes.'

This moment marked a shift in Morrison's politics. He made a choice to be tough on national borders and in doing so showed little humanity. It also sent a signal that he was now more closely aligned with the Liberal Party's hard right, although they would never accept him as a member. But there would be no going back to his original moderate roots. Morrison's heartless response to what had happened off Christmas Island left many people mystified as to how he reconciled such a position with his Christian faith. Morrison has since justified his stance as necessary in order to stop the people-smuggling trade:

Those who were thinking of making the voyage and, more
importantly, those who were thinking or running the smuggling,

needed to understand that if we were elected, their worst nightmare
had arrived. That was the only way to stop them. When you
are dealing with life and death consequences there are no simple
answers ... one of the things I learnt from my father is that crooks
are crooks, and they will keep going until you stop them. It was
never about having a position on the victims of the crooks.

Several days after airing his disapproval over how 'taxpayers' money' had been spent on the funerals, and under intense pressure from colleagues and the media, Morrison attempted to wind back his comments, but he refused to withdraw them. 'The timing of my comments over the last twenty-four hours was insensitive and was inappropriate,' he told 2GB. 'I have to show a little more compassion than I did yesterday. I am happy to admit that.'

As the furore continued, Morrison came under renewed pressure when some of his colleagues leaked damaging details of an internal discussion in which he had allegedly also recommended the Coalition capitalise on growing public concern about Muslim immigration. According to several former colleagues who were present at that meeting, Morrison told the shadow Cabinet that there was a sense of worry within the community about Muslim arrivals, and the Liberals could use it as a way to attack Labor. At the time, the only member of Abbott's ministry to publicly detail the conversation and confirm Morrison's contribution, albeit hedging in regard to the substance of it, was then finance spokesman Andrew Robb, who said: 'I'm sure he meant we should engage in a constructive way. If I'd thought he was saying anything else, that meeting would still be going on.'

Morrison the politician survived the controversy, but he lost his reputation as a moderate, compassionate Christian.

* * *

Luckily for Morrison, the Gillard government was in a death spiral, allowing him to quickly recover. Between 2008 and 2013, more than 50,000 asylum seekers would arrive in Australia by boat. In May 2011, the Gillard government announced that unlawful arrivals would not be processed in Australia, denying them the legal protections granted to refugees. Instead, they would be sent to Malaysia, where a deal had been brokered whereby that country would accept 800 asylum seekers for processing by the UN. In exchange, Australia would take 4000 approved refugees, certified by the UNHCR. The policy was challenged in the High Court, with the full bench blocking the removal of asylum seekers to Malaysia.

Unlikely bedfellows the Greens and the Coalition had tried to find a way to block the so-called 'Malaysia solution', with Scott Morrison working feverishly to woo several crossbenchers to demand amendments or vote against the legislation. The court's decision forced Labor to negotiate with the Opposition to pass enabling legislation in the Senate, but Abbott remained utterly defiant. Privately, Cabinet was split on the policy, with some ministers arguing the Coalition should support it with amendments. Ministers report that Morrison was open to the Opposition doing so, but Abbott refused to do anything to stem the flow of boats. Ultimately, the government was forced to withdraw the bill. Such chaos had become the theme of the forty-third parliament.

Behind the scenes, Morrison was working on a new policy to further wedge Labor on asylum seekers. He sought advice from his old friend and ally Stuart Robert, a Queensland MP and former army officer who was also Morrison's flatmate in Canberra during parliamentary sitting weeks. Robert introduced Morrison to retired major-general Jim Molan, a former military attaché in Jakarta and, in 2004, chief of operations of allied forces in Iraq. Along with Abbott's adviser Andrew Shearer and Morrison's chief of staff Bob Correll, a former high-ranking immigration deputy secretary who'd been sacked by Labor immigration minister Chris Bowen two years earlier, they drew up a blueprint for what would become Operation Sovereign Borders, which would see border protection come under the command of a three-star military officer.

In June 2013, with support for Julia Gillard waning, Kevin Rudd challenged her in order to retake the ALP leadership: he won by fifty-seven votes to forty-five. Rudd had remained popular with the general public during Gillard's stint in the top job and his return to the prime ministership delivered a boost to Labor's primary vote. And while the Coalition remained ahead in the two-party-preferred poll, Rudd was ahead of Abbott as preferred prime minister.

At this time, Scott Morrison and Malcolm Turnbull had lunch at Beppi's, one of Sydney's top Italian eateries. Four years had passed since Morrison, then a backbencher, had visited Turnbull's office to withdraw his support for Turnbull's leadership. Now, he appeared to be regretting that decision. According to Turnbull, Morrison floated the idea of reinstalling Turnbull as Coalition leader as a way of countering Rudd's popularity with the public. Turnbull has since insisted: 'I told him I'd keep my head down – it was all too late; we had to do the best we could with Abbott.' Indeed, there was no time: on 4 August, Rudd called the next election.

At the polls on 7 September 2013, Labor recorded its lowest primary vote in a century. There was a two-party-preferred swing to the Coalition of 3.6 per cent. The Rudd government was out, Tony Abbott was prime minister and Scott Morrison was to be sworn in as immigration minister six years after he was first elected as the Member for Cook.

Few people in Canberra or across the wider public knew who Scott Morrison was. He was an outsider, someone without a power base, not in the Liberal leadership group. Colleagues from this time say that while Morrison was regarded positively, he wasn't considered a heavy hitter. 'He had no media profile, he was clunky, a bit goofy and wasn't a great media or parliamentary performer,' observes a former Abbott government frontbencher. Yet with all of this working against him, he was nonetheless thrust into the public spotlight as the man who would stop the boats. Countless colleagues point to this as Morrison's 'lightbulb moment', when he realised his opportunity to rise through the ranks had arrived. And that's exactly what he did.

A matter of days after the election, the Coalition implemented its tough new asylum seeker policy – Operation Sovereign Borders – in an effort to fulfil its election promise and 'stop the boats'. Scott Morrison was the public face of the secretive, military-led operation to prevent asylum seekers from reaching Australian shores. The policy would be implemented by former Special Air Service commander and deputy national security adviser Angus Campbell, who was the deputy chief of army at the time. The Coalition's plan effectively was to militarise the fight against people smuggling by flooding Australia's waters with patrol vessels which would find asylum-seeker boats and, when it was safe to do so, drag them back out to sea. Visa conditions and offshore processing would also be toughened.

Initially, Morrison agreed to hold weekly press briefings to update journalists and the public on the operation which was, after all, a key election promise. But at the first briefing on 23 September, he baffled the attendant media by refusing to reveal if any asylum-seeker boats had been turned around, claiming that was an 'operational matter'. Instead, Morrison said, the government would provide an update on how many boats had arrived, including the numbers of asylum seekers on board. It clearly was a deliberate strategy. The masterminds of Operation Sovereign Borders didn't want to give any advantage to the people smugglers by releasing information about tactics, fleet numbers or the location of intercepts.

Over the next few months, Morrison further reduced the flow of information regarding Operation Sovereign Borders. Public briefings were initially replaced by email updates and eventually abandoned altogether, with Morrison saying the so-called establishment phase of the operation was over. Australians were merely told the number of asylum seekers arriving in Australia by boat was dropping, with little evidence given to substantiate the claim. As scrutiny grew, Morrison increasingly used the catchphrases 'operational' and 'on-water' matters to deflect difficult questions, a tactic he would take with him as he climbed the ladder of government, adapting the terminology to suit his other portfolios.

One-time Border Force boss and deputy Customs chief Roman Quaedvlieg insists that Operation Sovereign Borders wouldn't have been a success if the government had failed to hammer home the message that Australia was 'closed'. As a former marketing man, Scott Morrison was the perfect person to take on this role. Lost on no-one was the irony that Morrison's messaging was in stark contrast to the slogans he'd championed at Tourism Australia, inviting foreigners to visit.

While information in Australia was scarce, Morrison worked overtime to make sure that people in remote Middle Eastern villages or bustling Asian cities knew that Australia would send them back home if they attempted to arrive here by boat. Cabinet colleagues say Morrison was keen to impress the base with his tough policies and ensure he didn't flinch while implementing this uncompromising stance.

Cabinet ministers from the time describe Morrison as both hardworking but somewhat naive regarding the processes of government and managing a bureaucracy. And many senior bureaucrats felt uncomfortable with the harder edges of the Operation Sovereign Borders policy. 'Day in, day out, they would push back and say it's too hard, it's not working,' says one former Liberal insider. Sometimes, Morrison would bring these views to Cabinet without a solution. Senior ministers recall Tony Abbott demanding he return with a different answer.

In 2014, the Coalition's approach appeared to be at serious risk of faltering when Indonesia demanded Australia change its asylum policy due to Navy boats breaching Indonesian territorial waters on several occasions. Indeed, Indonesia was becoming increasingly annoyed with Australia's conduct in trying to stop the people-smuggling trade. Consequently, Australia's bilateral relationship with that country suffered a serious setback. It was Jim Molan who found a solution via a group of Indonesia army generals whom he knew personally from his time as a military attaché in Jakarta; it offered Australia a way to negotiate through the back door.

It's clear that policy problems and solutions such as this shaped Morrison's understanding of and approach to future problems in the portfolios he oversaw. As he has navigated government and risen through the ranks, Morrison has proven himself to be the great pragmatist and problem-solver. Senior public servants recall him arriving at meetings with pens and blank sheets of paper and asking for their most absurd ideas. Nothing, however bizarre, was off-limits. He has since developed a strong working relationship with some of Canberra's most senior public servants, who describe him as flexible when it comes to initial policy formation, though ultimately unwilling to accept 'no' for an answer.

* * *

Little was known about the boats that never made it to Australia but were turned back towards their port of origin, a fraught operation that relied on the cooperation of South-East Asian governments. What was clear was that the policies of successive governments not to allow anyone who arrived by boat to settle in Australia left several thousand asylum seekers on Nauru and Papua New Guinea's Manus Island. Many asylum seekers died while languishing in these detention centres.

As immigration minister, Morrison searched for another country in which to resettle the 1852 asylum seekers in need of a safe haven. In 2014, he brokered a deal with Cambodian Minister of the Interior Sar Kheng to allow refugees processed on Nauru to resettle in Cambodia in exchange for $40 million in foreign aid. The pair celebrated the agreement with a glass of champagne, with both the agreement and the celebration heavily criticised at the time. It turned out to be an expensive and unpopular deal, with only a handful of asylum seekers volunteering to live in Cambodia.

Also in 2014, towards the end of his time as immigration minister, one of Morrison's constituents from the seat of Cook gave him a trophy in the form of an asylum-seeker boat with the words 'I Stopped These' emblazoned on the side. Impressed, Morrison commissioned more with the same slogan, to hand out as gifts to the team involved in implementing the Operation Sovereign Borders policy, including Quaedvlieg. Quaedvlieg later tweeted a photo of the trophy, which he described as a 'bit gimmicky' and claimed downplayed the role of those on the frontline of the boat turnback policy, whose safety was at risk.

State Library of Victoria

Shutterstock

ALIA

MARY GILMORE

JENNIE

Politics in the DNA: Scott Morrison's great great aunt, the socialist Dame Mary Gilmore, appears on Australia's $10 note, and, according to former prime minister John Curtin, 'helped mould the national character'. While Morrison's politics differ quite significantly from his ancestor's, he believes her radical outlook was symptomatic of her generation's fight for a better life.

Above: Scott Morrison's mother, Marion Elsie Smith, and father, John Douglas Morrison, married in 1963 and moved in with John's Aunty Frank, who lived in a house in the beachside suburb of Bronte in Sydney's east, where Morrison grew up. Morrison believes his parents would have had to move to western Sydney if it weren't for Frank's gracious offer.

Left: One of the greatest influences on Scott Morrison is his father. John Morrison had a passion for community service, and served on Waverley Council for two decades, including a stint as mayor. Scott describes his father as 'larger than life' and the 'knockabout bloke', adding that 'everyone knew who Dad was'.

Right: Morrison's youth was largely shaped by his parents, the church and his local community. His boyhood wasn't one of struggle, nor was it grand in any sense. His parents worked hard to provide their children with considerable opportunities. They instilled a strong sense of community in their children, with less regard for the concerns of the wider world.

Left: Scott Morrison met Jenny Warren on a church youth group trip to Luna Park. Jenny has since described the young Scott Morrison as 'really confident' and 'good looking'.

Morrison (top row, second from left) attended Sydney Boys High, a selective-entry institution. But he was more sporty than academic, making the Firsts in both rowing and rugby union. One former classmate recalls, 'We were probably the sporting jocks to tell you the truth.'

Kristi Miller/Newspix

Only after a fourteen-year battle with infertility did Jenny fall pregnant with her and Scott's first child. She gave birth to Abbey Rose Morrison, pictured here, in 2007. Morrison said that being blessed with a baby reminded him that God was 'in charge', a belief he reiterated when addressing parliament following the birth of his second daughter, Lily, in 2009.

Michelle Mossop/Australian Financial Review

As Managing Director of Tourism Australia, Morrison presided over the advertising campaign that asked the world, 'So where the bloody hell are you?' But Morrison's controversial stint in the role and his poor working relationship with federal tourism minister Fran Bailey would lead to his removal from the position in August 2006. Tourism Australia issued a statement saying Morrison had 'agreed to depart'. While the board praised his service, Bailey's silence was deafening.

Morrison didn't live in the electorate of Cook in the Sutherland Shire prior to his preselection, but has since made 'The Shire' not only his home but part of his persona. And while Morrison has been called out as being overly eager to convince others that he is a Shire man through and through, he cannot be faulted for the way he has embraced his electorate. 'I have always been most at home in suburbia,' Morrison says. 'That's why I like The Shire so much … It's classic suburbia.'

While Morrison acknowledges that his faith is an integral part of his life, he insists the Bible is not a policy handbook, saying, 'My personal faith in Jesus Christ is not a political agenda.' It is, however, widely believed that Morrison's strong faith worked in his favour in the 2019 election campaign, as it gave religious communities confidence he was on their side.

On the campaign trail, Morrison contrasted his brutal attacks on Bill Shorten with his soft, daggy dad image. His closest friends defend this selling point, claiming that it is true to Morrison's character – albeit a little overdone. However, colleagues from Canberra roll their eyes when asked about the daggy dad persona. 'It's completely exaggerated,' says one long-serving Liberal Cabinet minister. 'He's actually a highly political person and he plays all the political games.'

AAP/Lukas Coch

Left: 'Anything but immigration,' Jenny had said to her husband prior to Morrison's appointment as Shadow Minister for Immigration and Citizenship. Jenny's reservations were well-founded – immigration is considered one of the most challenging and vexed portfolios in politics. Morrison did not survive it unscathed, with his strongest critics arguing that his hardline stance on asylum seekers ran counter to his claimed Christian belief in justice for all.

Right: Morrison's critics labelled him 'Scotty from Marketing', which was meant to be a derogatory term but turned out to be the perfect moniker. In the lead-up to the 2019 election, Morrison seemed to be successfully pitching himself as a suburban dad who had taken over the Coalition leadership in a Steven Bradbury–style win. 'Morrison was on the TV every night hitting balls and looking like a moron and some of our people couldn't believe their luck. But Morrison's images were always positive, always ran first and some of us were worried,' says one Labor campaigner.

AAP/Mick Tsikas

AAP/Lukas Coch

Morrison was sworn in as Prime Minister by governor-general Sir Peter Cosgrove in a small night-time ceremony. With Morrison were his numbers men, Stuart Robert and Ben Morton, as well as Jenny and his two daughters, eleven-year-old Abbey and nine-year-old Lily, who'd all made the trip down from Sydney to be by his side and pose for the traditional photos on the steps of Government House.

Pictured here with Gillon McLachlan: After Scott Morrison became the Liberal Party's new leader in the spill of 2018, a ballot was held for the position of deputy leader, and was won by Victorian Liberal Josh Frydenberg. After the vote, Morrison asked Frydenberg what portfolio he wanted. Frydenberg wanted to be treasurer. Morrison knew well the power that came with overseeing the Treasury portfolio and he was happy for Frydenberg to take the job. Theirs would become the partnership behind the government's JobKeeper scheme which was rolled out once the pandemic hit in 2020.

There's no denying that the 'women issue' has plagued Morrison for much of his prime ministership, particularly in early 2021. In mid-March, thousands of women called for gender equality and justice for victims of sexual assault at protests across Australia under the banner March4Justice. Much of the anger was directed at Morrison, who made matters worse when, while attempting to deflect the issue by praising Australia's democracy, told parliament that protests elsewhere were being 'met with bullets'. On Twitter and in certain parts of the media, his comment was painted as a perceived threat. It wasn't, of course, but it was way off the mark.

Chapter Nine

Trust

Eight months after the 2013 federal election, the wheels started falling off the new government. Tony Abbott's first attempt at budget repair in May 2014 was roundly rejected by voters: it was unequitable, broke promises, and introduced new taxes while reining in spending on schools, pensioners and hospitals. His government would never recover. Abbott's fighting instincts had suited him in opposition, but now he was finding it difficult to distinguish what his government stood for instead of what it was against. There also were complaints about his tendency to make 'captain's calls', making decisions without consulting Cabinet colleagues.

According to confidants, Morrison first raised the idea of a change of Liberal leadership within twelve months of Abbott's historic election win. Morrison had voted for Abbott to replace Turnbull as Opposition leader, but he is driven by polling and by June 2014, things were looking grim. Newspoll had the Coalition trailing Labor by a margin of forty-five to fifty-five, and Abbott was trailing Opposition leader Bill Shorten as preferred prime minister. Like many of his colleagues, Morrison didn't want to be a one-term Cabinet minister. Unlike many of his colleagues, Morrison understands the power of the media and ingratiated himself with key News Corporation journalists in the press gallery as well as conservative radio hosts. It's wise for an ambitious minister to cultivate the media, but this can raise the ire of other MPs. Towards the end of 2014, many of Morrison's Cabinet colleagues started to suspect that he was, in some way, responsible for fuelling doubts about Abbott's leadership and Hockey's ability as treasurer. Abbott was unperturbed. He told colleagues, perhaps naively, that he was encouraged by the competition between his ministers.

In late December, Abbott announced a major ministerial reshuffle, which he said would 'refresh and reset the government' after a bruising first year. In that time, Morrison had delivered one of the more difficult and personally taxing policies: Operation Sovereign Borders. The hardline approach to asylum seekers had drawn widespread criticism from refugee and humanitarian groups, but it had largely stopped asylum-seeker boats from reaching Australia's shores and was therefore considered a huge success by the government. Those closest to Morrison say he was desperate for a promotion and believed himself deserving of one. The job he most wanted was treasurer, with the incumbent Joe Hockey severely wounded after the reaction to his first budget. But instead, Morrison was appointed the Minister for Social Services and tasked with delivering unpopular changes to pensions and unemployment benefits that were proving difficult to get through the Senate. The portfolio also was expanded to include families, child care and the Paid Parental Leave (PPL) scheme, and it saw Morrison invited to join the government's key Expenditure Review Committee, which helps craft the budget. It was spun as a reward for Morrison, who would now have a role in shaping the government's economic agenda, but in Cabinet terms it was a sideways step. As one colleague recalls, 'He was terribly unhappy, but he hid it well.'

Most of Morrison's colleagues believe he was pushing for either the defence or treasury portfolios, and that while he had made mistakes in immigration, particularly with his choice of language at times, he had done the job asked of him and should have been rewarded. And the prevailing view among the Cabinet ministers was that Morrison was sidelined in social services to take him out of the limelight. 'Abbott and [chief of staff Peta] Credlin thought, "We don't want another power centre," and Morrison knew that was the reason,' says one minister. But those familiar with the inner workings of the Abbott government deny this was the case. They argue that Morrison had performed well in immigration but needed a domestic portfolio to boost his economic credentials. As one insider says, 'Tony was conscious that the hard edge of immigration would stick with Morrison and he needed to soften those edges. He also wanted to reform social services and knew Morrison had the communications ability to sell it.'

In the weeks leading up to the ministerial rearrangement, Morrison and Turnbull met up for dinner. According to Turnbull, Morrison was already of the view that Abbott would have to go by the middle of 2015 if his performance didn't improve. According to Cabinet ministers who served alongside him in the Abbott government, being overlooked in the reshuffle only made Morrison's need to get rid of Abbott all the more urgent. That summer, Morrison's political allies fielded calls from him as he prosecuted the argument that Abbott should be given less time than originally thought to improve the prospects of the government 'He seemed to have made up his mind, he [Abbott] had to go,' one Cabinet colleague recalls.

While Morrison primarily seemed angry about his new role in social services, he also was fearful that if Abbott were to remain prime minister, the Coalition would be voted out at the first opportunity. As has been the case over much of his professional career, Morrison was willing to align himself with the person who would give him the best chance of success: Turnbull. He also had a second target in his sights.

* * *

Under Abbott, NSW Liberal MP Joe Hockey had been appointed treasurer and miraculously managed to hold on to the high-profile role after the December 2014 ministerial changes – miraculously because much of the Abbott government's misfortune had been triggered by its first budget.

Few Liberal MPs would deny that the decisions taken for that first budget in 2014 were anything less than electorally catastrophic or that the situation was significantly worsened by Abbott and Hockey repeatedly denying that they had broken any election promises. And the Abbott–Hockey defence wasn't just a public front but a narrative the pair reiterated to Cabinet ministers who were staring at the red ink on their portfolio balance sheets. 'We were thinking, "How are we meant to pretend there are no cuts when that clearly wasn't true?",' says one former Abbott government minister.

Abbott had been just as responsible as Hockey for many of the unpopular measures, but the treasurer was the public face of the budget and made numerous gaffes in his endless battle to defend his legacy. Hockey declared the age of entitlement was over and characterised Australia as a nation of 'lifters' (those who were employed), not 'leaners' (those receiving welfare). While attempting to sell the indexation of the petrol excise, he tried to argue that the tax would only really affect high-income earners because 'the poorest people either don't have cars or actually don't drive very far in many cases'. To this day, that comment is used inside ministerial offices to gauge the extent to which a minister has cocked something up. When questioned about skyrocketing house prices that were preventing a generation of workers from entering the property market, Hockey advised people to 'get a good job that pays good money'. It all contributed to the perception that Joe Hockey was not in touch with middle Australia, a connection that Scott Morrison liked to pride himself on. And when Hockey was snapped smoking a cigar on a Parliament House balcony during the budget preparations, it further fuelled the idea that he was ill-suited to the role of treasurer and too removed from the Australian public.

Colleagues of Hockey from this time describe him as fun and amicable, but many agree he was not a good fit for the Treasury portfolio. 'He was bombastic and not across any of the detail required for the role,' says one. Another says there was a common perception that Hockey was prone to pretending he understood economic theories that, in reality, he struggled with: 'He'd use jargon he thought would impress people, but it just made it clear he had no idea what he was talking about.' It seemed to many that Hockey was out of his depth, both naive and too self-assured. 'He genuinely believed his easygoing nature would be enough to protect him,' quips one former fellow Cabinet member.

But Hockey did possess two things that Scott Morrison wanted: the Treasury portfolio and more influence in the

NSW Liberal Party. One of the best characterisations of the Morrison–Hockey power tussle comes from a long-serving Liberal minister, who describes Morrison as a predator intent on dominance:

> *I could see Joe lacked the equipment he needed to protect himself.*
> *He was a like an injured elk in the forest hoping no-one would*
> *notice him. I thought, 'You're doomed.' But Hockey was aware of*
> *Morrison's ambitions, and regularly described him to colleagues as*
> *the 'most dangerous man in politics'.*

In a story that has become folklore in Canberra, Morrison is said to have approached Tony Abbott at the beginning of 2015 and demanded he get rid of Hockey. The story goes that Abbott proceeded to take full responsibility for the 2014 Budget and told Morrison that if Hockey went, he would have to go too. Morrison has always disputed this story, but ministers repeat who-said-what by rote. True or not, when it first became known, the story damaged Morrison's relationship with Abbott's office, which was now firmly of the view that he was trying to help Malcolm Turnbull return to the top job. What is certainly true is that Morrison had started compiling lists of which of his colleagues would support Abbott and who would support an alternative candidate for the leadership.

One of Abbott's greatest flaws, if you can call it that, is his loyalty. He liked Hockey and he was unwilling to drop his political ally to save his own prime ministership. That loyalty extended to Abbott's controversial chief of staff, Peta Credlin, whose wielding of power angered Liberal ministers and backbenchers. Some also blamed Abbott's misguided loyalty for his bizarre decision to grant Prince Philip a knighthood on Australia Day, which was widely regarded as an unusual priority. Liberal MPs could barely hide their derision – even Abbott's backers in the media thought it was an absurd idea. 'I think there was an element that he had told the Queen that he would, so he thought he'd better,' says one Cabinet minister. It was the tipping point.

* * *

Malcolm Turnbull has confirmed he had dinner with Morrison and their mutual friend Scott Briggs, chairman of the Cook electoral council, in early January 2015. Morrison may not have wanted the public to know that he was pushing for Abbott to go, but he certainly appeared to be lobbying colleagues on the need for change. It's a path favoured by political leadership candidates who want the top job for themselves one day: they pretend otherwise, acting as if they are being recruited for the role rather than actively pursuing it. Turnbull recalls Morrison suggesting that they commission polling from the Liberal Party's go-to pollster and strategist Mark Textor as to what policies the party would need to change if Abbott was deposed.

Colleagues report that Morrison viewed Abbott's position as untenable, but he was desperate not to be seen to be masterminding a plot to overthrow the prime minister. It's a widely held view among members of the former Abbott government that Morrison was torn between wanting the leadership for himself and accepting – albeit reluctantly – that it was not yet his time. At the dinner with Turnbull and Briggs, displaying his obsession with research, Morrison argued that Turnbull would not be accepted by certain sections of the right-wing media that Morrison himself had wooed. He was also suspicious of deputy leader and foreign minister Julie Bishop, regarding her as an obstacle to his own rise. Bishop, who doesn't have a high opinion of Morrison, has reportedly told colleagues that she was always confused as to why he loathed her so much. According to their Cabinet colleagues, she always viewed Morrison as deeply untrustworthy, and he felt the same way about her.

Morrison understood that if Turnbull were to take over the party's leadership, it would give him his best chance of taking over from Hockey as treasurer. It would also put him one step closer to the prime ministership. It wasn't the perfect scenario for a man who wanted to become prime minister, but it would have to do for now.

Weeks of rumours came to a head on 6 February 2015, when Liberal backbencher Luke Simpkins told his colleagues he had submitted a motion to the government whip to spill the positions of party leader and deputy leader. Morrison wasn't the one who pulled the trigger, but there was a high degree of suspicion among Abbott's supporters concerning his level of involvement. 'Tony didn't want to believe there were bigger powers at play, he wanted to believe it was some disgruntled backbenchers, but it was clear Scott was absolutely all over it,' says one former Abbott aide. Simpkins was backed by other Western Australians, including veteran Canning MP Don Randall and Steve Irons, another former flatmate and close friend of Scott Morrison's. The day before the spill, Turnbull, Bishop and Morrison agreed to vote against the motion but they would not necessarily encourage their factional allies to do the same.

On 9 February, the spill was defeated by sixty-one votes to thirty-nine. The Prime Minister's Office had briefed members of the Canberra press gallery that fewer than twenty MPs would vote for the spill, and instead almost double that number wanted him gone, even without a formal contender. The result appeared to gift Abbott more time to resuscitate his ailing prime ministership, but it would only be a matter of months before he would be replaced.

Within the Prime Minister's Office, there was growing angst about what role Morrison had played in the spill. The social services minister had been notably absent from the airwaves in the days before the vote, whereas a number of other ministers had publicly thrown their support behind the prime minister. Morrison also had not been among the protective throng of loyal MPs who had walked Tony Abbott to the party room vote. While it was unavoidable that he would lose Abbott's trust, he clearly didn't want to be directly linked to the attempted leadership coup, knowing that such a blemish on his reputation would haunt him and potentially prevent him from becoming prime minister in the future.

* * *

Morrison knew that if he kept his head down, he was likely to become treasurer should Turnbull eventually become prime minister, which seemed somewhat inevitable. Just as he had done as immigration minister, he was determined to work hard in his new portfolio of social services and continue to make a name for himself in politics.

As Opposition leader, Tony Abbott had unveiled a plan to pay working mums their salary up to a cap of $150,000 a year for six months after the birth of a child. The Paid Parental Leave scheme was meant to entice professional women to have more children and would be funded by a proposed increase in company tax, but it was expensive and viewed as unequitable because it meant that wealthy families would be better off than so-called battlers. Morrison, who regarded himself as having a unique understanding of middle Australia, had despised the policy, as had many of his colleagues. His new role as social services minister gave him a seat on the Expenditure Review Committee, which ticks off any policy that has implications for the budget. Using this new-found influence, he was able to lobby Abbott and Hockey to dump the toxic policy under the cover of budget repair. The experience also served as a kind of apprenticeship for the role of treasurer.

It was in the months following that first failed leadership coup that a series of leaks emerged from the Expenditure Review Committee, targeting the treasurer and foreign minister. In February 2015, it was reported that a plan to accelerate the taper rate for wealthy pensioners had been blocked by Hockey, who favoured a broad cut in the indexation rate of all age pensions. Then, in March, Bishop was left red-faced when *The Australian* revealed that the Expenditure Review Committee had just approved a cut to foreign aid for the May budget. And in April, it was reported that Hockey had missed a crucial five-hour Expenditure Review Committee meeting due to a delayed flight, meaning the committee had been unable to finalise key budget decisions. It's unclear who was responsible for the leaks but, unfairly or not, many of his Cabinet colleagues pointed their fingers at Morrison.

With Hockey still damaged from the 2014 Budget fallout, Morrison manoeuvred his way into the role of chief salesman in the lead-up to the 2015 Budget. He gave more than a dozen interviews while Hockey was kept out of the spotlight ahead of the Abbott government's make-or-break second budget. While colleagues questioned how much they could trust Morrison, they were wooed by his negotiation skills. Morrison re-engaged with the Greens and the welfare lobby to seek support for an assets test that would boost pensions for low- and middle-income earners but take away the part-pension for wealthier people. As social services minister, Morrison could see the advantage in pitching himself as someone who could embrace policies that blended conservative compassion with economic pragmatism. This contrasted with Hockey, who had been framed as heartless and cruel. To achieve this, Morrison lobbied for millions of dollars in increased childcare spending to lessen the blow of the 2014 Budget. But it was tied to cuts to family tax benefits that would affect hundreds of thousands of households, which had been blocked by Labor in the Senate.

The 2015 Budget, which was presented to the House of Representatives on 12 May, was well received, at least compared with the 2014 Budget. But leaks, disunity and scandals continued to damage the Coalition, and the appetite to remove Hockey and his protector Abbott only grew. The bitterness between Hockey and Morrison was so overt that, ahead of Hockey's post-budget address at the National Press Club, a senior member of Morrison's staff walked the halls of the press gallery, briefing journalists on questions that would expose Hockey's weaknesses on the national stage.

Chapter Ten

Thirty Newspolls

In the lead-up to the Liberal leadership challenge of September 2015, Scott Morrison publicly supported Tony Abbott, but in private, few of his colleagues believed it. The Prime Minister's Office had become somewhat suspicious of Morrison since what had been called the 'empty chair' spill seven months earlier: Abbott had faced a spill motion but there were no other contenders for his job. For one thing, the media were repeatedly tipping Morrison to take on the Treasury portfolio if Malcolm Turnbull were to become prime minister. Furthermore, for months Morrison had spent evenings dining with Turnbull while in Canberra for parliamentary sitting weeks, including private dinners at Turnbull's apartment on

Kingston Foreshore. Internal party brawls over factions and leadership often can be predicted weeks before they occur by watching the goings-on after dark in Canberra's inner south. MPs, staffers and party insiders usually stay and eat in the lakeside suburbs of Kingston, Manuka and Barton. This area is also home to many members of the press gallery, who are prone to looking in the windows of local restaurants as they walk by to see who might be sharing a bottle of red or some Shantung lamb.

Morrison hadn't changed the position he'd held for the past year: Abbott needed to go. One night in mid-September, a group of plotters met at the Queanbeyan home of then Eden-Monaro MP Peter Hendy – Turnbull and Hendy were joined by fellow Liberals who shared the appetite for change, including Arthur Sinodinos, James McGrath, Scott Ryan, Mitch Fifield and Wyatt Roy. Further up Canberra Avenue, Morrison was at Parliament House, shoring up support for Turnbull. He didn't physically attend the dinner at Hendy's house, but the plotters knew he was on their side. It was a dangerous game. Morrison knew he was no longer trusted by Abbott, but he also knew that he couldn't risk being seen as duplicitous and publicly needed to keep his hands clean.

On 14 September, Turnbull visited Abbott after question time and told the prime minister he was going to put up his hand for the Liberal leadership. Following a heated exchange, Turnbull went to the Senate Courtyard – the site of much parliamentary treachery – and announced his intentions to the media. He gave Abbott's thirty consecutive Newspoll losses as the reason for challenging the prime minister, and he also promised a different style of leadership and policies that would respect the intelligence of voters. The Abbott and Turnbull camps then feverishly hit the phones to get promises of votes.

In a final desperate act, Abbott offered Morrison the position of Liberal deputy leader and suggested they run on a joint ticket; such a role would give Morrison the pick of any portfolio, meaning he could finally become treasurer. But Morrison wanted to be on the winning team and Turnbull had already promised him the Treasury job. The following morning, Malcolm Turnbull defeated Tony Abbott by fifty-four votes to forty-four. Morrison had voted for Abbott but he did not instruct any of his supporters to do the same, which ultimately delivered crucial support to Malcolm Turnbull.

Anyone who has observed party leadership spills over the years knows that the strongest feelings are reserved not for the ones who declare their hand early on, but for those who try to play both sides. For instance, in August 2018, when Malcolm Turnbull was deposed, he and his office felt more betrayed by frontbenchers like Greg Hunt and Mathias Cormann than by Peter Dutton, the man who orchestrated and ran in the failed coup. Such was the case with Abbott and his closest supporters, who believed Morrison had deceived them. To this day, Abbott supporters contend that Morrison was directly asked by both Abbott and his office whether he thought the prime minister was in any trouble but failed to be up-front. 'At least Malcolm was open about his ambition,' says one former Abbott staffer. Morrison sees it differently: his strategy was to keep a low profile because he didn't want to be caught up in the bitter fallout of the spill.

* * *

To his colleagues, Morrison seemed like a much more natural fit with the Treasury portfolio than his predecessor, Joe Hockey, who was dispatched to Washington to take on the role of Australian Ambassador to the United States. One Cabinet minister says that Morrison 'was much more capable than Joe. He was much more methodical, much more across the detail, and if he wasn't across the detail, he would ask questions about it and respond sensibly'. Importantly, say some of his peers, he never panicked but instead remained calm and analytical. Hockey, on the other hand, 'was a good salesperson but he wasn't good on detail'.

However, Morrison quickly attracted criticism for running policy through the media instead of tabling ideas in the Cabinet. Colleagues from this time referred to him as 'the Tabloid Treasurer'. One long-serving minister who worked alongside Morrison in the Turnbull Cabinet says:

All he was doing was going for a headline in the Daily Tele, *which was his bible, more so than the Christian Bible. He'd come running*

into meetings with a mad idea. It would take him a long time to
see that his idea didn't hold water, then he'd blame his staff or a
bureaucrat. He never went past the headline.

Another colleague describes Morrison as a 'populist' who would come up with seemingly easy solutions to hugely complex issues, adding: 'History shows that these so-called solutions have disastrous consequences, but they might be popular on the front page of newspapers for a minute.'

When MPs come to journalists with unsanctioned stories, it's usually for one (or more) of three reasons. There are those who feel that proper processes have been ignored and genuinely want to expose wrongdoing, such as whistleblowers. Then there are those who like to leak to ingratiate themselves with the external media and press gallery journalists and to boost their profiles. And some use the media to trial policy or publicise their ideas, offering up yarns to newspapers in exchange for favourable coverage. Morrison's colleagues argue he adheres to a toxic mix of the final two rationales.

Since arriving in Canberra, Morrison has cultivated his home-town newspaper the *Daily Telegraph* as well as fellow News Corp publication *The Australian*. There is nothing wrong with this, of course; any MP with a hint of ambition would do the same. But Morrison has taken it one step further. 'He has an inclination to approach policy problems utterly from a media a point of view,' says one former Cabinet colleague. 'He would workshop policy ideas with newspaper editors instead of his Cabinet colleagues.' Another former Coalition minister describes Morrison as being 'beholden to the readers of the *Tele*' in the same way other MPs feel bound to factional bosses or union heavyweights. Just as when he had angered Fran Bailey when unapproved tourism stories appeared in the newspapers, Morrison wasn't concerned about annoying his Cabinet colleagues by promoting new policies in the media.

Morrison's preference for frontrunning economic policy through the media infuriated prime minister Malcolm Turnbull, who would complain about his treasurer to the other Cabinet ministers. One example from those early days of the Turnbull government involves Treasury officials trying to float an idea they had taken to the previous treasurer. Under the proposal, which Hockey never took to Cabinet, the rate of the GST would rise from 10 per cent to 15 per cent, generating about $40 billion more in revenue over the four years of it being phased in. About one-third of the cash would go to the states and territories, with the rest enabling tax cuts and extra welfare measures. Hockey had only ever discussed the plan with Tony Abbott, whose leadership was already in strife and who wasn't prepared to pursue such a divisive policy. So when Scott Morrison became treasurer, department officials again pitched the idea of boosting or broadening the GST. Turnbull was open to the idea of tinkering with the GST, or at least was prepared to have it discussed in Cabinet. But, in early November 2015, the Treasury proposals suddenly appeared on the front page of the *Sunday Telegraph*. Any talk of the government increasing taxation was lethal, and this leak gave Labor a free whack at the government and damaged any chance of it attempting GST reform. 'It totally fucked us up,' says one Cabinet minister, explaining that such tactics 'stymied good policy debate'.

It's arguable that Morrison didn't see it this way. In taking policies straight to the media, he may have felt that he was gauging the public's interest so that the government didn't waste its time trying to sell unpopular proposals. But that's not how his colleagues saw it, and they grew increasingly wary of Morrison. 'It was an absolute nightmare,' says one long-serving Liberal minister. 'He saw it as essentially a form of policy development.' To make matters worse, Morrison would deny he'd had any role in backgrounding newspapers on policy proposals. One former colleague describes him as being like a naughty boy who walks out of a pantry covered in crumbs yet denies he has eaten any cookies: 'He is a terrible liar. Even if you catch him red-handed, it wouldn't matter.' Another minister takes a more pessimistic view, describing him as 'volatile, sly and untrustworthy'.

* * *

In 2016, eight months after becoming treasurer, Morrison handed down his first budget. It would be the first budget in more than sixty years whose release was brought forward.

This had been Turnbull's plan and not even Morrison knew about it beforehand. The treasurer had just left the studio of a Sydney radio station, where he'd assured his interviewer that the budget would be presented on the traditional date of the second Tuesday in May, when Turnbull let Morrison in on the plot via a Cabinet phone hook-up. Bringing the budget forward by a week would allow Turnbull to recall both houses of parliament for an unscheduled sitting to deal with industrial relations legislation. Anticipating that the Senate would reject the legislation in question, Turnbull planned to use the stalemate to trigger a double-dissolution election for 2 July, just ten months into the term of his government.

It was the sort of parliamentary trickiness that Turnbull loved but punters despise. 'All this mad lawyer stuff like proroguing [ending a session of] the parliament that they thought was so clever, was confusing the hell out of the punters,' says one Liberal MP. Despite the confusion around this mechanism, Turnbull's plan worked, insofar as it allowed him to go to an early election to break the impasse over the industrial relations legislation. Budgets are always important but this one would shape the government's narrative in the lead-up to the July poll. Morrison had coveted the job of treasurer and now he was under enormous pressure to deliver.

Like many treasurers before him, Morrison wanted to be the architect of tax reform. With any GST proposal considered unpalatable, he toyed with the idea of superannuation changes and reining in housing concessions such as negative gearing. Morrison, the arch defender of middle Australia, believed Labor would gain ground by pitching these policies as overly generous to the well-off. According to one Cabinet minister, the treasurer was particularly passionate about the government doing more to help younger Australians buy their first home. He floated the idea of reforming negative gearing, which allows home owners to offset the net rental loss on a property against their income, or even allowing younger Australians to use their superannuation to buy property. Acquiring real estate is considered the great Australian dream. But any policy that made it easier for some voters to buy homes had the potential to hurt another cohort of aspirational voters who were using generous government concessions to build their own wealth. There was significant political risk in playing around with this arrangement. Besides, there were other priorities.

The Coalition was severely damaged by the first Abbott–Hockey budget, which had been designed to get the government back on track after years of what then treasurer Joe Hockey called Labor mismanagement. But dumping the unpopular measures that still lingered was hardly going to be enough for Morrison's budget to succeed – without isolating its base, the government had to show that it was fair, that the lesson had been learned. To distinguish himself from Hockey, Morrison, with the help of assistant treasurer Kelly O'Dwyer, engaged welfare groups and unions as part of their consultation in the lead-up to the 2016 Budget. Treasury officials report that Morrison was a hard worker during this period, and more than willing to listen to policy ideas pitched by bureaucrats.

Morrison's budget ultimately included a cut in the company tax rate from 30 per cent to 25 per cent over a decade, starting with small and family-run businesses. To counter the sweetener for the so-called big end of town, the Turnbull government also promised to launch a crackdown on global tax avoidance and wind back some of the more generous superannuation concessions exploited by wealthier Australians – a policy that would come back to bite it. Morrison's ambition for large structural reform was thwarted by pragmatism: an election was just around the corner and the government didn't want to scare voters.

One of Morrison's great blind spots as a politician has always been regional Australia. This is mainly because, as Morrison admits, he is most at home in suburbia – conveniently, so are most of Australia's marginal electorates. In the months leading up to the 2016 Budget, Morrison ignored warnings from his National Party colleagues that they would revolt unless the government disowned a Hockey-era policy that would see the $18,200 tax-free threshold for working backpackers scrapped, forcing them to pay 32.5 cents in tax on every dollar earned.

Farmers were concerned the tax grab could damage Australia's competitiveness as a backpacker destination.

But Morrison was insistent that foreign workers should 'pay their fair share' of tax in Australia. 'If you work here, you should pay your tax here,' he repeatedly said.

Nationals MPs told the treasurer that they would campaign against the tax in regional seats that were subject to three-way contests with the Nationals. With an election approaching, the issue was proving messy for the government.

Ultimately, however, Morrison would choose pragmatism and politics over policy, and announced a review of the working holiday visas, effectively postponing the change until after the election.

Delivering his budget night address, Morrison encouraged his mates in the media not to explain the budget as a battle between winners and losers:

> The Australian people have moved on from all of that. They want a plan for getting us through this economic transition, and the old way of looking at winners and losers and who's targeted and who's not targeted, that's not what this budget is about.

It was the sort of political messaging Morrison would later fully embrace as prime minister, deriding those in the media as the ones creating divisions in society and himself speaking directly to the Australian people. Of course, his call was roundly ignored. Yet despite this, the budget was considered relatively fair, particularly when compared with the previous two budgets overseen by Hockey. This perception didn't stop Labor campaigning as the party of equality, framing the Coalition as only representing big corporate interests. But early polling nonetheless suggested that Morrison's budget had been well received.

* * *

Scott Morrison showed his tendency to overreach early in the 2016 election campaign when, in late May, he launched an attack that backfired spectacularly. While standing alongside finance minister Mathias Cormann, Morrison claimed there was a $67 billion black hole in Labor's costings. The figure appeared to be a back-of-the-envelope calculation that included all of the Opposition's spending commitments as well as government cuts that Labor disagreed with – Morrison and Cormann imaginatively argued that Labor's resistance to the cuts meant that it was money they would spend if elected. The strategy had been sanctioned by the government's campaign team, but no-one had thought to probe the enormous figure the treasurer declared. When confronted by journalists, Morrison retreated somewhat, now claiming that the funding shortfall was somewhere between $32 billion and $67 billion. What's $35 billion between friends?

Turnbull was ropeable, but he also struggled during the campaign. Unlike Abbott, he found it difficult to talk in three-word slogans and had a tendency to waffle. He also lacked the mongrel leaders need for a successful election campaign, those who constantly whack the other side day after day, even when it's believed that one of their policies has merit. Lifelong Liberal Party servant and key Howard adviser Tony Nutt was heading the campaign, alongside polling boss Mark Textor. Each morning, Nutt and Textor would brief the Coalition leadership team, which included prime minister Turnbull, deputy prime minister Barnaby Joyce, treasurer Morrison (to whom Nutt had been something of a mentor), Julie Bishop, Arthur Sinodinos, Fiona Nash, Mathias Cormann, Christopher Pyne, Peter Dutton and Mitch Fifield.

Many of the members of this leadership group have since admitted that they were concerned with the direction of the campaign. The pre-election polls showed the Coalition and Labor to be neck and neck, with the Opposition's so-called 'Mediscare' campaign playing to an existing belief about the Coalition's approach to privatisation. The Coalition largely ignored Labor's accusation that the government intended to privatise Medicare, regarding it as preposterous. Also, Turnbull wanted to run a positive campaign, believing the public would embrace it. But the Mediscare rumour gained traction. Voters are prone to saying they want a positive approach when questioned in focus groups or during phone polling, but emotionally they are influenced by negative campaigning.

Another policy damaging the government was its superannuation changes. As part of the 2016 Budget, the government had introduced a $1.6 million cap on the amount of tax-free superannuation savings a person could hold in retirement, and it decreed that an individual would pay tax at a rate of 15 per cent and 10 per cent on income and capital gains respectively on the balance of their superannuation fund. The government also had announced a $500,000 limit on after-tax contributions. While it had been estimated that these changes would adversely impact only about 4 per cent of superannuation accounts, many of those accounts belonged to Liberal voters. A small but vocal group of wealthy retirees subsequently launched a coordinated attack on the Turnbull government which attracted support from conservative commentators. Morrison was roasted by Sydney shock jock Ray Hadley, who warned him that the superannuation changes could be the 'rock on which you perish', although Morrison insisted the policy would only negatively impact a small cohort and the savings would be redirected to fund superannuation tax cuts for those at the bottom of the wealth pile. It was a progressive policy package but it disproportionately affected the Liberal Party's base, particularly in the Victorian seats of Higgins, Kooyong and Goldstein, the Western Australian seat of Curtain, the division of Ryan in Queensland and the NSW divisions of Bradfield and North Sydney.

The leadership team's fears were validated. The federal election of 2 July 2016 saw the Coalition win seventy-six seats, the slimmest of majorities in the 150-seat lower house. They picked up just one seat, Chisholm in Victoria, which was claimed by Julia Banks. Three of their seats fell in Tasmania, four in New South Wales, two in both Queensland and South Australia, and one each in the Northern Territory and Western Australia. The election losses were blamed on poor campaigning by Turnbull, a collapse in donations, and the failure to counter Labor's Mediscare campaign, which alone was estimated to have cost the Coalition up to seven seats. Liberal backbenchers were also scathing in their criticism of the superannuation changes, putting Morrison under intense pressure to roll back the reforms. He reacted by doubling down on the policy and releasing data that apparently showed the Coalition improving its margin in many of the electorates where affected residents lived, including Julie Bishop's seat of Curtin and Kelly O'Dwyer's seat of Higgins, where angry constituents had threatened retaliation.

Morrison's then Cabinet colleagues insist he was spooked by the results of the election. Several confirm that, in one particularly fiery Cabinet meeting, Morrison attempted to shift much of the blame for the toxic superannuation policy onto O'Dwyer, who was one of the architects of the retirement fund changes – a position that was challenged by Turnbull. 'He essentially said it's all Kelly's fault and that no-one should suggest he had anything to do with the superannuation reforms,' says one minister.

* * *

The near loss at the 2016 election sapped Turnbull's authority within his own party. Many of Scott Morrison's colleagues point to this moment as the first time he genuinely believed he would take over as the next Australian prime minister. Turnbull's grip on the Liberal leadership was now weak, and it was clear that the conservative wing of the party was never going to give up its quest for retribution over the coup of September 2015. Tony Abbott had remained in parliament since then, which signalled that he wanted one of two things: to return to the top job or to ensure that Malcolm Turnbull lost the prime ministership to someone else. As one long-serving Liberal MP puts it:

After the 2016 election, Morrison thought Malcolm was never going to make it, and if Malcolm wasn't going to make it, he better position himself in the event that Malcolm went under. He didn't need to do anything to push him. He just waited to see what Abbott and Dutton would do.

Chapter Eleven

Becoming Prime Minister

Shortly after Tony Abbott won the 2013 federal election, government MPs and their partners met at Government House in the Canberra suburb of Yarralumla for a soiree of sorts. Those in attendance were in a celebratory mood. Abbott had joined Sir Robert Menzies, Malcolm Fraser and John Howard as the only Liberal Party leaders to have defeated an incumbent Labor government. That night, one of Morrison's closest friends, Stuart Robert, brought up the idea of a succession plan. His colleagues were shocked – Abbott had been in the job for only a few weeks. Those familiar with the conversation say

215

Robert insisted that despite Abbott's win, party members had to think about the longer term. 'He said we have to think about future leaders and train up good people like Scott Morrison to follow Abbott,' one MP says. 'It was telling.'

Fast-forward three years to August 2016, when downhearted Coalition MPs were returning to Canberra for a new parliamentary term. Support from the crossbench coupled with narrow victories in the Queensland seats of Flynn and Capricornia had helped the Coalition form government after the July election, but there was an aura of instability around the federal parliament. The first few months after an election victory are often smooth sailing for governments; traditionally, it's the losing side that is tearing itself apart. Instead, Turnbull's Coalition had set itself a series of policy traps and the narrow win was proving problematic.

They faced a litany of issues. On 9 August, a distributed denial-of-service attack – a hack which makes it impossible for an online service to be delivered – on the ABS website disrupted the census. The double-dissolution election had severely weakened the Coalition's position in the Senate, making it difficult for the government to deliver its union reform bills. On the policy front, school funding, the divisive superannuation changes and a potential royal commission into the banking sector dogged the government. But few issues were as fraught as that of same-sex marriage.

During the election, the Coalition had campaigned on a national vote to decide on whether or not to allow same-sex couples to marry, but after the poll, the party room remained bitterly divided about the process. Turnbull, a long-time supporter of same-sex marriage, wanted the issue resolved not only because he believed same-sex couples should be allowed to marry, but because the issue had been used as a political weapon by both progressives and social conservatives. According to Cabinet members at the time, there was a level of acceptance by some staunch conservatives of the need to move on from the subject, so much so that behind the scenes even Mathias Cormann and Peter Dutton were working on ways to tackle the issue – although you would never have known it.

By late 2016, Cormann had softened on the idea of holding a postal ballot on same-sex marriage, which made the whole thing more palatable to conservatives. More moderate Cabinet members despised the idea and continued to push for a free vote. They argued that Australians had elected them to parliament to decide and a public vote would be cruel and create division. After months of debate and backroom negotiations, Cabinet finally agreed on a voluntary postal survey to gauge the mood of the public. Anticipating strong private-sector support for same-sex marriage, Scott Morrison, as treasurer, was strongly in favour of allowing the 'yes' and 'no' camps to have an equal allocation of public funding in an attempt to even up the fight.

Morrison's views on same-sex marriage were well known. A year after he was first elected, in 2008, parliament was asked to vote on a bill to eliminate discrimination against same-sex couples and the children of same-sex relationships in a range of laws such as those applying to taxation, superannuation, social security, veterans' entitlements, immigration and families. It would mean that all couples would be recognised, regardless of the gender of a partner. The bill was ultimately passed, but Scott Morrison argued against the reform on the basis that it sought to 'undermine the primacy of marriage'. Morrison said that while he supported the intent of the bill and opposed discrimination, there were 'moral absolutes that protect our society which should never be compromised'. He went on to say:

> The language in this bill is seeking to rewrite how we describe marital relationships in our laws. This language I cannot tolerate. Where do we draw the line? I fear that, as a result of the language in this bill and those that follow, it will not be long before we will be debating in this place a harmonisation of laws bill that seek to standardise this language across all statutes, including the Marriage Act. I cannot stand idly by and allow this march to undermine marriage ...

The postal survey was to be sent out on 12 September and the outcome announced on 15 November, including seat-by-seat data, although Morrison argued against releasing electorate-specific results. The issue continued to divide Cabinet, with those ministers against the change no doubt fearful that, if they voted 'yes', they would have to justify an opinion that contrasted with that of the bulk of their constituents. But if Morrison hoped his viewpoint would prevail, ultimately he would be disappointed. In August 2017, as treasurer and overseeing the ABS, he issued the following directive:

> *Today I have issued a direction to the Australian Statistician, asking the Australian Bureau of Statistics to request statistical information from all Australians on the electoral roll as to their views on whether or not the law, in relation to same sex marriage, should be changed to allow same sex couples to marry. This information will be sought on a voluntary basis. This direction will be registered on the Federal Register of Legislation and will apply from the day after registration.*

The following month, Morrison declared he would be voting against same-sex marriage in the postal plebiscite and told his fellow Australians it was 'OK to say no'. Morrison has proven to be the ultimate political pragmatist on most issues, but his closest colleagues agree that same-sex marriage was the only policy area on which he had a strong ideological view. Someone who has known him for more than two decades says, 'He is a highly political person who doesn't have any sort of strong values, but the only thing he always had a strong view on was gay marriage. He was vehemently opposed.'

On 15 November 2017, the results of the public poll were announced. More than 7.81 million Australians – representing 61.6 per cent of participants – voted in favour of allowing same-sex couples to marry, compared with 4.87 million people – 38.4 per cent – who voted 'no'. Of the 150 electorates involved, 133 voted 'yes' and seventeen 'no' – most of the latter were in western Sydney and most of those were represented by Labor MPs. In Morrison's seat of Cook, 55 per cent of respondents voted in favour of allowing same-sex couples to marry.

According to Turnbull, the opponents of same-sex marriage, including Scott Morrison, were 'utterly deflated' by the result. Morrison is said to have told Turnbull that he felt as if Australia had changed; he no longer felt it was the same country he had grown up in. Morrison appeared to be unwilling to accept that same-sex marriage was no longer viewed as a radical idea. As their opponents mounted a defence of Western civilisation, of traditional marriage and of a Judeo-Christian heritage, those campaigning for change mostly favoured restraint. They based their campaign on the belief that homosexuality had already gained wide acceptance and, therefore, support for same-sex marriage wasn't necessarily an indication that society was undergoing a dramatic shift to the left. Importantly, their campaign wasn't based on fear but on the national ballot being a vote on equality and fairness.

On 8 December, parliament was asked to vote on whether to legalise same-sex marriage. Only four MPs voted against the bill. Two did so because they had vowed to vote whichever way their electorates did, while another two MPs – Liberal Russell Broadbent and crossbencher Bob Katter – simply opposed it. More than a dozen MPs who had advocated a 'no' vote, including Scott Morrison, Tony Abbott, Kevin Andrews and deputy prime minister Barnaby Joyce, abstained from the vote in an attempt to balance their personal views and the views of the majority of Australians.

Morrison would later justify his decision by saying he didn't want to 'stand in the way' of the government resolving the issue. But a number of colleagues saw this as an unsatisfactory excuse. Many of those who voted for same-sex marriage still personally opposed it, but they did so in order to respect the wishes of their constituents. In the case of Morrison, he seemed unable to put the views of his electorate ahead of his own, despite his previous claim that the Bible was not a policy handbook. It was ironic that many of the people who were disappointed with Morrison's inability to separate his personal faith from his politics on this occasion were the same groups that had called for him to show more of that faith as a Christian when it came to the treatment of asylum seekers.

* * *

As treasurer, Morrison can be credited with reducing the tax rate for small- and medium-sized businesses, drops in the unemployment rate, and ensuring Australia retained its AAA credit rating. As with his previous two portfolios, he was outcome driven and determined to deliver public-pleasing policies. But after a near-death experience at the 2016 election, the government had little appetite for big ideas.

In the lead-up to the 2017 Budget, Morrison, just as he had a year earlier, privately lobbied for radical changes to negative gearing. He still believed housing affordability was one of the biggest issues facing the country, particularly the suburban Australia he claimed to represent. While his colleagues had long argued this was primarily a concern for younger Australians (who don't usually vote for the Coalition), Morrison knew that older voters continued to be frustrated that their children were struggling to get into the housing market. Limiting the ability of investors to buy more properties had to help first-home buyers enter the market. And so, just before the budget announcement, stories began to appear in the media suggesting the government was now open to tinkering with the tax break – a proposal to cap the size of the associated deductions was even floated in *The Australian* that February. Behind closed doors, the Cabinet agreed to some changes to negative gearing, including stricter lending rules for investors and the abolition of a tax concession that allowed landlords to treat the costs of travel to inspect their properties as a deduction. But Morrison did not get Cabinet's full imprimatur for his policy and by April, he reverted to language he had used earlier that year when he described Labor's own push to scrap negative gearing as 'a blunt measure' that would increase rents.

Neither was the Coalition going to risk a cost-cutting budget. Instead, Morrison risked angering conservative

Liberals with a decided lack of restraint when it came to spending, and new taxes on big banks. He injected billions of dollars in extra funding into schools and launched a crackdown on multinational tax avoidance.

Morrison also implemented a $8.2 billion rise in the Medicare levy to fund the National Disability Insurance Scheme (NDIS). To justify the increase, he got personal. At the post-budget breakfast on 10 May 2017, Morrison talked about his brother-in-law Gary Warren, a former fireman who was living with an aggressive form of multiple sclerosis. Speaking to a large audience in the Great Hall of Parliament House, which included Warren, and an even larger audience across Australia, he told this story:

> Gary and Michelle Warren are extraordinary Australians ... They live in Peakhurst Heights in southern Sydney in the same home Gary grew up in. They have four sons. Gary's mum lives upstairs. Her and Roy, who we lost not that long ago, raised their family in this house. Gary's younger sister is my wife, Jenny.
>
> After Gary left school he trained to become a fireman ... He was passionate about being a fireman. He did it for twenty years. He's a very physical guy, Gary. I remember going on hikes, canyoning – I wasn't doing that, but he was. But in 1999, Gary was diagnosed with progressive MS, the aggressive form of MS, and he knew it at the time. The oldest son at that time was just eight years old; the youngest son had not been born ...

Gary was able to draw down, after he left the fire brigade, on an annuity but he has … sought to work every single day from then until now. Because of his annuity he hasn't had to draw down on a disability support pension. He hasn't claimed on Newstart. The family is supported by the carer's payment and, equally, a mobility payment – as should be the case. Gary has worked at the triple zero call centre for the ambulance service. He's worked for call centres at Fair Trading and court systems in New South Wales …

A few months ago they bought their first home, an incredible achievement … Gary is now in the chair, before that he had a Segway … But for the last five years that's how he's got himself around. And recently when the van was off the road, that he used, Gary had to catch public transport. At the time he was working in Parramatta. That's an hour and a half both ways from where they live … That's being committed to working. But Gary told me just how helpful his fellow commuters, his fellow Australians, were. 'People,' he's told me, 'are enormously generous – not just happy to help, but keen to help.' And he said, 'It's not flash being disabled. It's not flash. But if there's anything good about it,' he said, 'it's that you're disabled in Australia.'

Morrison was clearly affected by Gary's story, delivering these words with tears welling in his eyes. It was a politically savvy move, neutralising Labor's complaint that Australians would have to pay more through the higher Medicare levy.

Morrison, more than most, understands the power of personal stories in politics and the importance of shaping a narrative to sell policies.

* * *

Selling the 2017 Budget proved to be fairly straightforward, but the government soon had a big problem on its hands. Calls had been growing from the public and within the Coalition's own party room for a royal commission into the banking sector, spurred by stories of the mistreatment of customers and a general failure to put their needs first. Labor had tried to harness the public's anger by promising to set up a royal commission into the finance sector if it won the 2016 election, and while the ALP had remained in Opposition, the proposal itself was still popular across the community. In an attempt to hold back the rising anger over the maltreatment of ordinary people by overpaid executives, the government announced a series of banking sector restrictions. One such change was the Banking Executive Accountability Regime (BEAR) which included new rules on the structure of senior bankers' pay and boosted the powers of the banking regulator to dish out fines and discipline shoddy practitioners. The government also legislated better protections for finance-sector whistleblowers who highlighted misconduct. But this did little to stem voters' disaffection when it came to the banks.

Inside the Liberal Party, the appetite for a royal commission was spreading from the backbench into the Cabinet. Initially, there was solidarity among the ministers about resisting calls for a royal commission, as they didn't want to be seen to be bending to Labor's will. Then a small but vocal group of ministers told prime minister Turnbull that a probe into the banks was unavoidable. They were concerned that the government was using up precious political capital by protecting the scandal-plagued banks and receiving little in return. Some ministers quietly came up with ways to provide the government with opportunities for a tactical withdrawal.

Around this time, a senior Cabinet minister who believed a royal commission was now inevitable gave a member of the press gallery a gentle nudge to call Kate Carnell, the small business and family enterprise ombudsman. Carnell had earlier headed a probe into the lending practices of the big banks, initially insisting that her investigation would provide 'direct and timely assistance' in a way a royal commission could not. But a flood of evidence of poor banking practices and unconscionable behaviour had forced Carnell to have a rethink and she had come around to the idea of a banking royal commission. She was privately lobbying senior ministers who believed her change of heart would give the government cover to change its mind. Carnell was a former Liberal chief minister of the Australian Capital Territory, and conservative politicians were more likely to listen to her than to more progressive voices.

By August 2017, the mood had shifted further with the news that criminal syndicates had run millions of dollars through Australia after the Commonwealth Bank allegedly breached money laundering and counterterrorism financing regulations more than 53,000 times. Fuelled by constituent concerns and a growing fear that Coalition MPs could cross the floor, frontbench MPs started pushing Turnbull and his economic team, which included Morrison, finance minister Mathias Cormann and assistant treasurer Kelly O'Dwyer, to agree to a royal commission. O'Dwyer was the first one in the group to come around to the idea, while Morrison, with his self-claimed unique insight into the public mood, had resisted it – he called it 'a stunt', insisting that the government couldn't back down now.

Morrison at first had most of the senior Cabinet ministers on his side in believing the royal commission would not only be expensive, it wouldn't reveal anything that the government didn't already know. Banks were on the nose, that was already obvious. By backing down and launching a probe, the government risked the humiliation of being forced to take action by a handful of Coalition backbenchers. Plus, a royal commission was backed by Labor, and the government didn't need the Opposition looking like it was calling the shots.

Despite this, one by one, ministers started to waver as the political pressure intensified. Morrison maintained his strong opposition to the probe, but by late November 2017, the government's thin majority was exposed as Labor and some Nationals MPs schemed to set up a royal commission by voting in favour of a private member's bill. A policy U-turn to hold a royal commission would be embarrassing, but losing a vote on the floor of parliament to establish such a commission, backed by Coalition MPs, was out of the question.

There was a feeling among senior ministers that the government would receive some cover if the banks and other leading financial experts requested the inquiry. An agreement was then reached in late November when the banks wrote to Scott Morrison requesting a royal commission as a way of ending the deadlock. The letter was signed by ANZ chairman David Gonski and chief executive Shayne Elliott, Commonwealth Bank chairwoman Catherine Livingstone and chief executive Ian Narev, National Australia Bank chairman Ken Henry and CEO Andrew Thorburn, and Westpac chairman Lindsay Maxsted and CEO Brian Hartzer:

> We are writing to you as the leaders of Australia's major banks.
> In light of the latest wave of speculation about a parliamentary
> commission of inquiry into the banking and finance sector, we believe
> it is now imperative for the Australian Government to act decisively
> to deliver certainty to Australia's financial services sector, our
> customers and the community.

But it wasn't that simple. The day before the request was released to the public, a draft version of the banks' letter was sent to Scott Morrison's office to prevent catching the government by surprise. This wasn't a 'gotcha' moment. By requesting the investigation, the banks were able to have a say in the timeline and terms of the probe.

On 30 November 2017, Turnbull and Morrison fronted the media to announce the Royal Commission into Misconduct in the Banking, Superannuation and Financial Services Industry, arguing that the speculation and uncertainty over a probe was affecting confidence in the Australian economy. 'The nature of political events means the national economic interest is now served by taking what I describe as a regrettable but necessary action,' Morrison said at the time.

* * *

While many of Morrison's colleagues believe the Coalition's narrow win at the 2016 federal election reignited his ambition for the top job, few accuse him of undermining or damaging the government's chances of winning. According to several Cabinet ministers, Turnbull would often complain that Morrison was an incompetent treasurer, insisting that he was being forced to do the job of both prime minister and treasurer, but not many shared Turnbull's view. His colleagues in general may not have trusted him, and increasingly they were frustrated by his propensity to trial policies in the media, but he was viewed as a hard worker and a strong communicator. Besides, another minister was proving more of a headache for the Turnbull government.

As his prime ministership continued, Turnbull increasingly became dependent on senior conservatives such as close friends Peter Dutton and Mathias Cormann. Dutton and Cormann were both from the Liberal Party's right, but they offered some protection to the moderate Turnbull, whose very existence grated on his more conservative colleagues. Cormann was exceptional at negotiating government legislation through the Senate, while Dutton acted as a buffer between Turnbull and the more extreme elements of the right. Deep down, Turnbull and his office were always wary of Dutton, more so than Cormann, but a level of trust developed based on the fact that their private conversations never ended up in the media, unlike those conducted with Morrison.

Turnbull's reliance on Dutton and Cormann came at a cost, however. His traditional allies, the more moderate Liberal MPs, felt they were being sidelined and that their warnings about Dutton were falling on deaf ears. Turnbull's closest confidants would caution him that Peter Dutton, while useful, could not be trusted, but Turnbull dismissed their concerns. As one senior Cabinet member puts it:

Malcolm couldn't believe that anyone in their right mind would think that they would be a better prime minister than Malcolm. He was unbelievably naive. As a politician, Turnbull can be as Machiavellian as the rest, but he had a blind spot when it came to lesser mortals going for his job.

According to a senior Cabinet minister, Turnbull dismissed concerns about Dutton by saying: 'Not even he is stupid enough to think he could be prime minister.'

In early 2018, the warning bells rang louder. Throughout his prime ministership, Turnbull lived with the knowledge that a group of like-minded conservative government MPs came together for lunch each Tuesday when parliament was sitting. The group became known as the 'Monkey Pod', after the type of timber used for the table in the room in Parliament House where they met. In April 2018, the group, which included Angus Taylor, Kevin Andrews, Michael Sukkar, Zed Seselja, Craig Kelly and Tony Abbott, transformed itself into the Monash Forum based on a shared love of coal-fired power. Its members now had a policy they could fight for that reflected their right-wing ideology. This couldn't have come at a worse time for Turnbull who, that same month, was approaching the unfortunate milestone with which he'd challenged Tony Abbott.

On 8 April, the Coalition under Malcolm Turnbull notched up its thirtieth consecutive Newspoll defeat by Labor. The following morning, senior Cabinet ministers were sent out to front the media and support their prime minister. The media, of course, began asking the MPs about their leadership ambitions, and most knew how to respond tactfully, backing in the current leader and then deflecting the question by telling the interviewer how hard they were working in their own portfolios. But that weekend, Peter Dutton made it clear he wanted the top job should Turnbull fall. 'Of course I want to be prime minister one day,' Dutton told *Guardian Australia*. 'I think it's best to be honest about that. That's an ambition long-held and is only realistic if stars align and an opportunity comes up.'

Within days, Morrison similarly indicated that he, too, wanted the job. However, he did so more tactfully, telling the ABC's *7.30* program that it would only be an option: 'Down the track, I am sure if an opportunity presented itself. But not while Malcolm Turnbull is the prime minister.'

As deputy leader, Julie Bishop was alarmed by these pronouncements and immediately called Turnbull, but her warning was brushed off. Other ministers, backbenchers and staff also sounded the alarm, but Turnbull just couldn't see it. Morrison, however, could see how events would unfold. He didn't need to agitate for change, nor did he need to chase the leadership as forcefully as Dutton. He chose a more tactical approach: to wait. Turnbull may not have identified his strategy, but other colleagues were aware that Morrison was positioning himself for an inevitable clash. As one senior Cabinet minister describes it:

> *It was about that time that Scott clearly saw that Dutton was undermining and made the decision to sit back and let it unfold. I knew Scott was positioning [himself] so that if Malcolm was under threat he would come through the middle. He was just going to play them both.*

Between April and August 2018, Dutton flexed his political muscle in Cabinet and had a number of national security victories, including a decision to ban the Chinese telecommunications company Huawei from involvement in Australia's 5G network. Meanwhile, outside of Cabinet, Abbott and other outspoken conservatives were publicly fuming over Turnbull's energy policy: the National Energy Guarantee (NEG). This wasn't just a simple disagreement over policy. Rather, it had the potential to topple the prime minister – energy policies had ended Turnbull's time as Opposition leader and dealt enormous damage to Labor's Kevin Rudd and Julia Gillard during their prime ministerships. It was in late 2017 that Turnbull attempted the risky task of coming up with an energy plan that would unite the warring conservative and moderate factions of his party. The resulting NEG was intended to deal with rising energy prices, reduce emissions and give the energy sector greater certainty in regards to investing. The plan also was meant to guarantee reliability by forcing companies to use a percentage of electricity from dispatchable sources such as coal, gas and pumped hydro, which can be used at short notice to keep the lights on.

The energy sector also would be encouraged to invest in renewable energy to ensure Australia was able to reduce its carbon emissions by 26–28 per cent below the 2005 levels by 2030. In addition, subsidies for renewable technologies would be phased out when those technologies were deemed competitive. To help push the policy, Turnbull had appointed eager young Liberal Josh Frydenberg as Minister for the Environment and Energy. Frydenberg was a workaholic and respected by both the left and the right wings of the party.

In early August 2018, the Coalition party room approved the prime minister's plan for the NEG, although any celebrations would have been a little premature. A majority of MPs had backed the policy because they wanted the issue dealt with once and for all. But Abbott and a number of other MPs, including Craig Kelly, Tony Pasin and George Christensen, rebelled against the proposal and threatened to cross the floor on any bill setting out an emissions reduction trajectory – that group itself was split between those who genuinely despised the energy plan and those who saw the rebellion as convenient cover for creating trouble for Turnbull. Buoyed by the apparent party room win, Frydenberg lodged the legislation in the Table Office for discussion that evening. But the leader of the house, the moderate Christopher Pyne, who was tasked with arranging and managing the government's parliamentary schedule, could see trouble brewing and intervened to keep the bill from being brought up for debate.

After days of negotiations, it became clear that opponents of the NEG simply wouldn't agree to in any way legislate an emissions reduction target. On 17 August, as the issue threatened to turn into a full-blown crisis, Turnbull backflipped on this aspect of his proposal. Moderates were disappointed but they realised that such a concession was possibly the only way the government would agree on an energy plan; they saw it as a way to move on. Importantly, as confirmed by a number of Cabinet ministers, Peter Dutton agreed with the policy amendments and indicated he would publicly back the changes. But efforts made to convince the disgruntled Abbott and his allies were futile. And as senior ministers – among them Scott Morrison – advised the prime minister not to push ahead with debate on the matter, reports of a looming leadership challenge appeared in the media – although many Liberals, including Turnbull, dismissed the reports.

By 20 August, the media was awash with reports that a challenge was imminent, making for an awkward leadership meeting that Monday morning. Turnbull's colleagues, staff and his supporters on the backbench scoped out the situation and dutifully confirmed the threat to the prime minister. Dutton and his allies had run the numbers and believed the Minister for Home Affairs would prevail in the contest they had pencilled in for the following month. Their plot had been exposed early, but the groundwork had already been laid.

Both privately to Turnbull and publicly, Scott Morrison gave an assurance that he was supporting the prime minister, even if his allies inside and outside parliament were pushing him to run. On the night of 20 August, a group of Morrison supporters, including Alex Hawke and Stuart Robert, dined together in Kingston, having worked the phones over the weekend. During those calls, which were ostensibly about the approaching spill, they did not explicitly ask for support for

Scott Morrison, but several of those contacted report that the callers attempted to gauge interest in a Morrison candidacy.

* * *

On 21 August, Turnbull attempted to take matters into his own hands by declaring that both his position and that of the deputy leader were open, paving the way for an immediate leadership ballot. He made this decision without consulting Julie Bishop or any of the senior moderates in his Cabinet, who today insist they would have talked him out of it. Morrison also was caught by surprise that morning.

Turnbull had been forewarned about the growing support for Morrison, not just the small group of factional allies that had met in Kingston the night before but from a wider group of MPs Morrison appeared to control, including the NSW MPs Lucy Wicks and Ann Sudmalis, Western Australians Steve Irons and Ben Morton, and Victorian MP Chris Crewther. The group of relatively unknown and unaligned politicians had a potentially central role to play in whether Turnbull remained prime minister. On the eve of the spill, Turnbull's office tested scenarios that took into account Dutton's level of support with and without Morrison's allies, and believed Turnbull would win the ballot on that Tuesday morning either way.

When Turnbull declared the Liberal Party leadership vacant, Peter Dutton was the only other nominee – no-one challenged deputy leader Bishop, despite speculation that health minister Greg Hunt wanted her job. Turnbull defeated Peter Dutton by forty-eight votes to thirty-five. Morrison gave his word to Turnbull that he had voted for him to remain as prime minister and few challenge him on this. But there is a strong view among both Dutton and Turnbull supporters that some of Morrison's closest allies, including Ben Morton, Stuart Robert and Alex Hawke, voted for Dutton in order to inflict significant damage on Turnbull and leave the leadership door ajar for Morrison.

Although Turnbull had been wounded in the vote, his closest supporters still thought he might be able to unify the government, at least until the next election. That was until Turnbull, encouraged by Morrison, invited Dutton to rejoin the Cabinet, despite his treachery. Dutton declined, making it clear that he would come for Turnbull again and again, ruining the government along the way. One of Turnbull's then Cabinet allies says: 'I started thinking, if Malcolm will be attacked again, I can't see us surviving, and even if we do survive, the government is fucked.'

At this point, Christopher Pyne, having observed many leadership challenges in Canberra, realised two things. First, he believed that the Coalition could not win an election under Peter Dutton and therefore he needed to buy time so he could come up with a new plan. Second, with Turnbull seemingly done, there were only three candidates who could feasibly run for the leadership: himself, Scott Morrison and

Julie Bishop. Pyne quickly ruled himself out and decided Bishop would struggle to beat Dutton in a party room vote, so it had to be Morrison.

With Dutton out of the ministry, Turnbull announced that Morrison would act as home affairs minister 'pending other arrangements'. While the portfolio was temporary, Morrison was excited to be back in charge of the borders. The following day, 22 August, he called one of his closest friends, who was on a European holiday, and the conversation soon turned to the Liberal leadership. Morrison told the friend he hadn't yet made up his mind about whether or not he should challenge, but he admitted that his supporters were running the numbers on his behalf. He said it would be preferable if the government could limp to the end of the week so that Liberal MPs could return home to their electorates and take a collective deep breath. However, it's not clear if Morrison thought that strategy would give him time to build support or if he thought it would help Turnbull retain the prime ministership.

Another of Morrison's confidants claims that, also on 22 August, he urged Morrison to approach Turnbull and seek an endorsement or a blessing for him to take over as leader. Morrison apparently responded: 'There is no chance of that happening.' Morrison had one eye on the leadership but he wasn't yet ready to show his hand.

With Dutton free of the ministry, he addressed the media to pitch his policy initiatives should he become prime minister, starting with a promise to remove the GST from household power bills in a bid to alleviate price pressures on consumers. Such a policy would have deprived the states and territories of $30 billion. It was immediately slammed by the Turnbull camp and Labor, but it was also used by Morrison later in the week to try to sway undecided colleagues to vote for him. Morrison believed that the Treasury portfolio was a better training ground than other portfolios for an aspirant prime minister, an argument that he used to draw colleagues to his cause.

That afternoon, finance minister Mathias Cormann, communications minister Mitch Fifield and jobs and innovation minister Michaelia Cash went to the prime minister's office to tell Turnbull he no longer had their support. The trio joined a long list of frontbenchers who had already resigned that week, including James McGrath, Zed Seselja, Michael Sukkar, Concetta Fierravanti-Wells and Angus Taylor. Cormann's betrayal came just hours after he had stood alongside Turnbull at Parliament House to announce that the government was abandoning its planned tax cuts for larger companies, which had failed to pass the Senate. Cormann was asked whether he supported the prime minister, to which he replied: 'I was very grateful when Malcolm invited me to serve in his Cabinet in September 2015. I have served Malcolm loyally ever since. I will continue to serve him loyally into the future.'

Morrison similarly had been grilled on his loyalties. Putting his arm around Turnbull, he'd said: 'This is my leader, and I'm ambitious for him.' Turnbull replied: 'Good on you. Thanks ScoMo.'

Turnbull wanted to go straight to an election, and he even made an appointment to see the governor-general the next day, but he was talked out of it. Colleagues describe his office as 'descending into madness'. Significantly, Turnbull's determination to destroy Dutton gave Morrison a distinct advantage. As one senior minister says: 'It's a miracle he [Turnbull] didn't turn against Morrison but he was just so focused on Dutton.'

Intensifying this already fraught period was Labor's release of advice from the constitutional lawyer Bret Walker SC which it had been sitting on for months, stating that Peter Dutton was ineligible to sit in the forty-fifth federal parliament due to the fact that his family trust had received support from the Commonwealth through its childcare business. Section 44 of the Constitution states that a person is not eligible to sit in the parliament if they have a direct or indirect pecuniary interest in a contract with the public service of the Commonwealth. Solicitor-General of Australia Stephen Donaghue soon cast doubt on the claim, but it sent a scare through the Dutton camp.

Turnbull insisted that the majority of the party room sign a petition for a meeting to bring on a second vote. If the Dutton forces could get the numbers, Turnbull would agree to a spill motion, and if it was carried, he would stand aside. It was at that point, on the morning of 23 August, that Turnbull gave his blessing for both Scott Morrison and Julie Bishop to run for the leadership in the event of another vote. The petition was the brainchild of Pyne, who wanted to ensure Morrison had enough time to build support to beat Dutton. Pyne was a staunch Turnbull supporter but he could see that the current prime ministership was doomed. He also believed that Morrison offered the party a stronger chance at the next election, while Bishop, although popular with the public, would be unable to garner enough support from key factions to win the party room ballot. Pyne was right. When Bishop hit the phones that Thursday afternoon, she discovered that not only were her colleagues already wedded to an alternative candidate, but that one of the contenders was Scott Morrison. Bishop has since told colleagues that Liberal MPs reported that Morrison and his supporters had been active as early as the previous weekend in sounding out support.

Morrison, whose parliamentary career had seen him shift from the Liberal Party's moderate faction to the centre-right, would need the support of the moderates to win. But there was a lot of work to be done to get all the members of that faction onside. There were many young and ambitious MPs whom Dutton had promised to promote in exchange for their vote. The moderates also were split over whether or not to support Bishop, but in that case, pragmatism won out. Leaked WhatsApp messages later revealed that Liberal moderates had decided to vote against her to ensure Peter Dutton was kept from power. Pyne, Paul Fletcher and Simon Birmingham had earlier devised this strategy to keep Dutton out of The Lodge. They had divided up the names of their colleagues and hit the phones to build support for Morrison. Morrison's allies changed the name of their group WhatsApp message to 'Team ScoMo' and locked in the support of the centre-right.

By the morning of 24 August, Dutton's supporters were visibly nervous, and with good reason. Heavy-handed tactics such as threatening preselection challenges had backfired on their camp. Instead, the not-so-rusted-on Dutton supporters were wooed by Morrison's centre-right and left credentials. Morrison's aides had worked late into the previous night to ensure they had the numbers, whereas many of Dutton's closest political allies had been spotted at Canberra eateries – it is disputed whether the attitude of the Dutton camp represented a premature celebration or despondency.

One of the last people Morrison spoke to before the Friday morning vote was his wife, who had made a last-minute dash to Canberra with their two girls. Scott would later tell Jenny: 'At the end of the day, you are always here … and that's what matters most.' His final act before entering the party room was to pray alongside his friend and political ally Stuart Robert.

The first vote on whether or not to spill the Liberal leadership resulted in forty-five for the motion and forty against: Turnbull was gone.

In the second ballot, to determine a new leader, Dutton received thirty-eight votes to Morrison's thirty-six, with a bloc of moderates swinging behind Morrison, and Bishop received just eleven votes and was eliminated. A final ballot was held to determine which candidate had majority support to become leader. Dutton was defeated by a margin of forty-five votes to forty. Scott Morrison was now Australia's thirtieth prime minister.

After his victory, Morrison stuck to what he knew best, invoking his faith in an effort to bring the wounded members of his party together. He related the biblical story of God asking Joshua to bring down the walls of Jericho, a tale of how one's obedience to God, even when faced with seemingly insurmountable odds, will be rewarded.

Chapter Twelve

Nothing to Lose

After Scott Morrison had been anointed the Liberal Party's new leader, a ballot was held for the position of deputy leader. Victorian Liberal Josh Frydenberg won that ballot in the first round, gaining forty-six votes compared with twenty votes for Steven Ciobo and sixteen votes for Greg Hunt, who'd backed Peter Dutton. Morrison, then fifty years old, and Frydenberg, forty-seven, represented generational change in the federal Liberal Party. Shortly after the vote, Morrison and Frydenberg went back to Morrison's ministerial office, where they sat together alone. The new prime minister asked Frydenberg what portfolio he wanted, a perk of winning the ballot for deputy. Frydenberg replied that he wanted to be treasurer – John Howard recently had reminded him that being treasurer was the second most important job in government and that he should put his hand up for the role. Morrison well understood the power that came with overseeing the Treasury portfolio – it's no secret that he himself found the role very fulfilling – and he was happy for Frydenberg to take the job.

The rise of Morrison and Frydenberg also marked the end of the bitter factional power struggle between Turnbull and Abbott that had eaten away at the federal Liberal Party for years, and that's the message the freshly minted prime minister and treasurer now wanted to send to a nation fed up with the constant changes at the apex of domestic politics. In the Blue Room in the ministerial wing of Parliament House, Morrison, with Frydenberg standing alongside him, outlined his vision. He promised to prioritise policies to bring down electricity prices, improve access to health care and immediately help the farmers battling a brutal drought, wrapping up the commitments in an appeal to what he saw as fundamentally Australian values:

> *If you have a go in this country, you'll get a go. That's what fairness*
> *in Australia means. This is something we hold very dear to us.*
> *We're on your side. We're on your side because we share beliefs and*
> *values in common, as you go about everything you do each day.*

That weekend, there was little time for Morrison to celebrate his victory. Instead, he bunkered down in his ministerial office while Malcolm Turnbull moved out of the prime minister's workplace. With Morrison were his numbers men, Stuart Robert and Ben Morton – he refers to Morton as 'The Apprentice'. Also there were his wife Jenny and his two daughters, eleven-year-old Abbey and nine-year-old Lily, who'd all made the trip down from Sydney to be by his side as he was sworn in by then governor-general Sir Peter Cosgrove. It was a small night-time ceremony, but Morrison and his family still posed for the traditional photos on the steps of Government House.

Subsisting on takeaway food and aided by a skeleton staff, Morrison got straight to work. He met with the secretary of the Department of Prime Minister and Cabinet, Martin Parkinson, and nutted out a new agreement with the National Party. The junior Coalition partner would be given five Cabinet positions and the same level of ministerial representation, despite NSW National Kevin Hogan having quit in disgust over the treatment of Turnbull. Hogan now sat on the crossbench, but guaranteed confidence and supply for the government; he even continued to attend the Nationals' party room meetings.

With the Nationals on board, Morrison spoke to a number of foreign leaders, most of whom would have been familiar with the protocol for welcoming a new Australian prime minister. Phone calls with New Zealand Prime Minister Jacinda Ardern and US president Donald Trump were at the top of his list. He was keen to avoid the feisty conversations that his predecessor Malcolm Turnbull had endured with Trump and instead tried to butter him up by talking about golf. 'I did tell him I was a rubbish golfer,' Morrison says. 'I am not quite sure that term is well known in the US so there are other phrases I have and I'll have to be careful of using Shire colloquialisms in international engagements.'

Morrison also found time to reach out to former Liberal prime minister John Howard and his long-serving treasurer Peter Costello, and then it was time to choose his Cabinet. Ahead of the ballot, Morrison told his colleagues he would not seek retribution against those who had opposed him in the leadership spill. True to his word, he allowed Peter Dutton and Mathias Cormann to keep their powerful Cabinet positions – with the leadership ballot decided by just a handful of votes, this was a strategic move, as Dutton still remained popular within the party room. With Malcolm Turnbull vowing to quit parliament, Morrison didn't have to grapple with what to do with the former prime minister. And in an effort to reset the top tier of government, he refused to bring back Tony Abbott.

Unlike Turnbull, Julie Bishop told colleagues she wouldn't desert the Liberal Party and spark a by-election. But she loathed Scott Morrison and had no desire to serve in a Cabinet led by him. After the spill, Bishop returned to Perth, where she fielded calls from colleagues urging her to consider fighting to remain in her role as foreign affairs minister. Meanwhile, publicly, Morrison described her as a 'rock star', saying: 'She has been an amazing contributor and driver of foreign policy, and an advocate for Liberal values from one end of this country to the other and one end of this world to the other.' But it was useless. Cabinet members from the time believe the animosity between the pair would have made it impossible for Bishop to remain on the frontbench. It was clear she wouldn't be welcome, nor did she want to stay.

As well as sticking to his word and (for the most part) not punishing the MPs who had voted against him, he also rewarded those who had. Christopher Pyne, who had delivered the crucial moderate votes to Morrison and helped ensure that Frydenberg, not Hunt, won the deputy leader position, was rewarded with the defence portfolio. Stuart Robert, who was considered Morrison's best friend in the parliament, was returned to the ministry after having been forced to resign two-and-a-half years earlier over accusations of improperly using his role as assistant minister of defence to broker a mining deal while supposedly on a 'personal' trip to China. Another mate of Morrison's, Steve Irons, was appointed assistant minister to the prime minister. NSW MP Sussan Ley, who had turned on Turnbull after she was dumped following a travel rorts scandal, was also returned to the frontbench, while NSW moderate MP David Coleman, who had stood against Morrison in Cook all those years ago, became immigration and multicultural affairs minister. Morrison's key numbers man, Alex Hawke, was promoted to special minister of state.

Morrison's peace accord with Dutton's backers didn't extend to Concetta Fierravanti-Wells and James McGrath, who were stripped of their frontbench positions – the bad blood between Morrison and Fierravanti-Wells stretched right back to the Cook preselection. But Angus Taylor, another Dutton supporter, was appointed Minister for Energy and Emissions Reduction. Searching for a truce with the Catholic schools' sector over a funding disagreement, Morrison replaced Simon Birmingham as education minister with Victorian Dan Tehan, a Catholic; Birmingham was offered trade. Michaelia Cash moved to small business, Mitch Fifield was returned to communications and Greg Hunt kept the health portfolio.

As important as ministerial appointments are the roles inside the Prime Minister's Office. For his media team, Morrison hung on to Andrew Carswell, whom he'd poached from the *Daily Telegraph* when he was treasurer, as well as his media adviser, Kate Williams. Joining the pair was Nick Creevey, who had worked for Birmingham, and Ben Wicks, who had been with Hunt. Morrison also retained his chief of staff, John Kunkel, an economist who, while in his previous post at the Minerals Council, had helped Morrison acquire the lump of coal he waved around in parliament during a bemusing question time performance in February 2017. Kunkel has a PhD in trade policy from the Australian National University and is considered a master of economic and strategic issues. He was also head of government affairs at mining giant Rio Tinto. Peter Conran, who worked as a senior adviser to John Howard between 2001 and 2007, was mobilised from retirement into the role of Cabinet secretary.

The key advisory role of principal private secretary went to Yaron Finkelstein, who had worked for David Kemp and later the former Liberal leader Brendan Nelson. He also had served as an executive at Liberal pollsters Crosby Textor – Morrison, a polling aficionado, first met Finkelstein during that time and was wooed by his political antenna. Morrison also hired former Ambassador to Myanmar Michelle Chan as his national security adviser, after a stint at the Office of National Assessments. He also poached Jimmy Kiploks, a senior defence bureaucrat, from Marise Payne and appointed Brendan Tegg, who'd worked for him when he was immigration minister, to oversee border security issues.

* * *

Had Julie Bishop decided to fight to keep her position as foreign minister, she wouldn't have stayed in the post for long. Six weeks into the PM's job, Morrison made his first major foreign policy announcement, declaring he would relocate Australia's embassy in Tel Aviv to Jerusalem. At the time, the prime minister said the move was simply intended to bring Australia into line with a decision by US president Donald Trump, who had just recognised Jerusalem as the legitimate capital of Israel. In reality, Morrison had been heavily swayed by Dave Sharma, who was contesting the upcoming by-election in Turnbull's now-vacated seat of Wentworth, which the Liberals held by a 17 per cent margin. It was a must-win poll for Morrison as a loss would rob him of his one-seat majority in parliament. Sharma, a former Australian Ambassador to Israel, had argued that recognising Jerusalem was consistent with a two-state solution – an independent Palestine alongside Israel – to the long-running deadlock in the Middle East. Wentworth has a large Jewish constituency – about 13 per cent – and a policy shift would help the Liberal Party's chances. Julie Bishop, now on the backbench, didn't want to enter into a public spat but was said to be gobsmacked by the move. She had fought against the proposal when foreign minister, and she told colleagues that had she still been in the post when Morrison made the Jerusalem announcement, she would have quit.

What began as a political ploy for a by-election battle soon blew up into an international dispute. Indonesia, which has the world's largest Muslim population, warned that the decision threatened global stability. Morrison had forewarned Indonesian President Joko Widodo by text message before announcing the policy shift. It was Indonesian Minister for Foreign Affairs Retno Marsudi, who had shared a close friendship with Bishop, who fired back: 'Indonesia asks Australia and other countries to continue supporting the Palestine–Israel peace process in accordance with the principles that have been agreed and to not take steps that may threaten the peace process and world stability.'

Jerusalem wasn't the only issue now threatening to hurt the Liberal Party's chances in Wentworth. The seat had been Liberal since the party's inception – prior to that, the affluent harbourside suburbs of Double Bay, Point Piper and Vaucluse were represented by the conservative party of the day. But Liberal voters were angry. Their man in Canberra, Malcolm Turnbull, had had his prime ministership cut short and they wanted revenge. To make matters worse, Turnbull had flown to New York with his his wife, Lucy, shortly after his resignation and he remained silent in the lead-up to the Wentworth poll. While Turnbull turned down numerous offers to throw his support behind Sharma, his son, Alex, urged Australians to donate to the Labor candidate, Tim Murray.

Liberal MPs criticised Turnbull senior (and junior) for their behaviour, but in Canberra, their party was doing little to improve its chances of winning. A snippet of the Philip Ruddock report on religious freedom that recommended allowing religious schools to retain the power to kick out gay students was leaked to the media. Then there was a cock-up in the Senate which saw the Coalition vote in favour of a motion by One Nation's Pauline Hanson that had borrowed the white supremacist slogan 'It's OK to be white'.

Caught up in the chaos, the National Party had become consumed by talk of a leadership spill to bring back former leader Barnaby Joyce to replace Michael McCormack. Julia Banks, the Liberal MP for Chisholm, announced she wouldn't stand at the next election, citing the bullying and nastiness of the spill. Then her colleague Ann Sudmalis called it quits too. The Morrison government appeared to be terminal.

The week before the by-election, the Liberal Party knew it was in strife. Defence minister Christopher Pyne was telling anyone who would listen that the Liberals were on track to be smashed by the independent Kerryn Phelps. And smashed they were. On 20 October 2018, the constituents of Wentworth backed Phelps, the former boss of the Australian Medical Association, to replace Malcolm Turnbull. Less than two months into his prime ministership, Scott Morrison had lost his one-seat majority, plunging Australia into a hung parliament.

* * *

In the final months of 2018, the government looked to be on track for a hammering at the next election as the Coalition ended the year in a poll slump. Morrison indicated he would bring the 2019 Budget forward to April to allow for a mid-May election. In a further blow to the government, National Party MP Andrew Broad quit in December following a string of revelations of adultery and sleazy behaviour. The government looked rudderless, defining itself by scandal, not policy.

One small but on brand success for the government was its response in September to a strange crisis involving sewing needles being found in punnets of strawberries produced in

Queensland and Western Australia. It was a crisis without a script, but Ben Morton recognised it as being ripe with opportunity. Morton had heard from his wife that the issue, which arose shortly after the leadership spill, was top of mind for parents in his WA electorate of Tangney, so he dutifully suggested that the federal government should join the hunt for the saboteur/s. Morrison quickly announced new laws that would see anyone who contaminated strawberries face increased jail time. It was the sort of low-hanging fruit the government needed to give it some sense of unity and direction.

That summer, with the Morrison government likely entering its final months, long-serving MPs considered their futures. One of Cabinet's most senior female members Kelly O'Dwyer decided to call it quits to spend more time with her two children. She stressed that the decision didn't reflect on Morrison's leadership or the Coalition's election prospects, but regardless it was a bad look for a party that had been accused of having a women problem. By March 2019, Christopher Pyne, Steven Ciobo, Julie Bishop, Michael Keenan and Nigel Scullion also had announced they would be leaving politics after the May election. It appeared that not even government MPs thought the Coalition could win.

Morrison, however, remained somewhat optimistic of the Coalition's chances. His deputy, Josh Frydenberg, had spent the summer at the Victorian beachside town of Lorne, penning opinion pieces about Labor's economic policies. It was one area where the government knew it had a strong track record compared with Labor and Frydenberg went hard on this point in the media. Morrison, as a former treasurer, also knew the importance of economic success come election time. In fact, he'd always taken a strong interest in his previous portfolios, never fully leaving them when he moved into a new role. During the chaos of the August 2018 leadership spill, he had been delighted to take on Peter Dutton's portfolio of home affairs, if only for a few days.

In January 2019, Morrison played to another strength, pushing to assert so-called traditional national values in the run-up to Australia Day. He promised to strip local councils of the power to hold citizenship ceremonies unless they held them on Australia Day, a move triggered after a handful of councils voted to shift citizenship events to another day out of respect for Australia's Indigenous people. It's the sort of politics Morrison is good at. He firmly believes the majority of Australians are proud of their country and unite around shared values. So he figured that the citizenship policies gave him a double hit: he would be seen to be standing up for so-called middle Australia, but secondly and more importantly, the announcement would give him a chance to wedge Labor and its leader Bill Shorten for not immediately backing the move, which he described as common sense.

As part of his Australia Day pitch, Morrison also announced a plan to impose a dress code on citizenship ceremonies. Those closest to him say the move was designed to reflect the kinds of Australians he had met while holidaying in regional NSW over the summer break. It's not clear if casually dressed would-be Australians was an issue that ever needed addressing, nor is it clear if the new regulations have been strongly enforced since being imposed. But it did give Morrison the opportunity to declare himself 'a prime minister for standards'.

When parliament returned in February, Morrison again saw opportunity where others tried to create political pain. Labor teamed up with the crossbench and the Greens to pass the Medical Evacuation Bill (the 'medevac' bill), which made it easier for refugees in offshore detention to be brought to Australia for medical treatment. The bill's passage delivered the first major loss by a government on the floor of the House of Representatives since 1929. But Morrison remained mostly sanguine following the historic defeat, perhaps because he understood that voters cared little about parliamentary procedures and power. A staffer who was sent to inform him about the loss said he simply shrugged before moving on to the next crisis. Rather than bemoan the result, Morrison went on the political offensive and pitched Labor as soft on border control. He claimed the vote proved Labor didn't have the 'mettle' to make the difficult calls to protect Australia's borders and could not be 'trusted' to stop deaths at sea.

Labor was confident it could win the election but it still struggled to campaign effectively against Morrison. He didn't have the same public profile as his predecessor, Malcolm Turnbull, who was well-known before he arrived in

Canberra, and constituents were still making up their mind about their latest prime minister. Labor strategists identified that Australians remembered him from his time as the country's hardline immigration minister but little else.

With border security now back in the spotlight, Morrison decided he needed to play to another perceived Liberal strength if he had any shot of retaining the prime ministership. Frydenberg's first budget, which he announced on 2 April 2019, delivered personal income tax cuts to low- and middle-income Australians worth $158 billion over ten years. The government also promised the return of a balanced budget, an attempt to highlight the Coalition's record of producing surpluses and paying off national debt. Frydenberg declared the budget was 'back in the black' and 'back on track', with a surplus forecast to reach $7.1 billion the following financial year. The COVID-19 pandemic would later deny Frydenberg his promised surplus but it worked as an election pitch. Morrison and Frydenberg also had to counter Labor's pledge to lift wages and help low- to middle-income earners through tax cuts. To do that, the Coalition also promised $285 million worth of one-off payments to pensioners, carers and single parents to cover the cost of electricity bills.

In the days after the budget was handed down, internal polling conducted by Crosby Textor showed that it had been positively received by voters – men and women. Importantly, it was playing well in marginal seats. Research in twenty key seats showed that the Liberal Party's primary vote had jumped from 38 per cent to 41 per cent off the back of the budget, seemingly putting the government in a more competitive position for the election.

* * *

With an election campaign due within days, Liberal Party Federal Director Andrew Hirst prioritised the economic narrative, believing it would be the key to a Coalition win. But while Newspoll gave the Coalition a small post-budget boost, the polls still suggested the Morrison government was on track to lose the election on 18 May.

On 11 April, Scott Morrison rose before dawn and at about 6.45 am he departed The Lodge in C1, destined for nearby Government House. Over a cup of coffee, Morrison met governor-general Peter Cosgrove to officially prorogue the forty-fifth parliament and send Australia to the polls. Back at Parliament House, Morrison had a quick bite of toast with Vegemite ahead of the 8 am press conference where he would make his pitch to the Australian public. Addressing the media, as well as Australians who were enjoying their breakfast, Morrison echoed former Liberal prime minister John Howard by framing the election around trust and promising to 'make your life easier' through continued economic growth.

It is crystal clear, at this election, it is a choice between me as prime minister and Bill Shorten as prime minister. You vote for me, you'll

*get me. You vote for Bill Shorten and you'll get Bill Shorten. The
choice to be made by Australians on 18 May is like it always is at
every election, and that is: who do you trust to deliver that strong
economy which your essential services rely on?*

Morrison then borrowed from Howard's 2004 election
victory by kicking off the campaign in western Sydney. His
first stop was Penrith, in the heart of the Labor-held marginal
seat of Lindsay. It wasn't the Blacktown Workers Club, but
it was home to Howard's battlers and was a suburb firmly in
Morrison's sights.

The post-budget boost in the polls slightly reinvigorated the
Coalition team, but the outlook was still grim. The Coalition
embarked on its election campaign behind Labor, both in the
opinion polls and the betting markets. Few, if any, Liberal
MPs believed the government would retain power – except
Scott Morrison, of course. Even Josh Frydenberg privately told
colleagues it was unlikely the Coalition would remain in office.

Malcolm Turnbull had been popular in Frydenberg's home
state of Victoria, where the Liberal team had been smashed
at the state election the previous November, after Morrison
had become prime minister. So a confident Bill Shorten
kicked off his own campaign in the eastern Melbourne seat
of Deakin, which was held by Liberal Michael Sukkar by a
margin of more than 6 per cent. Political insiders saw this
as a cocky move, but Labor strategists were soon questioning
their own messaging. The Opposition spent the first week of

the campaign spruiking its big-ticket policy promising more money for cancer patients – it was hardly controversial, but it meant lots of hospital visits and sad tales of sick Australians. Meanwhile, says one Labor campaigner, 'Morrison was on the TV every night hitting balls and looking like a moron and some of our people couldn't believe their luck. But Morrison's images were always positive, always ran first and some of us were worried.'

Morrison's critics had labelled him 'Scotty from Marketing', which was meant to be a derogatory term but turned out to be the perfect moniker. His political messaging was sharp and his tourism years had taught him the importance of positivity. He also ruthlessly attacked Labor leader Bill Shorten, who was already unpopular with voters. Shorten had come close to winning the 2016 federal election, which many political insiders believe gave him the confidence to pursue a higher-taxing agenda targeting tax loopholes such as franking credits and negative gearing. But Morrison characterised Shorten as the 'bill' Australia simply couldn't afford. It was a smart strategy that set its sights on the big policy Shorten was trying to sell, which involved stronger intervention in wealth redistribution to assist the lower paid and sick.

Shorten also greatly underestimated his new opponent. Asked at the time how Morrison stacked up against the previous two prime ministers he had faced, Shorten seemed to mock Morrison's enthusiasm in the face of predicted defeat, responding:

Abbott has a strong intellect which I don't think people realise. What he thinks is unusual … but he is not an idiot and he is very good at just punching a message. Turnbull looked like a prime minister. And the current fella, well, he's not going to die wondering.

He offered this assessment with his trademark smirk. It was clear he truly believed Morrison wasn't up to the job and he was going to rely on Australians making the same assessment.

Labor strategists, however, were struggling to figure out Morrison. When Turnbull's leadership had appeared unstable, they had prepared, reluctantly, for a Julie Bishop win. It was a scenario they feared. She was popular with the public, a woman and a great campaigner. Dutton had been viewed as an easier opponent than Bishop, although he still had his strengths. While a polarising figure, he was popular with a certain section of the middle class, particularly tradies, who saw him as strong – Shorten, by contrast, was sometimes described by these demographics as appearing weak. But the new prime minister? 'Morrison we just couldn't get a read on. We struggled to characterise him,' says one Labor campaigner. He was less recognisable and that meant he carried less baggage. Labor reminded focus groups that Morrison was the guy who'd been involved in the Tourism Australia controversy, an attempt to portray him as dodgy. But political messaging has to be sharp and punchy. It doesn't work if you have to teach people about the subject before landing a blow.

Labor then decided to back in research that showed that many voters characterised the Coalition government firstly as chaotic and secondly as out of touch because its policies often helped the big end of town. Both of these attack lines had worked against Turnbull, a wealthy investment banker who had led a coup to overthrow Tony Abbott. But used against Morrison, this strategy fell flat. He seemed to be successfully pitching himself as a suburban dad who had taken over the Coalition leadership in a Steven Bradbury–style win. Bradbury was a speed skater who in 2002 became the first Australian to win a gold medal at the Winter Olympics after his four rivals all collided and fell over, allowing him to glide past to claim victory. Of course, Bradbury's win in Salt Lake City wasn't all circumstantial. Like Morrison, he had earned a place among the final contenders and then positioned himself perfectly for when his competitors tumbled.

Coalition strategists realised that Labor had underrated Morrison. 'It had been such a chaotic year in the lead-up to that election that it lulled Labor into a false sense of security,' says one Liberal strategist. Still, the polls continued to predict that the Coalition's time was up. After the first week of the election campaign, everything pointed to a Labor victory, with the Opposition ahead on a two-party basis by 52 per cent to 48 per cent according to Newspoll. Not one national poll had the Coalition in front, while Labor's internal polling, conducted by YouGov Galaxy, broadly reflected the public surveys.

* * *

Over the early days of the campaign, Shorten suffered a series of stumbles that played poorly on the news and also affected his momentum and confidence. First, he said there would be no changes to superannuation – except, of course, for the major ones he'd already announced. Then, when pushing for a transition to electric vehicles, Shorten appeared not to be across the details of his own policy when he said it took eight to ten minutes to charge such a car, when in fact it can take hours.

Unlike Turnbull in 2016, Morrison clung to Shorten's gaffes, constantly using them to attack the Opposition. He likened Shorten to former Liberal Party leader John Hewson, who in 1993 struggled to explain whether his proposed GST would apply to birthday cakes. 'Malcolm believed that people would naturally relate to the sun god [Turnbull] whereas Scott was far more of a brawler,' says one of Morrison's election team. 'He started to lay punches on Shorten that he [Shorten] simply failed to recover from.'

Shorten's first week jitters didn't stop there. He was campaigning in the South Australian seat of Boothby when he was grilled on the Opposition's emissions-reduction policy. Ten Network journalist Jonathan Lea repeatedly asked Shorten how Labor would achieve its ambitious targets and at what cost to the economy. Shorten was at first evasive and then became visibly agitated with Lea:

Lea: 'You have focused almost exclusively, since your budget reply speech, on health. When can voters expect to learn more about Labor's emissions-reduction target, how you're going to get there, and the cost to the economy?'

Shorten: 'Well first of all, I haven't spoken exclusively about health.'

Lea: 'Well to be fair, some of your staffers said the same in private conversations. You've focused pretty exclusively on it since Sunday.'

Shorten: 'I don't know what private conversations you have with people or what you want to reveal. But let me just go to the record. I just said, four minutes ago, that Mr Morrison loves to boast about his strong economy. I'm pretty sure we were all here when I said that. But let me say it again, because I think it's a really good point to make. Mr Morrison loves to boast about his strong economy. But his strong economy is your classic Liberal strong economy. It's built upon two propositions: one, low wages, they're proud of it. They almost have a religious fervour, don't they, about being happy when the wages are low and corporate profits are up. Did you know that since the last election, corporate profits have gone up 39 per cent? But in fact wages have moved on average 5 per cent? And the second leg that he relies upon for this Liberal strong economy is the ... reduction in real spending on services. In particular, health, but also I mentioned education, I mentioned TAFE. I mentioned child care ...'

Lea: 'You're not answering the question, Mr Shorten.'

Shorten: 'Oh, okay. I'm going to give someone else a go.'

Lea: 'Answer the question … When can people know, Mr Shorten, the cost to the economy? You didn't answer the question.'

Shorten: 'You know what, Jon? I'm going to go to the next person.'

Lea: 'No, you should answer the question, That's why we're here, to ask questions. And you're not answering the question. When can people expect to know, Mr Shorten, the cost to the economy? Why can't you answer the question, Mr Shorten?'

Shorten: 'Because I'm going to give your colleagues half a go.'

And on it went. Veteran campaigners in Labor's headquarters were relieved when the Easter break arrived, so that the nervous Shorten could reset. By contrast, Morrison looked calm and relaxed.

In political circles, Morrison is often described as a confidence player. Free from pressure, he can perform well and often defies expectations. So it was at the beginning of the 2019 election campaign: he had nothing to lose and unexpectedly finished that first week in front of his opponent. When one of Morrison's closest confidants called him, they could hear the enthusiasm in the prime minister's voice. He understood the benefit of being seen as the underdog and said that the Liberal team were 'buoyed' by how everything was going.

The Easter period offered Morrison and Shorten a break from engaging with the relentless news cycle. Voters were visiting family or relaxing at favourite locations and had switched off from the election campaign. Importantly, the holiday gave the respective leaders the chance to spend some time with their own families ahead of a gruelling schedule in the lead-up to polling day. On Easter Sunday, Morrison allowed the media into his local Pentecostal church in southern Sydney, where he sang, eyes closed and waving his hands in the air, alongside fellow worshippers. Labor's campaign team rightly steered clear of using the footage to score political points, which would've allowed Morrison to launch an impassioned defence of his faith. But a few weeks later, their candidate strayed from the agreed script, with Shorten criticising Morrison's silence over the Israel Folau controversy. This prompted Morrison to offer a lengthy and nuanced rebuttal, and the promise of greater religious protections for Australians. A subsequent review of Labor's campaign would find that, on the whole:

> ... *people of faith did not desert Labor, but Labor lost some support among Christian voters, particularly devout, first-generation migrant Christians. Bill Shorten called Scott Morrison out on his failure to condemn Folau's remarks. This led to Shorten defending criticism he was seeking to embarrass Morrison because of his religion.*

On the campaign trail, Morrison contrasted his brutal attacks on Bill Shorten with his soft, daggy dad persona. His closest friends defend this selling point, claiming that it is true to

Morrison's character — albeit a little overdone. They insist he really doesn't have highbrow tastes. Unlike Turnbull and Abbott, who both won Rhodes Scholarships and attended Oxford University, Morrison studied his Bachelor of Science in Applied Economic Geography at UNSW. He prefers a beer over a glass of wine, and favours Australian songstress Tina Arena over the Sydney Symphony Orchestra. Even those of his colleagues who roll an eye at the cap-wearing, suburban prime minister they see on the television claim that, however cringe-worthy it can be, it isn't a huge stretching of the truth.

One of Morrison's closest confidants believes the party leadership and Morrison's time as a senior government minister changed the way Morrison holds himself and how he conducts himself. He said Morrison is now more inclusive and consultative. However, he also says that, as with Trump:

> … the gravitas of being the leader hasn't altered him. There are parts of you that are essential to who you are and they simply shouldn't change. People can relate to the caps, the footy, the church, the childhood sweetheart, and those parts that are uniquely him.

* * *

Shorten emerged from the Easter break refreshed and with sharper messaging, but his campaign team were still finding it difficult to land a blow on the prime minister. Not that they hadn't tried to find a weak spot. Not long after Shorten won the party room ballot for leader of the ALP, his office commissioned Labor's so-called 'dirt unit' to find skeletons in Morrison's closet. It shouldn't come as a surprise to learn that the major parties each have backroom operations where eager partisan folk diligently search through documents and make calls to find problematic tales about certain MPs and candidates. One Labor insider says the ALP attempted to elicit ammunition from Michael Towke, whom Morrison had beaten in the Cook preselection. They also phoned former Liberal minister Fran Bailey, who oversaw Morrison's removal from Tourism Australia, as well as government contacts in New Zealand in the hope they'd share juicy details of Morrison's early departure from the Office of Tourism and Sport. However, says the insider, 'People simply didn't want to go to war with him. They seemed to be scared of him and wanted to stay out of the way.'

When interviewing Morrison's colleagues, friends and professional contacts for this book, a trend emerged. Morrison is a polarising figure. His male peers speak of a hardworking, down-to-earth man who is driven by outcomes. But there are many people who loathe Morrison, and they are overwhelmingly women. Few feel confident speaking publicly, fearing blowback as Morrison is considered to have a glass jaw. Some were so irritated by him, they simply don't want to relive the experience.

Meanwhile, inside the Liberal campaign, Morrison was heavily involved in directing traffic. Between events, he spent time talking to newspaper editors and briefing key journalists, campaign strategists and pollsters. Instead of relying on a national message and banking on a countrywide swing, the Liberals also ran a small-target operation. Morrison methodically followed the polling in twenty marginal seats and was prepared to instantly adapt his campaign to woo voters in those electorates. He is at heart a marketing man and he well understood the strategy he needed to apply and the product he needed to sell.

Liberal research soon discovered that Labor's franking credit policy was proving contentious and might offer the Coalition a narrow path to victory. Franking credits were introduced in 1987 to address double taxation on dividend income. They allow investors to claim a credit equal to the amount of company tax already paid on those dividends. In 2001, the Howard government supercharged the scheme, making franking credits a fully refundable tax offset. This means that if someone's tax bill is less than their franking credits, the excess credits will be refunded by the government. But Labor had promised that, if elected, they would scrap the cash payments for excess franking dividends, albeit with an exemption for pensioners. Turnbull was the one who had labelled the proposal a 'retiree tax', but Morrison now hammered home this point. At community halls and senior citizen centres across Australia, he held heavily vetted information sessions at which retirees begged Morrison to do more to protect their retirement income.

The strategy ultimately would prove effective. On polling day, Labor would suffer swings against it at booths where people aged over sixty made up more than 15 per cent of the population. The Opposition would be hurt in key seats that included Reid, Lindsay, Banks and Longman. Labor's election review later disputed this, arguing that the voters most affected by the franking credits policy actually swung to them. But the party did concede that the volume of spending and tax changes created a sense of risk in the minds of the main beneficiaries of Labor's policies: economically insecure, low-income voters.

But all of that was yet to come. By the final week of the election campaign, the public polls still had Labor in front, although inside both the Shorten and Morrison camps there was a growing expectation that neither party could win a majority. With only a few days to go until the poll, Morrison gave a speech at the National Press Club in Canberra. He noticed his friend David Gazard in the audience and later rang him from C1 to discuss the campaign. Morrison apparently said, 'We are right in this. We can win with a majority, we can win in minority, we can lose in minority and we can lose in majority. That's how close it is.'

Gazard believed him and urged the prime minister to start thinking about potential negotiations with the crossbench in the event of a hung parliament. Gazard's brother-in-law Rob Oakeshott was running as an independent in the NSW seat of Cowper. Labor had preferred Oakeshott as second on its how-to-vote card, making him one of several independents who potentially would be kingmakers. But although Oakeshott had helped deliver a minority government to Julia Gillard in 2010 when he was the MP for Lyne, Gazard didn't think his brother-in-law would necessarily back Labor a second time. There was even a suggestion of offering an independent such as Oakeshott the job of speaker.

On 17 May, the day before the election, the published opinion polls still had the Coalition losing, but the Liberals' internal polling painted a different picture. Labor were on track to lose Herbert in northern Queensland and Lindsay in western Sydney, meaning the Opposition had to convert nine seats to form a majority government. Labor was in front in the marginal Victorian seats of Chisholm, Dunkley and Corangamite, but that wouldn't be enough. The Liberals still looked popular in Tasmania and Western Australia, and internal polling suggested that between 10 per cent and 15 per cent of voters hadn't yet made up their minds. Morrison headed for Tasmania, where he spent the final morning of the campaign.

No senior minister seriously believed the Coalition would win a majority, including deputy leader Frydenberg. But on election day, the increasingly confident Morrison told the pragmatic Frydenberg that he would campaign until he dropped. The previous evening, he had sent his deputy a text saying he believed in miracles and the result was in God's hands.

* * *

On the night of 18 May, Morrison invited his family, closest advisers and friends to Kirribilli House. Some who were present at the prime minister's residence that night say that Morrison was obsessed by the data rather than the media coverage. He wanted live results from key scrutineers, not the opinions of politicians and pundits – as a former state director of the Liberal Party, he understood the raw data. Supporters and staff – including David Gazard, Scott Briggs, Yaron Finkelstein, Andrew Carswell, John Kunkel and Morrison's university friend Adrian Harrington – were crammed around a desk, watching the results come in. By 7 pm, the mood in the room was upbeat. An hour later, Morrison told his team that he thought they were going to win.

Shortly after 10 pm, Morrison's car headed across the Sydney Harbour Bridge, bound for the Sofitel hotel in the CBD where the Coalition faithful had gathered. Both prime ministerial candidates had prepared for positive and negative outcomes, but few had thought Morrison would need to spend much time rehearsing his victory speech. Labor were reluctant to admit defeat, but eventually, at about 11.20 pm, Shorten called Morrison. In a private room at the Sofitel, Morrison announced to his team, 'Bill's conceded.' Against all odds, the Coalition had won the election and Morrison would get another term as Prime Minister.

A short time later, standing on a stage with his wife and two daughters in front of a cheering crowd, Scott Morrison declared:

I have always believed in miracles! I'm standing with the three biggest miracles in my life here tonight, and tonight we've been delivered another one. How good is Australia? And how good are Australians? This is the best country in the world in which to live. It is those Australians that we have been working for, for the last five and a half years since we came to government, under Tony Abbott's leadership back in 2013. It has been those Australians who have worked hard every day, they have their dreams, they have their aspirations. To get a job, to get an apprenticeship, to start a business, to meet someone amazing. To start a family, to buy a home, to work hard and provide the best you can for your kids. To save your retirement and to ensure that when you're in your retirement, that you can enjoy it because you've worked hard for it. These are the quiet Australians who have won a great victory tonight.

Chapter Thirteen

Aloha

In November 2016, Julia Banks found herself walking out of the House of Representatives just as Scott Morrison was also heading out the doors. Banks had only been elected four months earlier, with her victory in the ultra-marginal seat of Chisholm in Melbourne's east the only instance of a Liberal Party candidate snatching a seat from Labor in the federal poll. A corporate lawyer, Banks was a hard worker and keen not to put a foot wrong in Canberra in those early days. So as she and Morrison exited the chamber, she asked him if he thought it would be acceptable for her to close down her electorate office between Christmas and New Year. Banks was worried that a constituent might reach out to her office for help with Centrelink payments or their power supply over that time. She told Morrison she would still have staff answer the electorate office phones but she wanted to give them time with their families. Morrison, Banks later told colleagues, had smirked and said his own electorate office effectively operated on summer hours during December and January because the public didn't want to see or hear from MPs between December and Australia Day.

It's an outdated rule of politics but one many MPs prescribe to: those twelve or so weeks between Melbourne Cup Day and Australia Day aren't to be embraced with the same enthusiasm for work as the rest of the year. It's for this reason that the events of December 2019 came as no surprise to Banks.

A prolonged drought and scorching temperatures had created tinder-box conditions across much of Australia by the spring of that year. It was those factors, combined with unusually low humidity and wild winds, that sparked a rare fire in the Gold Coast hinterland in September 2019. The usually lush farmlands and forests of Queensland's Scenic Rim had slowly turned a dull brown after years of little rain, and a single spark was all that was needed to start an inferno. A carelessly discarded cigarette is believed to be the cause of the blaze that flared on 2 September. It would mark the start of an unprecedented bushfire season in Australia that would claim thirty-three lives and destroy more than 3000 homes. Within a week, eighty fires were burning across Queensland and another forty were raging in Morrison's home state of

New South Wales. Australia has always suffered from the brutality of bushfires, but never before had it experienced fires on such a scale so early in spring.

In late October, a lightning strike to the north-west of Sydney sparked an unprecedented bushfire in both its size and ferociousness. A month later, the blaze had consumed 85,000 hectares and was threatening lives and property. The worst nightmare of those in charge of battling the outbreaks was soon realised when several of the fires around Sydney came together to create the biggest forest fire in Australian history. This coincided with the country recording its hottest day on record, with a nationwide average maximum temperature of 40.9 degrees Celsius. And summer had only just begun.

Months earlier, a group of twenty-three former fire and emergency services leaders had tried to persuade Scott Morrison that Australia needed more water-bombers to tackle the bigger, faster and hotter blazes that were expected in the upcoming bushfire season. The group, led by former NSW Fire and Rescue chief Greg Mullins, had first sought a meeting with the prime minister in April, then again in May, immediately after the federal election. Its members were fearful that Australia would struggle to borrow firefighting equipment from the United States if needed, as the bushfire seasons in the two countries had begun to overlap.

The request for more water-bombers had been ignored.

* * *

Following his miracle election victory, Morrison had had a taxing year that had denied him precious time with his wife and children. Trying to balance his role as a father with that of prime minister, he made a promise to his family that he would take them to Hawaii for a holiday over the Christmas period, when he expected that few people would want to see or hear from a politician. And so, with Australia stifled by soaring temperatures, on 16 December 2019, Scott, Jenny, Abbey and Lily boarded a Jetstar flight to Honolulu. It was the family's second Pacific trip that year, having visited Fiji following the May election. It would be a decision that Morrison would ultimately live to regret, one that would see the public and his colleagues question his leadership and judgement soon after his election win.

For the most part, Australian prime ministers have tended to avoided international holidays while in office. While escaping to a European winter or an African jungle might be the perfect antidote to public life, Australians can be quite judgemental about such seemingly extravagant vacations. The tall poppy syndrome is rife in this country, especially among working Australians who spend the year saving for an annual break at one of the many beautiful caravan parks favoured by millions of families each summer. This perception is not necessarily fair, but typically it is something that all prime ministers have understood.

John Howard, arguably one of Australia's most unpretentious leaders, spent almost every summer break at Hawks Nest, a seaside town three hours' drive north of Sydney. Howard, wife Janette and their three children, Melanie, Tim and Richard, would rent an apartment, aptly named The Lodge, directly opposite the beach.

For years, Tony Abbott and his family holidayed with old friends at Berrara on the NSW South Coast. They'd stay at the Berrara Beach Park, an upmarket holiday park where caravans had been replaced by plush cabins right on the water's edge. During his first Christmas as prime minister, Tony Abbott did brave an international holiday, flying economy with his family to Switzerland to visit eldest daughter, Louise, who was working at the Australian embassy in that country. But at the time Abbott's office made it clear he wasn't interested in an upgrade to the pointy end of the plane.

In 1974, prime minister Gough Whitlam was on tour in Greece when Cyclone Tracy hit Darwin. He briefly returned to Australia to tour of the devastation before jumping on the next plane back to Europe, prompting criticism he was more interested in looking over the ruins of ancient Olympia than Darwin.

Kevin Rudd learned the hard way that Australians, while aspirational, despise champagne socialists. In 2011, Rudd and his wife, Thérèse Rein, purchased a $3.1 million holiday house at Castaways Beach, south of Noosa in Queensland. The lavish abode might have been less than two hours' drive from the family's Norman Park home, but it was clearly out of the reach of the average Aussie worker, and their purchase garnered negative media suggestions that Rudd's new neighbourhood would have him bumping shoulders with the rich and famous, including the likes of Sir Richard Branson and Bob Ansett.

During the 2019 election campaign, Morrison had been acutely aware of the need to seem grounded and unpretentious. He capitalised on his footy-loving everyman persona, which told voters he was just like them. But mere months later, it appeared that Morrison had forgotten the need to be seen as down-to-earth when he jetted off to Honolulu in a business class seat. For Australians in top-tier tax brackets, a family holiday to Hawaii on budget airline Jetstar is hardly a lavish affair, but for workers bringing in an average wage, such a trip is seen as a once-in-a-lifetime holiday. And while Australians are fairly understanding types and appreciate, for the most part, that prime ministers work hard and are entitled to a break over summer, this was no ordinary summer – by mid-December, Australia had endured weeks of unprecedented bushfires that were smothering Sydney in a choking haze.

The final work commitment Scott Morrison had planned in 2019 was to deliver the Mid-Year Economic and Fiscal Outlook, which revised down the government's revenue by $3 billion on earlier projections. That was bad enough, but after Morrison had taken Jenny to the Sydney Coliseum Theatre in Rooty Hill to see his favourite singer, Tina Arena, before heading to the airport for the family's international flight, things got much worse. When prime ministers do take a break from their daily duties, traditionally it has been announced via a statement from the Prime Minister's Office. The communiqué not only explains why the prime minister is going to be absent from talkback radio and the nightly news, it signals who will be in charge in their absence. However, in this case, Nationals leader and Deputy PM Michael McCormack was appointed acting prime minister but would not publicly confirm or deny his role, instead referring questions to the Prime Minister's Office. In turn, responding to questions from press gallery journalists about Morrison's whereabouts, that office asserted that any suggestion he was in Hawaii was wrong and then pointedly refused to disclose where he was.

Denying journalists such basic information as the location of the prime minister rarely stops a story from building; in fact, it usually has the opposite effect. And so the pressure mounted. Lara Worthington nee Bingle, the model who had fronted Tourism Australia's controversial 2006 campaign, tweeted: 'Scott Morrison: WHERE THE BLOODY HELL ARE YOU??? #AustraliaBurns #AustraliaFires.' Some of the staff inside the Prime Minister's Office began challenging the holiday denial strategy, concerned that Morrison's location would eventually be discovered anyway by the story-hungry media. McCormack only made matters worse when he refused to say where Morrison was, or even if he was still in the country.

With the bushfires worsening, television footage from 2010 was aired that showed Scott Morrison criticising then Victorian police chief Christine Nixon, who'd infamously eaten at a gastropub on the evening of 7 February 2009 when the Black Saturday bushfires were raging:

She's clearly made a bad judgment call. That happens to people from time to time, but this was a very serious issue. I think there are very serious concerns in the community about exercising judgement, and it's incumbent on all of us in public life to make decisions following that in the best interests of the ongoing nature of the program.

While Labor leader Anthony Albanese refused to criticise the prime minister publicly, the actions of the two men couldn't have been more different. With Morrison nowhere to be found, Albanese was spotted at a Woolworths in Sydney's inner west, stocking up on water and snacks for the volunteer firefighters battling blazes in the Blue Mountains. The contrast was just as striking in regards to former prime minister Tony Abbott, who as a volunteer firefighter battled the blazes burning south of Canberra.

Morrison hadn't yet been gone a week when thousands of protesters rallied outside his Sydney residence, Kirribilli House, concerned about the effects of climate change. That same day, 19 December, a photo was published showing Morrison in board shorts on Waikiki Beach at sunset with some Australian tourists, making the shaka or 'hang loose' hand gesture. There was no doubt the prime minister was receiving daily briefings on the unfolding disaster in Australia, but the beach image nonetheless was very damaging. For one thing, the Prime Minister's Office was now forced to admit that Morrison was in Hawaii, despite days of denials. With egg on their faces, his media team confirmed he would arrive back in Australia on 23 December.

On the night of 19 December, a truck carrying volunteer firefighters flipped after colliding with a tree to the south-west of Sydney. Geoffrey Keaton, thirty-two, and Andrew O'Dwyer, thirty-six, both fathers to young children, were killed in the crash, and three other passengers were injured. The calamity prompted Morrison to cut short his holiday. He issued a statement the following day:

> *I deeply regret any offence caused to any of the many Australians affected by the terrible bushfires by my taking leave with family at this time. I have been receiving regular updates on the bushfires disaster … The Commonwealth's responsibilities have been well managed by the Acting Prime Minister, Minister [David] Littleproud and Minister [Marise] Payne. As noted, given the most recent tragic events, I will be returning to Sydney as soon as can be arranged.*

* * *

Through his absence and subsequent defensiveness, a pattern emerged of Morrison sheltering behind rhetoric instead of acting. Questions about his whereabouts had been deflected, relegated to something that was only of concern to journalists. It's a strategy he has relied on throughout his career. While priding himself on his marketing prowess, when cornered, Morrison often attempts to spread the blame and downplay a story's significance, including his own role. He most commonly falls into this trap when speaking with more 'friendly' media sources like commercial radio, when he attempts to reach the public over the heads of journalists and commentators.

On 19 December, speaking from Hawaii for a 2GB interview, Morrison declared:

I'll be getting back there as soon as I can. The girls and Jen will stay on ... the rest of the time we had booked here. But I know Australians understand this and they'll be pleased I'm coming back I'm sure. They know that, you know, I don't hold a hose, mate, and I don't sit in a control room. That's the brave people who ... are doing that job. But I know that Australians would want me back at this time out of these fatalities. So I'll happily come back and do that.

His tone suggested he was doing Australia a favour, his turn of phrase shorthand for blame-shifting. Morrison had made a bad situation even worse, something he would do again and again. In comparison, almost a decade earlier, when an asylum-seeker boat sunk off Christmas Island and forty-eight people died, then prime minister Julia Gillard had cut short her own annual holiday and struck a completely different tone, stating that she was focused only on the rescue and treatment of those injured.

Compounding the controversy, on his final day in Hawaii, as he was waiting for the next flight to Australia, Morrison was photographed with his wife at a bar watching the sunset on Waikiki Beach. The images only increased the rage back home. In an age when most travellers have a smartphone, it's little surprise that Morrison was photographed in a tourism hotspot like Waikiki. What is surprising is that his office thought it would be able to keep his whereabouts out of the media, a task made practically impossible given a Labor staffer was staying at the same hotel as the Morrisons. Staff working for Morrison at the time recall days of discussions about how to handle his impending holiday, and there is a general consensus that the orders to divert and deflect came from the top.

Morrison jetted into Sydney on a Hawaiian Airlines flight just before 8 pm on 21 December. Up early the next morning, he was briefed on the bushfires at the NSW Rural Fire Service headquarters before visiting evacuation centres with NSW Premier Gladys Berejiklian. But nervous government MPs were feeling the heat, with their constituents angered by the prime minister's recent absence. It didn't help that ministers who contacted the Prime Minister's Office to express their frustration were soon put in their place – even the most constructive advice was deemed unnecessary.

Morrison's deputy Josh Frydenberg did all he could to protect his boss, calling every single member of the Liberal and National party room to reassure them that the pain being felt by the government would not be permanent. Morrison 'really appreciated that', says a Liberal insider. 'It helped calm everything.'

* * *

Over Christmas 2019, the fires burning along the coast south of Sydney dramatically escalated, as did the blazes burning in thick bushland in Victoria. At seaside holiday spots in eastern Victoria and southern New South Wales, thousands of residents and holiday-makers were forced to shelter on the beach and were warned that they might need to enter the ocean to protect themselves if the fires approached – many of them eventually would be evacuated by Navy ships. Then, on New Year's Eve, an emergency warning was issued to the 750 residents of Cobargo, an historic dairy-farming town situated just inland from Bermagui in southern New South Wales. A firestorm swept through the township, killing 29-year-old dairy farmer Patrick Salway and his 63-year-old father, Robert, who died while desperately trying to save their home from the inferno. The fire also destroyed dozens of historic buildings, leaving lives and livelihoods in ruin.

On 2 January 2020, Scott Morrison made an ill-fated trip to Cobargo. Entering disaster zones is always challenging for politicians: to stay away, as Morrison had done at the start of the bushfires, is seen as insensitive and heartless, but turning up comes with its own risks.

In 2011, as foreign minister, Kevin Rudd picked up a foot infection after wading through floodwaters in Brisbane to help some Korean students evacuate from the disaster. In such situations, politicians can cop flack for potentially getting in the way of rescue teams or for bringing news crews into already chaotic environments. In Rudd's case, his good intentions were overshadowed by his decision to ignore the advice of Queensland's Chief Health Officer Jeannette Young, who'd warned people to stay out of potentially contaminated waters. Julia Gillard, who was prime minister at the time, was criticised too, for her choice of clothes and wooden demeanour while visiting victims of the floods. And back in 2002, John Howard's decision to embrace survivors of the Bali bombings at a memorial service at the Australian consulate in Denpasar was seen as detracting from the main event. It's almost impossible for politicians to get it right.

Morrison had known he would be taking a risk by entering Cobargo and other fire-damaged communities just forty-eight hours after the devastation of New Year's Eve. In fact, his office had even checked polling booth figures from the last election – Cobargo sits in the bellwether seat of Eden-Monaro, where constituents traditionally elect members to the government benches. Surrounding areas may host swinging voters but the town of Cobargo isn't Liberal heartland. Arriving in the devastated community to find it was still under a blanket of thick red smoke, Morrison wanted to speak with the locals and offer his support. But it did not go well. A number of locals swore at and otherwise abused the prime minister, aggravated by a combination of anger over Morrison's Hawaii holiday and an alleged lack of emergency relief funding. Such interactions with the public are normally choreographed, with the people whom Morrison meets heavily vetted, but he just couldn't have that level of control in a disaster zone. Instead, vulnerable and grieving victims came face to face with the prime minister and told him how they really felt.

At one point, Morrison took hold of a young mother and forced a handshake onto her. He did the same thing with a volunteer firefighter who clearly didn't want to shake the prime minister's hand – it was later revealed that the man had lost his home to the fire. These interactions were not indicative of Morrison's entire visit to the bushfire zone, but they were the moments that made global headlines and, coupled with his early inaction, framed his response.

In the wake of the Cobargo visit, Josh Frydenberg called Ben Morton and the pair concluded that the prime minister mustn't retreat after the disastrous trip. Rather, they felt that he needed to get straight over to bushfire-ravaged districts in East Gippsland. Morrison took the advice and, carrying a shopping bag full of goods for volunteer-run relief centres, he met with bushfire victims and inspected smouldering ruins.

When Morrison was later quizzed about the anger expressed in Cobargo and the ongoing condemnation of his trip overseas, he again became defensive. Those closest to him believe that while he didn't like the criticism, he didn't need his mistake to be explained over and over. Instead, he wanted to rectify the situation, fast. 'He doesn't like to hear it but when it's said, he examines it,' says one Liberal MP. 'It was a tough time but he learned from it.' In the days after the Cobargo visit, Morrison also said he didn't take the abuse personally: 'Whether they're angry with me or they're angry with the situation, they're hurting. And it's my job to offer comfort and support.'

But the public's displeasure was obvious across Australia. In the first Newspoll of 2020, voters vented their fury at the prime minister, whose personal approval rating tumbled. Satisfaction in Morrison fell by eight points and the dissatisfaction with him increased by eleven points – within a matter of weeks, Morrison's lead over his Labor rival had been wiped out. Still, his colleagues hoped he'd learned his lesson, that he now understood the need for a prime minister to appear to be doing something even when unable to assist. They preferred to believe that he wouldn't make the same mistake again.

Chapter Fourteen

A Global Pandemic

On 25 January 2020, the day before Australia Day, health authorities confirmed the first case of coronavirus (2019-nCoV) in Australia. The patient was a man from Wuhan, the capital of China's Hubei Province and the epicentre of the virus, who had flown from Guangdong Province to Australia on 19 January. The mysterious pneumonia-like virus had first been identified in Wuhan, a city of 11 million people, in December 2019, with Chinese authorities confirming a month later that they had identified the novel virus, which became known as COVID-19.

Five days before the first case of the deadly virus was confirmed in Australia, health minister Greg Hunt received a phone call concerning the coronavirus from the country's chief medical officer. Brendan Murphy was known to be measured, not prone to hysteria, but there was something in the tone of his voice that made Hunt realise the virus posed a significant threat. Murphy went on to tell Hunt that Chinese authorities had confirmed human–to–human transmission for the virus and he thought Australia should list it as having pandemic potential under Australia's *Biosecurity Act*. Hunt agreed and a brief was prepared for him and Scott Morrison.

At that time, there were three direct flights from Wuhan to Sydney each week. The government arranged for border security and biosecurity staff to meet all passengers arriving on those flight and distribute a pamphlet in English and Mandarin that outlined the symptoms of coronavirus. It was viewed as a measured approach. With COVID-19 now designated as having pandemic potential, the government had the ability to use enhanced border measures such as screening, closures or forced quarantine, but this didn't seem necessary at that time. He may have been prime minister, but the years that Morrison spent working in tourism had made him acutely aware of the economic impact of stopping flights from China. There was also a diplomatic relationship to consider.

That week, a drained Morrison attended Cabinet's National Security Committee (NSC) to discuss the gravity of the coronavirus situation – he had been busy juggling the bushfire response in southern NSW, for which he was under pressure, and also supporting his mother, Marion, and brother, Alan, as they all grieved the loss of Scott's father, John Morrison, who had died after months of ill health. It was at those initial meetings of the NSC that senior ministers first debated whether or not to block flights from China. Speculation was also simmering about whether or not the virus had occurred naturally or whether it had escaped from the Wuhan Institute of Virology, a lab known to have worked on novel viruses and other dangerous pathogens. Morrison, however, was of the view that such theorising was somewhat unhelpful. In his opinion, as the virus was spreading, the response to it was more important that its origin.

On 29 January, the government agreed to evacuate some Australians from Wuhan and surrounding Hubei Province, flying the most vulnerable of some 600 nationals to quarantine on Christmas Island. In the background, senior ministers and health officials were continuing to debate the merits of closing the border to China entirely. Doing so would be viewed as a dramatic step, as the World Health Organization (WHO) didn't view border closures as an appropriate approach to virus management – at least not yet. So by evacuating some of its most at-risk citizens, Australia was hoping to prevent any blowback.

On the first day of February, a Saturday, Greg Hunt was walking laps around the cricket oval at Balnarring on Victoria's Mornington Peninsula when he received a call from Brendan Murphy. Hunt had spent much of the summer break working, so he was taking the opportunity to exercise on the sidelines while his son played a cricket match. Murphy had a clear message for him: there was evidence of human-to-human transmission of COVID-19 outside Hubei Province and it was time to close the borders to China. The Australian Health Protection Principal Committee (AHPPC), which comprises the chief medical officers of all the states and territories, already had discussed the development and agreed with the recommendation to halt flights from China. Hunt called Morrison and then asked Murphy to join them on the line. Murphy insisted a border closure was the best option.

From the first notification of the coronavirus threat, Morrison had agreed to follow the expert medical advice. His advisers say he understood the gravity of the situation but that he also appreciated that he lacked the scientific knowledge to make a call without the AHPPC. Up until this point, Morrison had showed an instinct for making tough decisions but also a wilfulness in backing his own judgement, even when it was wrong. Some of his colleagues believe his mishandling of the bushfires had robbed him of such resolute decision-making and that he was now more willing to listen.

Morrison convened a meeting of the NSC for 2 pm that day to formally consider the border proposal. At around 4.30 pm, the meeting adjourned after it had been agreed to ban all flights from China as well as any foreigners attempting to enter Australia who had travelled through China. However, the entry ban would not apply to Australian citizens, permanent residents and their immediate family members, nor to aircrews, who would all self-isolate for a period of fourteen days.

Greg Hunt later said:

The economic impact of closing the border with China seemed monumental. It was massive, but from the outset the PM said: 'If this is going to be what you think, then we are going to have to do everything we can.' The goal was to reduce the spread and build the capacity of our system. We were able to buy ourselves the best part of six weeks but we always knew that in a global pandemic, no-one escapes. From the start I said to Brendan [Murphy]: 'You must give your unvarnished medical advice.'

Morrison also vowed to follow Murphy's guidance. According to those close to Morrison, the pair share a similar pragmatism and approach to decision-making. Morrison respects Murphy's scientific credentials but also his political nous, which is not a trait shared by many bureaucrats. As one senior minister puts it: 'Brendan Murphy was exactly the person we needed. Confident, calm and creative.'

* * *

By late February, Australia had activated the Emergency Response Plan for Communicable Disease Incidents of National Significance, a blueprint for preparing sectors such as the police, child care, schools, transport and essential utilities to respond. However, despite the state of preparation, few restrictions were put in place in Australia. The virus was already spreading, with major outbreaks in Iran, South Korea and Italy. But health experts were still gathering data about susceptibility, incubation, duration, transmission rates and mortality in relation to COVID-19. So the government rejected calls to extend travel bans and tighten quarantine rules for other overseas travellers. Closing the borders to China had bought Australia precious time and the initial aim was to flatten the curve – the strategy remained one of suppression, not eradication.

By March, however, the situation began to change as the federal government learned more about the transmission of the virus, the possibility of a long incubation and its often asymptomatic infections. These characteristics meant the virus would be harder to track and its potential to spread was much greater than first thought. When worldwide coronavirus cases passed the 100,000 mark on 7 March, the worrying milestone prompted stronger action from the Commonwealth Government, which shut out foreign nationals entering from Iran, South Korea and Italy – Australians returning from those countries were required to self-isolate for fourteen days on arrival. It seemed a proportionate measure, but a mere week later, life in Australia would change dramatically.

A Council of Australian Governments (COAG) meeting of federal, state, territory and local government leaders was due to meet in Sydney on 13 March. The unfolding coronavirus crisis was on the agenda, but it was far from the only issue that leaders had come to discuss. The destruction and disruption caused by the 2019–20 bushfires was another weighty topic, with small businesses and residents in the affected communities continuing to struggle with the financial and emotional toll exacted by the fires. Then there was the drought, domestic violence and suicide prevention, as well as a new waste-management plan to debate. But the immediate priority became clear when, early on the morning of the COAG meeting, leaders woke to the news that global share markets had plunged over fears the coronavirus would destroy economic growth.

The main UK index had dropped more than 10 per cent and Wall Street had recorded its steepest daily falls since 1987. In addition, local newspapers now warned of more than 100,000 deaths in Australia if the pandemic was allowed to run its course. This came in the wake of a WHO statement several days earlier that officially declared the COVID-19 outbreak a pandemic, with more than 125,000 cases reported in 118 countries. The WHO nonetheless urged governments to 'strike a fine balance between protecting health, preventing economic and social disruption, and respecting human rights'.

Brendan Murphy briefed Scott Morrison and the state and territory leaders in the morning session of COAG. His message remained one of caution as he counselled against any extreme measures, although it was looking as if upcoming high-profile events such as Sydney's Royal Easter Show and Melbourne's Formula One Australian Grand Prix wouldn't go ahead. After hearing Murphy's briefing, the COAG attendees agreed that there was no need to dramatically change Australia's approach and they moved on to other agenda items.

Then, during a recess, Murphy spoke with members of the AHPPC, who informed him that new data was being made available every hour and it looked grim: cases were appearing in the community with no clear point of transmission, and concerning information was emerging on the incubation of the virus and its mortality rate. AHPPC positions are consensus positions. In relation to COVID-19, state health officers, particularly those in Queensland and Victoria, were increasingly becoming concerned about the silent spread of the virus, especially at major events – all it took was one asymptomatic person catching a crowded train or going to a football match.

Murphy pulled Scott Morrison and a handful of his key advisers to one side for an urgent discussion. According to one adviser in the room, 'that conversation changed everything'. Murphy wanted to address COAG again to update his recommendations, which now included social-distancing measures. Morrison, who had vowed to back his chief health officer, at first challenged Murphy as to why so much of the earlier advice now needed to be reversed. Part of Morrison's initial frustration was personal – he had planned to attend the Cronulla-Sutherland Sharks' round one rugby league match against the South Sydney Rabbitohs the following day as a clear signal to Australians not to be unduly scared of the virus. Regardless, says another onlooker, 'Unlike some other bureaucrats, Brendan Murphy knows politics. The PM trusts him very strongly, and when Brendan changed his advice the PM knew that he needed to act, even if he didn't like it.'

Advisers and hangers-on were then asked to leave the room as Murphy gave an updated assessment to the state and territory leaders. It was agreed that mass gatherings of more than 500 people would be banned, but only from the coming Monday, accounting for the fact it was already Friday afternoon and weekend plans were well and truly underway. It was also agreed to update the advice being offered to would-be travellers, urging them not to leave Australia for overseas destinations unless it was absolutely essential. And there would be a new National Cabinet that would include state, territory and federal leaders, essentially replacing COAG – a Morrison legacy that is expected to remain in place long after he ceases to be prime minister. The National Cabinet agreed to meet weekly initially to assess Australia's response to the coronavirus.

The National Cabinet was an example of the pragmatism Morrison had displayed throughout his political career. He believed that the only way to tackle the challenges of COVID-19 was to regularly meet with his counterparts to resolve problems instead of dealing with each leader unilaterally. Conveniently, the National Cabinet offered a degree of protection for political leaders in a crisis. There were risks, too, of course, with some senior government ministers initially feeling that the new forum robbed them of influence.

* * *

After the drama that day, Scott Morrison, his senior advisers and key staff retreated to Kirribilli House for further meetings, which were expected to run into the night. It was just after 4 pm when the Prime Minister's chief of staff John Kunkel received a call: home affairs minister Peter Dutton had fallen ill after returning from a trip to the United States and was now in hospital, having tested positive for COVID-19.

The previous weekend, Dutton had been in Washington, DC, where he met with senior Trump administration officials about data encryption and measures to combat child exploitation. Those he had been photographed with included US attorney-general William Barr and the president's daughter, Ivanka Trump. Back in Australia, Dutton had attended a full Cabinet meeting in Sydney on Tuesday 10 March before returning to Brisbane on a commercial flight. The prime minister's aides now scrambled for information about where Dutton had contracted the virus and when he may have been infectious. Brendan Murphy sought advice from his deputy, Paul Kelly, an epidemiologist as well as Dutton's treating doctor in Queensland.

One adviser recalls Morrison's staff frantically attempting to clarify whether the entire Cabinet would need to isolate after having been joined in a meeting by the home affairs minister three days earlier. At one stage, a seating chart and floor plan were produced to measure the size of the Cabinet room and the distance between the attendees. Queenslander Karen Andrews and Western Australian Christian Porter, who had returned to Perth, were considered to be most at risk due to their proximity to Dutton in that meeting.

Later, a recalculation showed Dutton was unlikely to have been infectious until after the Cabinet meeting, meaning there was no need for the prime minister and other ministers to immediately be tested. Instead, they were told to wait for any symptoms before taking a test, which was consistent with the public health message at the time. The medical advice was the same for then education minister Dan Tehan and former defence chief Angus Houston, who had been joined by Dutton the day before the Cabinet meeting for the opening of a new campus for the University of the Sunshine Coast; Tehan and Houston would only be tested if they displayed symptoms.

While ultimately there was relief, the scare brought home the risk of the coronavirus, particularly when the symptoms were mild. It had the potential to do significant damage both by making patients sick and by forcing hordes of Australians to isolate if they were deemed at-risk. Indeed, within days, the media cycle was dominated by COVID-19 news. It was as if things that once mattered no longer did. Tasmania and the Northern Territory closed their borders to residents of the other states, and Western Australia, South Australia and Queensland followed within a matter of days. But it was the international border that posed the greatest risk. Morrison responded accordingly, ordering a fourteen-day self-isolation for anyone arriving in Australia.

By 20 March, a travel ban was in place for all non-residents and non-Australian citizens, mirroring a similar ban in New Zealand. Morrison had strong instincts about sealing Australia off from the rest of the world, not just as a health measure but also as a political move, which he rightly predicted would have widespread support in the community. The closure was based on advice from Murphy and the AHPPC that about 80 per cent of the known COVID-19 cases involved someone who had contracted the virus overseas or who had had direct contact with someone who had returned from overseas.

By that weekend (21–22 March), just a fortnight into the National Cabinet process, the premiers started to get nervous. Speculation had been growing about the need for some kind of lockdown, which now seemed inevitable. Morrison spent that Saturday and Sunday in Canberra with Treasurer Frydenberg and other key ministers, working out the finer details of the government's second stimulus package. International borders and economic stimulus dominated the minds of the federal MPs, which is not surprising given the division of responsibilities in the Constitution. States, on the other hand, are responsible for frontline services such as hospitals, which were under pressure to respond to the growing number of coronavirus cases – that Saturday, New South Wales hit 533 cases of coronavirus and Victoria was at 296. So while Morrison juggled the economic issues, NSW Premier Gladys Berejiklian and Victorian Premier Daniel Andrews held private talks. They wanted stronger restrictions in place, including closing venues like pubs, shops and clubs – basically, all non-essential businesses.

Together, Andrews and Berejiklian represented the two largest states and they had significant sway in the National Cabinet, which was due to meet on 22 March following pressure from the two leaders. After consulting Andrews, Berejiklian contacted the Prime Minister the evening before the meeting to make it clear that New South Wales and Victoria were prepared to enforce their own lockdowns if the National Cabinet couldn't come to an agreement on the issue. She stressed the growing fear that Australians just weren't taking the social-distancing guidelines seriously – there had been a prime example earlier that day, with Sydney's Bondi Beach having to be closed after beachgoers failed to adhere to government spacing requirements.

Morrison listened to Berejiklian's warning but didn't grasp the seriousness of the threat from New South Wales and Victoria. He was focused on the economic stimulus and wanted clear air to announce the second-stage $66 billion package, which promised cash payments of up to $100,000 for small businesses, a $750 boost for some welfare recipients and the unlocking of $10,000 from superannuation accounts. However, his announcement the following day was overshadowed by a potential feud with the leaders of the two biggest states. Journalists had gotten wind of the growing angst in Victoria and New South Wales and had begun to make inquiries. Morrison was said to be furious with the leak and remained committed to the advice that was being prepared by the chief medical officers through the AHPPC.

Andrews and Berejiklian fronted the media following Morrison's economic announcement and confirmed that they would be pushing for harsher lockdowns in the scheduled National Cabinet meeting. The pair also shared concerns about schools remaining open. Public schools, which are also a state responsibility, were seeing reduced attendance as parents kept their children home, fearing they might catch the virus in the playground. Apprehension also was being expressed by teachers and other union members, who no longer felt safe. Andrews then announced that Victoria would shut down from 24 March to give parents some certainty; Berejiklian hinted that she might do the same but said she would make a further statement the following morning, a Monday. It was chaotic and resulted in mass panic as the public became very anxious about what closures were about to be enforced.

The National Cabinet meeting, needless to say, was robust. New South Wales and Victoria had the highest numbers of coronavirus cases and were forceful in their push for a lockdown. And some of the smaller states felt they had little choice but to be pulled into a lockdown even with much fewer cases – the consensus model didn't necessarily give all states and territories an equal voice. Eventually, at about 9 pm, the meeting wrapped up. The leaders had agreed that clubs, hotels, pubs, cinemas, casinos, nightclubs, indoor sporting venues and churches would close, while restaurants and cafes would be restricted to takeaway service only. Such strict measures would inevitably result in economic heartache for thousands of businesses, and another stimulus package was needed the very day that the Commonwealth had unveiled its latest plan for support.

The news triggered immediate job losses across Australia. The Centrelink website crashed as the number of unemployed Australians skyrocketed. In scenes unfamiliar to most Australians, there were also long lines of people outside Centrelink offices around the country.

* * *

Scott Morrison received constant updates and new cuts of data on the virus, but there were two moments he pinpoints when he saw not statistics but the actual devastating impact on human beings. The first came in late March 2020. Morrison had returned to The Lodge after a long day at Parliament House to find Jenny in bed with the television on. She was watching a Sky News UK report from the network's chief correspondent, Stuart Ramsay, about the worsening crisis in Italy. Ramsay was reporting from the emergency department at the main hospital in Bergamo, one of the hardest-hit medical facilities in Italy. He was surrounded by people in beds or on trolleys with plastic bubbles over their heads, all trying to breath. The sounds of heart monitors and breathing pumps filled the air. It looked like a scene out of a war zone. Dr Roberto Cosentini, the head of emergency care at the hospital, was saying he had never seen anything like it.

Morrison was mesmerised. He recalls just staring at the television: 'I was standing there. I just couldn't move. I knew these things to be true but I hadn't seen them. If you needed any steeling up and resolve about what we were facing and what the threat was, that report certainly crystallised it very sharply.'

A few days later, there was coverage of Centrelink queues snaking around blocks, another visual cue which prompted Morrison to take more action. 'We had planned and significantly lifted our capability to respond, but that still wasn't enough,' he says. 'What that said to us was if we think we can only deal with this through the government payment system, that's not going to work.' As a former adman, there's little doubt Morrison also understood the potential political impact of such scenes. It was that footage of so many people lining up for benefits that ultimately led the government to introduce its JobKeeper income support for out-of-work Australians, although the path there was not an easy one.

Secretary to the Treasury Dr Steven Kennedy had attended several Cabinet meetings in February as the coronavirus pandemic unfolded in China. He was acutely aware of the economic devastation of pandemics, having penned a paper on their macroeconomic impacts in 2006. A week before Australia's lockdown, the British Government had announced a wage subsidy scheme that would cover 80 per cent of the wages of millions of affected workers as long as companies kept staff on their books rather than fire them. Inside Parliament House and the nearby Treasury Department, the move prompted talks about whether or not Australia should implement a similar system. Kennedy began fielding calls about how such a scheme would work and developed some models alongside Deputy Secretary Jenny Wilkinson and senior executive Mark Cully from the macroeconomics team.

Like Morrison, Josh Frydenberg was shaken by the images of thousands of Australians queuing outside Centrelink and increasingly became convinced that a wage subsidy would be needed. Frydenberg didn't want to go down the path taken by the United Kingdom. He wanted Australia to adopt a flat rate that was temporary, targeted, scalable and relied on existing schemes. Kennedy agreed. Morrison was open to the idea but needed a bit more convincing. Cognisant of the scale of the crisis, and no doubt with strong recall of the criticism he'd faced following the bushfires, Morrison appeared to have mastered the art of listening and even adapting his viewpoint. One senior minister makes the following observation about those early days of lockdown: 'What Scott loved to do was hear things and talk them through. He was not afraid to change his position. He was very keen to get advice, challenge it and work it through.' This is in stark contrast to his time in the immigration, social services and treasurer portfolios, when colleagues recall a man who was so certain of himself and often unwilling to change his mind.

Frydenberg worked closely with Treasury on options for a wage subsidy, keeping up a constant dialogue with Morrison and finance minister Mathias Cormann. Eventually, Frydenberg took a figure to Morrison, recommending a fortnightly $1500-per-employee flat payment for businesses that had suffered a sharp drop in turnover. Those businesses would then pay at least that amount to workers who had been stood down since 1 March. Morrison agreed. This was somewhat problematic given Morrison had repeatedly opposed a wage subsidy scheme. This is a claim that he denies, insisting that he was only opposed to the UK scheme. But senior government advisers disagree, stating that the wage subsidy negotiations were initially tense and produced the most robust discussions between Frydenberg and Morrison, who traditionally had enjoyed a thoroughly workable relationship. It was Frydenberg's chief of staff, Martin Codina, who came up with the name 'JobKeeper'. Morrison says of the scheme:

It was incredibly unique, no-one did it like us. I thought it was true to Australian values in that it didn't matter what you were being paid beforehand. Income support shouldn't be in respect to what your previous wage was. People were all reduced to zero hours so why would one Australian get more than another … from an Australian taxpayer?

On 30 March, Morrison and Frydenberg fronted the media at Parliament House to announce the $130 billion wage subsidy package. It was the third economic package in the space of a month, it had taken weeks and weeks of consultation, and Morrison was tired. He describes those days as feeling like one long meeting after another. Colleagues and staff observe that Morrison was always in a better frame of mind after a quick swim, but that activity had proven elusive.

Morrison says he was 'extremely conscious' of the scale of what was unfolding. But he adds:

I didn't feel overwhelmed because my faith is a huge part of how I deal with things like that. We were working incredibly hard … We set up good strong data systems, not unlike what you do in a political campaign: constant information, constant reporting, making decisions over and over and over again. All that I needed to add was a lot of time on my knees praying.

* * *

By late August 2020, large parts of Australia were out of lockdown and the number of COVID-19 cases were in decline. Victoria was an exception. Earlier that month, the state had recorded more than 700 new cases of the coronavirus in a single day, which in turn saw the death toll rise weeks later. Back in March, the prime minister had warned Australians that the pandemic would be with them for six months. Now that deadline was fast approaching and there was no end to the epidemic in sight. A new view had gained widespread acceptance: that life would not even begin returning to normal until there was an effective treatment or vaccine for COVID-19.

Encouragingly, a vaccine being developed by Oxford University and pharmaceutical giant AstraZeneca was looking like a strong contender among the dozens of coronavirus vaccines in the trial phase. By mid-August, Australia was under rising pressure to lock in supply of a coronavirus vaccine after the United Kingdom and the United States moved to shore up their vaccine reserves, so the government announced that it had signed a deal with AstraZeneca to secure the company's vaccine if its trials prove successful. The recommendation had come from a newly established vaccine advisory group led by Brendan Murphy, who had finished up as chief medical officer and was now Secretary of the Health Department. The vaccine would be produced in Melbourne by local manufacturer CSL, potentially bypassing any supply or other logistical concerns. However, within hours of being announced, the deal started to unravel as it became clear it wasn't so much a deal as a letter of intent.

The following month, the federal government decided to bank on another locally made vaccine, committing itself to ordering 51 million doses of a preparation being trialled at the University of Queensland if it proved successful. In November, the government hedged its bets even further by signing a deal to access a vaccine by Pfizer, which was proving incredibly effective. The vaccine did come with some inherent difficulties, as initially it needed to be stored at minus-70 degrees Celsius. Also, Australia didn't have the technology to manufacture Pfizer's vaccine locally, meaning it would need to be manufactured offshore, transported to Australia and distributed domestically. Then there was the need for a second dose three weeks after the first shot. That initial deal saw Australia secure 10 million doses, but forced to join the queue for the subsequent shots. The announcements were well received by the public, but some pharmaceutical experts warned that Australia had joined the vaccine queue too late.

At the time, Morrison told reporters the investment would ensure Australia was 'leading the pack' as the world moved towards the vaccine phase. In reality, Australia was months behind countries like the United States, the United Kingdom, Japan and Canada, which all secured deals in the middle of 2020.

Watching the vaccine rollout unfold, Pfizer's former president of global research and development, John L LaMattina, later described Australia's efforts to procure doses of Pfizer as 'clearly lacking' and 'unconscionable', if somewhat understandable given Australia's initial success at containing COVID-19.

'In the case of Australia, enough vaccine to inoculate its entire population over the age of eighteen should have been done at once. Assuming that is about 20 million Australians, this would have cost about US$780 million,' he later told *The Guardian*.

In December, as thousands of UK and US citizens received their first dose, Australia's vaccine program hit its first major hurdle. The government cancelled its order for millions of doses of the COVID-19 vaccine being developed by the University of Queensland after some trial participants received false positive test results for HIV. It could not immediately be replaced with other successful vaccines, such as those produced by Moderna or Johnson & Johnson, which would only do deals with countries that had a no-fault compensation scheme in place. Such a scheme would allow patients to receive redress from the government for any injury or illness caused by a vaccine without having to go through the courts. Nations including the United Kingdom, United States, New Zealand, Canada and Brazil have no-fault arrangements in place, but Australia didn't want to budge on the matter.

By early 2021, while the United States and United Kingdom were battling new waves of the virus, Australia was proving to be one of the success stories of the fight against COVID-19. The low number of cases reduced the pressure on the government to vaccinate Australians with any urgency.

But health experts remained concerned about Australia's vaccine strategy. Jane Halton, who ran the Commonwealth Health Department for twelve years, has said Australia counted on vaccine options that simply didn't come through: 'Partly that is just bad luck. Now obviously the more you put in pre-purchase orders, the more you hedge those bets.' Her comments mirror those of senior ministers who were growing increasingly critical of the government's strategy. For most of 2020, the Commonwealth Government had been praised for its handling of the pandemic, including the early border closures, the economic stimulus and the policies to drive down case numbers. The delayed vaccine rollout threatened to undo that early success.

The rollout finally began in February 2021, with Scott Morrison promising that all Australians would be fully vaccinated by October. The time frame was based on advice he had received from medical experts and his vaccine advisory committee. Throughout the pandemic, he had backed the judgement of such experts and he felt he had no reason to doubt them on the vaccination drive. But within weeks it became clear that the rollout was failing to meet expectations – Morrison had set a goal of vaccinating 4 million Australians by the end of March, but at that point, fewer than 700,000 doses had been administered. Initially the government had planned to vaccinate Australians primarily through thousands of GP clinics, and this had added to the complexity of the distribution. From the start, the expected shipments didn't always arrive on time, forcing GPs to cancel appointments. Some states ended up with an oversupply of the vaccine but were unable to distribute the doses quickly enough after they arrived unexpectedly. The supply uncertainty also saw some states hold back doses to ensure patients would have a second dose available. While the CSL facility in Melbourne was able to produce the AstraZeneca vaccine, it took weeks for it to reach capacity, meaning Australia needed to rely on doses from Europe. To make matters worse, in March 2021, the European Commission, concerned with securing its own vaccine supply, blocked a shipment of 250,000 doses to Australia. And the following month, a shipment of 3.1 million AstraZeneca doses Australia had ordered from factories in Europe didn't show up due to supply shortages and export curbs.

While initially Morrison had hoped he could resolve the supply issues quietly, the AstraZeneca shortfall prompted a defensive outburst: '3.1 million of the contracted vaccines that we had been relying upon in early January when we'd set out a series of targets did not turn up in Australia. That is just a simple fact.' This had shades of Morrison's bushfire bungle when, while he was still in Hawaii, he'd claimed that returning to Australia early would be of little use as he wouldn't be the one holding the hose to put the fires out. It highlighted Morrison's willingness to take credit when times are good and shirk responsibility when times are tough. Initially, the federal government had been so keen to claim any praise for rolling out a vaccine that in February 2021, it had used the Liberal Party logo on a social media post about the government's vaccine deal. Indeed, over the first two years of his term, Morrison had regularly reminded Australians that he was the prime minister and therefore he had the final say. Yet when the vaccine rollout hit a roadblock, it became a supply issue: Australia had had a plan and it was the European Commission that had put a spanner in the works.

The vaccine rollout was beset by a new problem in early April, when the government's expert medical taskforce held an emergency meeting over Australia's reliance on the AstraZeneca vaccine, after the European Union's medical regulator found that rare cases of blood clots had arisen as a side effect in the weeks after the vaccine was administered. It prompted a change in the official advice and a political backflip. The government now recommended that people under fifty years of age take the Pfizer vaccine. Morrison was particularly unhappy at having to stage a snap press conference to announce the latest AstraZeneca guidance, meaning he was unable to say what impact it would have on the rollout. He could only simply concede that it would need to be 'recalibrated'.

The issue prompted a number of testy conversations between Morrison and the country's relatively new chief medical officer, Paul Kelly, who'd been appointed in December 2020. Kelly is an experienced epidemiologist with more than thirty years' research experience, but unlike Brendan Murphy, he lacks political nous. Government sources say that while Morrison respects Kelly's advice, he now seems to place less trust in his chief medical officer. This has led to some confusion and mixed messaging.

Ultimately, Australia's slow and clumsy vaccine rollout took the shine off the government's otherwise enviable reputation for managing COVID-19. And there were other issues. Morrison had led a successful pandemic response in Australia when compared with administration efforts in the United States, United Kingdom and Brazil, which had largely mishandled their strategies, with devastating consequences. Central to that success was the cooperation between the federal government and the states and territories, regardless of who was in charge in each jurisdiction. But, in late March, a federal government source leaked figures on the slow vaccine rollout to News Corp papers in an effort to frame the delays as a state issue – the statistics showed that New South Wales had only administered about 50 per cent of the doses it had received, while Queensland had administered about 55 per cent. Morrison, who was unaware of the leak until it appeared in the media, was furious.

For the most part, the prime minister had tried to avoid direct attacks on the states over their COVID-19 responses, even as his colleagues didn't show such control – in May 2020, as debate about whether schools in Victoria should be reopened had raged on, one of Morrison's frontbenchers, Dan Tehan, had accused Premier Dan Andrews of taking a 'sledgehammer' to the state's education. Morrison, too, was frustrated about what had become persistent school closures, believing that the education unions were pulling the strings, but nonetheless refused to criticise the Victorian approach. Within hours of his outburst, after a vigorous conversation with the prime minister, Tehan apologised to Andrews and withdrew his condemnation.

Morrison also had some robust conversations with Josh Frydenberg over his repeated criticism of the Andrews government lockdown. Frydenberg felt very worried about how the lockdown was affecting his home state. Worried parents had inundated him and other Victoria-based ministers, including Tehan, with text messages and emails about the impact it was having on their children's health. Morrison understood this personal frustration but he could anticipate the political impact of attacking a popular premier like Dan Andrews. He knew that there was no public appetite for such disputes.

For Frydenberg and Morrison, the disagreement marked another tense point in their otherwise strong relationship. Frydenberg made it clear to the prime minister that he would not be deterred from speaking his mind, not over something he felt so passionately about. Unlike other ministers, Frydenberg was elected by the party room in his own right, and Morrison knew that sometimes he had to back his deputy – even if they disagreed – in order to have his support in return. Frydenberg had, after all, shown Morrison tremendous loyalty during his bungled bushfire response.

* * *

Personal relationships have played a big part in helping Morrison stay focused on getting Australia through this unprecedented time. The prime minister greatly respected the advice of his previous chief medical officer, Brendan Murphy, and responded accordingly – at the state level, several premiers have given the impression of having a strong partnership with their respective chief health officers, but that hasn't necessarily been the case. Other unusual partnerships (for the political realm) also emerged during the pandemic, such as that between then industrial relations minister Christian Porter and Australian Council of Trade Unions Secretary Sally McManus. The pandemic response required temporary flexibility when it came to some employment protections, and cooperation between the pair was necessary to achieve this. Unions also had a strong role in advocating on behalf of workers as lockdowns were enforced.

Morrison also has formed some friendships across the political divide, no doubt assisted by his pragmatism-above-ideology approach. Inside the National Cabinet, he formed a close working relationship – some would say a 'friendship' – with Victorian Premier Dan Andrews. While there appeared to be an agreement that a working partnership would be mutually beneficial, some believe the two have a genuine respect for and appreciation of each other. These two highly partisan political tragics have fierce and loyal supporters who would be surprised to learn of their similarities, but those close to them are less surprised. They are both party men, having spent years working in the backroom operations of party politics, and as politicians, they are both strong communicators and campaigners. Privately, both are also dedicated fathers and husbands who have managed to steer clear of the trappings and temptations of parliamentary life. 'It's a relationship of convenience,' observes one senior Liberal minister. 'There is a grudging respect for each other's political talents.' Another Labor member of the National Cabinet, Northern Territory Chief Minister Michael Gunner, is also understood to have formed a respectful working relationship with Morrison.

Another relationship that has been key to Australia's success during the pandemic is that between Morrison and Frydenberg. When Frydenberg arrived in the federal parliament in 2010, Morrison was front-and-centre in the Abbott government as immigration minister. To Frydenberg, a backbencher, it was obvious that Morrison was tough, effective and relentless. It wouldn't be long before the pair worked together on the Expenditure Review Committee, with Morrison as social services minister and Frydenberg as assistant treasurer to Joe Hockey, who despised the ambitious Morrison. Frydenberg remained loyal to Hockey but never let it impact his bond with Morrison, whom he identified as a hard worker with the potential to make it all the way to the top job. Now, as treasurer and prime minister, the two men have a strong working relationship. Frydenberg and his wife, Amie, have welcomed Scott and Jenny Morrison into their home in Melbourne for dinner on numerous occasions.

And when in Sydney, Frydenberg has also taken up the offer of a room at Kirribilli House. As one senior Liberal says, 'It's unusual. Costello rarely walked through the door of Kirribilli when Howard was in office.'

While clearly not all Liberal leaders and deputies have had such a strained relationship as did Howard and Costello, some Liberal MPs believe that none have had such a purposeful working relationship since Robert Menzies and Harold Holt. Frydenberg has told colleagues that his professional relationship with Morrison has transformed into a genuine friendship. Both are men of faith from close-knit families and determined in their ambitions, so perhaps this friendship comes from a deep understanding of each other both as men and politicians. In Frydenberg, Morrison sees a similar ambition to that which he showed on his way up, but he also knows that Frydenberg, like him, is practical, hardworking and won't destabilise the government for a chance at the top job. Frydenberg is focused on what he wants, but he's not a plotter.

Frydenberg is viewed as Australia's next Liberal prime minister. It has been rumoured that should Morrison win the next election, due by the middle of 2022, he might even retire before his second term is up. Two of his closest confidants have confirmed that Morrison has indulged in such speculation over a quiet drink in a private setting, though both acknowledge that it's more of a hypothetical than a plan – the sort of thing someone says to downplay their own ambition, please a weary family, or try to convince oneself that it's the best course of action. In reality, such a decision is much harder to make. Every prime minister, in theory, would have preferred to leave at a time of his or her choosing rather than being dumped by voters or colleagues. But giving up the top job is difficult, particularly when your entire career has been geared towards getting it.

* * *

At first, the Coalition under Morrison seemed to turn the pandemic into an electoral winner, but 2021 changed that. The slow vaccine rollout forced he government to abandon its timeline to inoculate the population. And Morrison appeared unwilling to offer any guarantee that borders would reopen once a certain percentage of the population had received the vaccination. This was based on the fact that the government could no longer reliably predict the uptake or availability of the injections. This coincided with a shift in Morrison's language. His early confidence that Australia soon would open up again was replaced by a strong stance against opening the borders, driven by polling that repeatedly showed Australians wanted the borders to remain shut despite the large number of fellow nationals who remained stranded overseas. Morrison had previously criticised state premiers who'd enforced such rigid policies in 2020, but the slow vaccine rollout and public fear appeared to zap this early confidence. The Morrison government's election chances would be heavily impacted by the success of the vaccine rollout. The delay in that rollout halted any talk of an early election, with the government seemingly unwilling to go to the polls until the majority of Australians have been vaccinated against the virus.

By mid-2021, with the vaccine rollout facing significant delays, the federal government was also struggling with its public messaging. In the past, Morrison had proven himself to be a clear communicator but his comments around vaccine safety at this time seemed to only add to the chaos and confusion. The winter outbreaks in Melbourne and Sydney led to the federal government announcing a no-fault indemnity scheme for GPs, meaning any Australians under the age of sixty who wanted the AstraZeneca vaccine could do so in consultation with their GP. It was a way to get more people vaccinated while Australia waited for shipments of the Pfizer vaccine, still months away.

The proposal was immediately rejected by Queensland's chief health officer, Dr Jeannette Young, who said she did not want under-forties to get AstraZeneca. 'I don't want an eighteen-year-old in Queensland dying from a clotting illness who, if they got COVID, probably wouldn't die,' she said. The president of the Australian Medical Association, Dr Omar Khorshid, also refused to endorse the prime minister's announcement. It was a disaster.

Days later, finance minister Simon Birmingham added to the government's vaccine woes when he admitted that Australia was at the 'back of the queue' when it came to

Pfizer and other mRNA vaccines, a fact the government had keenly avoided admitting. It contradicted Morrison's claim eight months earlier that Australia was leading the pack when it came to Pfizer orders.

Amid reports that Australia had bungled its mid-2020 negotiations with Pfizer by sending junior bureaucrats, not the prime minister, to close the deal, inside the government, senior ministers, including Morrison, were concerned about the damage the delay was having, not just on the health and safety of Australians but on the Coalition's election prospects.

By July 2021, as Melbourne exited one lockdown and entered another and with Sydney in the grip of a deadly outbreak, the federal government announced it had secured a deal with Pfizer to increase supply to approximately 1 million doses a week, three times the May and June weekly average of 300,000 to 350,000.

The following day, Pfizer released a statement confirming the quicker delivery but insisting it wasn't an overall increase to its contract to deliver 40 million Pfizer doses by the end of 2021. A further 60 million doses were then locked in for delivery in 2022, with an additional 25 million to arrive in 2023. It was a sign that the government knew that its electoral success or failure hinged upon the vaccine supply.

The ghosts of prime ministers past popped up to haunt Morrison, with former Labor prime minister Kevin Rudd claiming senior business figures had asked him to intervene to help fast-track Australia's Pfizer vaccine supply. Morrison's predecessor, Malcolm Turnbull, also chipped in, describing the rollout as the 'worst failure of public administration in Australian history'.

Under pressure, Morrison did what he had done before and attempted to blame-shift, suggesting that the Australian Technical Advisory Group on Immunisation (ATAGI) had been 'very cautious' in its advice and therefore should shoulder some of the blame for Australia's vaccine rollout. It was an unusual move but followed a similar pattern to what Australians had come to expect from the prime minister in the face of immense pressure.

He wanted to craft the narrative that the delay, in part, had been inflicted upon his government, and it was not entirely untrue – it is accurate that some of the drama, such as the unforeseen events around the AstraZeneca vaccine, was out of his control. His argument had some merit, but voters and the Opposition care little for such nuance.

By late July and under mounting pressure, Morrison made the rare decision to apologise for the vaccine rollout after repeatedly refusing to say sorry for the missteps of his government. The prime minister, more than most, understands the intricacies of polling. He could sense the public mood was shifting and he had the data to back it up. It was an attempt at a political reset, designed to absorb the anger and restore some integrity for the government ahead of a looming election.

Chapter Fifteen

The Women Issue

The twenty-sixth of January is possibly the most polarising date on the Australian calendar. Australia Day is viewed by some as a celebration of the nation and by others as a day of national sorrow that marks the colonisation of an ancient culture. In the past, Scott Morrison has used the occasion as a tool to promote his brand of patriotic politics, which has also lead to criticism and accusations of igniting a culture war. In 2021, Morrison attempted to take the heat out of Australia Day by announcing that the country would make a small but significant change to its national anthem. Critics had argued that the line 'for we are young and free' was disrespectful to Indigenous history, so it would be changed to 'for we are one and free'. But this did little to stem the calls to move Australia Day from 26 January, to remove the association with the landing of the First Fleet at Sydney Cove in 1788.

One of those adding their voice to these calls was Grace Tame. Tame had been groomed and sexually abused as a teenager and had become a strong advocate for survivors of abuse, championing their right to speak out about the assaults they'd endured. On the night that Scott Morrison announced the 26-year-old as the 2021 Australian of the Year, Tame delivered one of the most powerful speeches ever given by an awardee, vowing to use her new position to call out misogyny and inequality. Months later, Tame would reveal that Morrison had privately responded to her powerful statement that night by remarking, 'Well, gee, I bet it felt good to get that out.' Like so many of his apparent faux pas, Morrison's comment could be dismissed as merely awkward, as not well considered, but it is yet another example of a consistent theme in how he deals with women.

The image of Morrison standing on a podium alongside a self-empowered survivor of sexual assault ultimately led to an explosive allegation of a rape in Parliament House and shone a light on the broader treatment of women in Canberra. Watching Tame that night was former Liberal Party staffer Brittany Higgins, who had been working for then defence industry minister Linda Reynolds in March 2019 when she alleges she was raped by a colleague in the ministerial wing of Parliament House. Higgins was just a few weeks into a new job as a media adviser for Senator Reynolds when she embarked on a drinking session in Canberra with some colleagues. The alleged offender offered to drop her home in a taxi but took her to Parliament House instead. It was there, in the office of her boss, that she alleges she was raped.

Higgins has said that, at the time, she decided not to pursue a complaint with the police as she felt it would affect her job and possibly jeopardise the Liberal Party's chances ahead of a crucial election. But now she feels as if she never really had a choice about making an official complaint. She has described a 'culture of silence' within Australia's political parties, based on a fear of letting the team down by speaking up.

It was the image of a smiling Morrison standing alongside Tame that was the tipping point. It made Higgins 'sick to her stomach'. She is reported as saying: 'He's standing next to a woman who has campaigned [for survivors' rights] ... and yet in my mind his government was complicit in silencing me. It was a betrayal. It was a lie.' On 15 February, Higgins went public with her story and announced that she was going to pursue a complaint of rape.

The following day, Morrison addressed the revelation. He said he had discussed the alleged rape with his wife:

Jenny and I spoke last night, and she said to me, 'You have to think about this as a father first. What would you want to happen if it were our girls?' Jenny has a way of clarifying things. Always has.

And so as I've reflected on that overnight and listened to Brittany and what she had to say.

It's not an unusual tactic for leaders to use. As prime minister, Malcolm Turnbull regularly referred to the advice his wife, Lucy, gave him. But Morrison's comments completely missed the mark. Some people interpreted his remarks as him saying that he had to be told by his wife that rape was bad. This was clearly not what he meant. His staff say he was deeply saddened by Higgins's accusation. But his response that day, as with his words to Tame after her speech, were sloppy and showed, perhaps, how uncomfortable he is responding to the issue of sexual assault.

However, days later, Morrison's office was accused of providing off-the-record information to journalists against Higgins's current partner as a way of discrediting her story. The government denied the accusation but nonetheless launched an investigation. Morrison initially claimed that neither he nor his office knew about the alleged rape until some days before Higgins chose to tell her story. But a leaked text message exchange between Higgins and another Liberal staffer in the weeks after the March 2019 incident challenged that narrative. Morrison then insisted he was angry with colleagues such as Senator Reynolds who, he said, had kept him in the dark for years. But this is challenged too, by two once senior ministers who served alongside Morrison in parliament and remain familiar with the inner workings of ministerial offices. 'To say he didn't know about Brittany Higgins is unbelievable,' one former minister claims. 'He should've been briefed within a minute of Linda Reynolds knowing. No adviser worth their salt wouldn't have told him.'

Another senior public servant and former prime ministerial adviser privately echoed this claim when addressing the question of whether or not Morrison would have known about a rape alleged to have taken place a few rooms away from his own office.

One strategy used by political staff is to keep their ministers in the dark about some highly sensitive matters to give them plausible deniability if asked about them in the media. It is therefore possible that while his office knew all about what had occurred, a decision had been made not to tell Morrison, as a form of protection. Higgins herself can't say with any certainty whether Morrison was informed of her allegation in the weeks or months following the alleged assault, but she claims the prime minister's principal private secretary, Yaron Finkelstein, called her in 2020 to 'check in'.

On 26 February, with the Higgins story still dominating the media cycle, the ABC published details of an anonymous letter sent to the prime minister, Senate Opposition Leader Penny Wong and Greens Senator Sarah Hanson-Young. It alleged that a sixteen-year-old girl had been raped in Sydney in 1988 by a man who was now a senior member of Scott Morrison's Cabinet. The letter also included a statement by the alleged victim, who had reported the crime to NSW

Police before taking her own life. Within days, then attorney-general Christian Porter outed himself as the Cabinet minister accused of rape, but he strenuously denied the allegations.

The two separate rape allegations dominated coverage of federal politics and overshadowed government announcements on the vaccine rollout. As a Christian who married his high school sweetheart, Morrison should have been the perfect leader to moralise about the toxic political culture at Parliament House. Unlike a number of his male colleagues, Morrison is still married to his first wife and has never been accused of inappropriate sexual behaviour.

In fact, in February 2018, when then deputy prime minister Barnaby Joyce admitted to an extramarital affair with his former media adviser Vikki Campion, Morrison was scathing about the situation. The affair prompted prime minister Malcolm Turnbull to introduce the so-called 'bonk ban', which prohibited sexual relationships between ministers and their staff. While Labor and many senior Cabinet members were initially cagey about whether to support the move, Morrison offered his unreserved support:

> *I'm happy to have a prime minister who's been prepared to call out a political culture in this country that has been going on for decades, if not generations. If you sleep with your staff, it's not private anymore. It's public because you're a minister in a position of responsibility and power over those who work for you. This is not moral police. It doesn't matter if you're married or single. You shouldn't sleep*

*with your staff. It's a bad practice ... it's not conducive to the good
running of your office and the performance of your duties.*

But while Scott Morrison's strong track record as a suburban
family man should have prepared him well for the significant
challenges of early 2021, he was ill-advised, and appeared ill-
equipped to deal with the controversies.

* * *

In mid-March, thousands of women, fed up with the culture
of silence that Brittany Higgins had spoken about, called
for gender equality and justice for victims of sexual assault
at protests across Australia under the banner March4Justice.
Much of the anger was directed at Morrison, who made
matters worse when, while attempting to deflect the issue by
praising Australia's democracy, told parliament that protests
elsewhere were being 'met with bullets'. On Twitter and in
certain parts of the media, his comment was painted as a
perceived threat. It wasn't, of course, but again, it was way off
the mark.

The Prime Minister's Office then took another misstep.
It assumed that only tertiary-educated women were angry
with Morrison's response – in other words, people who were
unlikely to vote Liberal anyway. But broader public concern
about the toxic mix of the Porter and Higgins allegations,
coupled with messy reactions by the prime minister, was

reflected in public polling. In late March, Newspoll declared Labor ahead of the Coalition for the first time since the bushfires of 2019–20. Internal polling commissioned by the Morrison government produced a similar result. What alarmed Morrison's team the most was its delay in realising that the issue had seeped into suburban lounge rooms.

When you speak to women who have worked alongside Scott Morrison throughout his career, you hear a consistent theme: broadly, he just doesn't seem to work constructively with them. A common sentiment expressed by female colleagues was that they felt excluded, overlooked and even ignored while Morrison was in the room. Not all women who've encountered him professionally make this observation, of course, but the vast majority share this view. One Coalition frontbencher, a woman, describes him as a 'deeply ingrained chauvinist' who is known to 'attack women in meetings and put them down'. Another Cabinet colleague, a man, says Morrison 'couldn't stand' some of his female colleagues – Julie Bishop was one, and Morrison 'hated' working with Kelly O'Dwyer, despite the pair once being close friends. There is a chance that these were simply personality clashes – politics is a nasty business and it's not unusual to dislike colleagues, regardless of their sex. But several government ministers agree that Morrison simply prefers to work with other men.

Early in his prime ministership, Morrison didn't deter women voters – quite the opposite. Liberal strategists believe that during the 2019 election campaign, female voters aged between thirty-five and fifty-four were actually wooed by Morrison. It's hard to pinpoint exactly what drew these women to Morrison, but the strategists believe that his marrying his childhood sweetheart, coupled with his family-friendly policies tackling cyberbullying and cost-of-living issues, resonated with the suburban female cohort. The events of early 2021 changed all that and the government quickly recognised the growing need to change the narrative.

The 2021 Budget announced on 11 May saw the government splash billions to frame itself as 'female-friendly' and hopefully rectify the political damage inflicted by its handling of the Higgins and Porter issues. There was loads of money for women's health, safety and economic security, as well as child care. It's difficult to know the long-term impact of Morrison's so-called 'woman issue' on the government's election chances, but the prime minister certainly saw the need to win back estranged female voters before they switched off for good.

By July 2021, polling showed the extent of the damage, with a drop in the Morrison government's primary vote from 41 per cent to 37 per cent among female voters since the 2019 poll. Such a swing was predicted to be significant enough to threaten his prime ministership. A subsequent survey by Newspoll one week later showed a similar trend, with Scott Morrison recording a 10-point slide from 27 per cent to 18 per cent in his approval rating, led by female voters.

One former long-serving Liberal minister describes public opinion as similar to wet cement in that it's all over the place until it sets, adding:

> When it sets, there is nothing you can do to shift it. With Scott, even though he mishandled it, I think the cement is still wet. If it sets for him, then he has got another term, but if it sets against him then he can use every trick but it won't work.

Conclusion

Scott Morrison would not be unhappy at being referred to as an 'accidental prime minister'. In many ways, his early life was extraordinary in its mediocrity. It wasn't a 'raised in a log cabin' story, nor was it one of exceptional privilege and good fortune. Morrison was smart without topping the class. He met a girl, graduated, married, worked hard and bought a house. This narrative is not only true, it's a political advantage for a prime minister who likes to sell himself as a regular dad from the suburbs. Viewing Morrison's life through this prism would give the impression that his rise to the prime ministership was some kind of lucky accident. However, this is not necessarily the case. Many of Morrison's opportunities and strokes of good luck have been delivered by a combination of hard work, hard-nosedness and an unrelenting focus on making it to the top. He has tied himself to success and made no bones about seeking to remove anyone who stands in his way. The upshot is that both of these perspectives ring true, and they make for a perilous combination.

In the 2018 leadership ballot and at the 2019 election, Morrison was grossly underestimated, something his detractors continue to do at the time of writing in mid-2021. For those who live and work in politics, Morrison is a polarising character, but it is how he is viewed in the wider community that will determine how long he will serve as prime minister. So, too, will the views of his Liberal Party colleagues. After years of disunity, he has managed to keep the party together. It is one of his greatest political strengths and will be key to him remaining prime minister.

Morrison's leadership could also hinge on his willingness to learn from his mistakes. Those who encountered him earlier in his career describe him as driven, determined, brimming with self-belief. But while the prime ministership and a number of missteps have smoothed some of his edges, it's that incredible self-belief that has the potential to damage his personal brand.

When Morrison is under pressure, he is quick to jump to his own defence when sometimes he would be better off acknowledging and accepting his mistakes. He dismisses genuine media inquiries that he simply doesn't want to answer as gossip; he shifted responsibility for aged care to the states; he blamed his office for keeping him in the dark over Brittany Higgins's allegation of rape at Parliament House; and he rejected calls for him to return from overseas to a bushfire-ravaged Australia by insisting he could do little to help as he doesn't 'hold a hose'. Deflecting responsibility is a tactic that may have worked during his rise to the top job, but in the national spotlight, it has the potential to bring him undone. If it were a singular event, it would be unlikely to shape Australians' view of him, but as a pattern, it is troubling.

To stay in office, Morrison instead will need to rely on the other skills that took him there: his ability to work hard, his determination and his focus. His opponents will only assist the marketing-man-turned-prime-minister if they continue to underestimate him.

Endnotes

Notes to the endnotes

Identity of sources: Many of the more than seventy subjects interviewed for this book were prepared to be quoted only on the condition that they not be identified by name. Accordingly, all quoted material that is not sourced in the text or these endnotes is attributable to personal communication, including but not limited to formal interviews and correspondence, from individuals for whom remaining unnamed was an express condition of including their contribution in this book.

Personal communication: All quotes that have named sources in the text but no corresponding endnote, including quotes attributed to Scott Morrison, are the result of personal communication, including interviews, with the author and to avoid repetition have not been relisted in these endnotes.

Introduction

P 4:   When he did finally return home … 'I don't hold a hose' …: Scott Morrison, radio interview with John Stanley, 2GB, 20 December 2019.

P 5:   the allegation that former Liberal staffer Brittany Higgins …: Lisa Wilkinson, 'Former liberal staffer speaks up about her alleged rape in Parliament House', *The Project*, 15 February 2021.

P 5:   he invoked his daughters in response …: Scott Morrison, doorstop interview, Parliament House, Canberra, 16 February 2021.

P 6:   the thousands of women who attended … should be thankful they were not 'met with bullets': Scott Morrison, Statements on indulgence – March4Justice, House of Representatives, 15 March 2021.

P 7:   *Wall Street Journal* columnist Peggy Noonan described how Trump hadn't been changed …: Peggy Noonan, 'America emerges disunited but intact', *Wall Street Journal*, 21 January 2021.

P 8:   The Organisation for Economic Co-operation and Development considers almost 60 per cent…: Organisation for Economic Co-operation and Development (OECD), 'Under pressure: the squeezed middle class', 2019.

Chapter One: Moulding the National Character

P 11:   According to Doug Anthony, the then deputy …: Troy Bramston, 'Harold Holt took his troubles to Cheviot Beach', *The Australian*, 16 December 2017.

P 13:   conspiracy theories, including claims he had defected …: Jackson Stiles, 'Harold Holt was a Soviet defector, claims film', *The New Daily*, 27 October 2014.

P 14:   The unusual path Gorton took to the prime ministership …: Norman Abjorensen, 'The accidental prime minister', *Inside Story*, 23 December 2015.

P 18:   'This is an important ritual, for us …': Scott Morrison, 'Until the Bell Rings', address to Menzies Research Centre, 6 September 2018.

P 19:   'He [Menzies] understood that for the individual …': Scott Morrison, ibid.

P 21:   'The young Lawson and I were both retiring …': Mary Gilmore, manuscript recollection of Henry Lawson, Mitchell Library, State Library of NSW, MLMSS 123, c. 1922.

P 23:   She explored the horrors of war in a book …: Mary Gilmore, *The Passionate Heart*, Sydney, Angus & Robertson, 1918.

P 24:   In 1942, on her seventy-seventh birthday …: 'She watched a nation grow', *The Sun* (Sunday supplement), 13 June 1948, p 2.

P 24:   then prime minister John Curtin said Dame Mary had 'helped mould the national character' …: Diane Langmore, *Prime Ministers' Wives*, McPhee Gribble Publishers, Melbourne, 1992, p 132.

P 25:   a letter to Mary Gilmore dated 30 July 1945 …: Nell Green, letter to Mary Gilmore, Papers of Dame Mary Gilmore, National Library of Australia, MS 727.

P 26:   Even to this day they look on the $10 note with great pride …: Scott Morrison, Federation Chamber, Adjournment – Dame Mary Gilmore DBE, House of Representatives, 29 November 2012.

P 30:   'I'm not one that rushes to the plane …': Scott Morrison, doorstop interview, Biarritz, France, 27 August 2019.

P 32:   described them both as 'striking personalities' …: Jonathan Foye, 'Church and state: Scott Morrison's faith and public policy', *Insights*, 31 August 2018.

P 35:   'That doesn't worry me … I have voted …': Tony Squires, 'Waverley's alderman Morrison will stand down – election countdown', *Sydney Morning Herald*, 3 September 1987.

ENDNOTES

P 36:   John denied there was a conflict of interest …: 'Mayor gets one of top police posts', *Sydney Morning Herald*, 2 January 1986.

P 36:   'After all those years, it's time to look at yourself …': Tony Squires, op cit.

P 39:   'I recall being completely in awe …': Scott Morrison, Main Committee – Apology to Australia's Indigenous Peoples, House of Representatives, 18 February 2008.

P 39:   'There was a large Indigenous family …' Scott Morrison, ibid.

Chapter Two: School, Sport and Spin

P 42:   'We went to public schools, like Jenny …': Scott Morrison, Coalition campaign launch, Melbourne, 12 May 2019.

P 44:   'Everyone is entitled to their opinion …': @ScottMorrisonMP, Twitter, 27 March 2015.

P 45:   Jenny has since described the young Scott Morrison as 'really confident'…: Jordan Baker, 'Meet Jenny Morrison, the "unrecognisable" woman behind the PM', *Sydney Morning Herald*, 12 May 2019.

P 47:   Scott Mason describes it as a 'disappointing but enjoyable season'…: Sydney Boys High School, *The Record*, 1985, p 112.

P 47:   a 'desire to secure possession at any cost'…: Sydney Boys High School, *The Record*, ibid, p 160.

P 52:   It was an experience that had a profound impact on Morrison, who, shortly after he was elected prime minister, said…: Annika Smethurst, 'I'm about fair go and family', *Sunday Telegraph* and *Herald Sun*, 26 August 2018.

P 53:   a 'unique capacity to communicate ideas in a persuasive and telling manner' …: Matthew Cranston, 'Scott Morrison is a property person's prime minister', *Australian Financial Review*, 27 August 2018.

P 54:   the famous 'shrimp on the barbie' Australian Tourism Commission ad …: Tourism Australia, 'Shrimp on the barbie – Paul Hogan', National Film and Sound Archive, 1983.

Chapter Three: Opportunities Either Side of the Ditch

P 60:   moving towards 'major events-related tourism activities …': Murray McCully, 'New Office of Tourism and Sport established', press release, 6 April 1998.

P 61:   an 'outstanding applicant' who possessed a strong knowledge …: Nick Venter, 'Blooded in battle', *The Dominion*, 8 May 1999.

P 61:   'I place a high priority on the contribution …': Murray McCully, 'Sports minister welcomes appointment of OTS Director', press release, 20 May 1998.

P 64:   'In order to fulfil my responsibilities …': Scott Morrison, email to Paul Winter, 29 October 1998, in New Zealand Auditor-General, 'Inquiry into certain events concerning the New Zealand Tourism Board', Wellington, 19 April 1999.

P 65:   described rather euphemistically by the auditor-general as 'problematic' …: New Zealand Auditor-General, ibid.

P 65: 'operating in a tactical rather than a strategic way': New Zealand Auditor-General, ibid.

P 65: He also wrote to his minister, encouraging him to take 'direct and immediate action' ...: New Zealand Auditor-General, ibid.

P 66: 'Mr Morrison was aware that the Board's directors ...': New Zealand Auditor-General, ibid.

P 66: comments which 'influenced the shape of the report'...: New Zealand Auditor-General, ibid.

P 66: 'In preparing your response you should ...': New Zealand Auditor-General, ibid.

P 67: He advised McCully that the allegations ...: New Zealand Auditor-General, ibid.

P 68: But an auditor-general report would later find there was never any clear ...: New Zealand Auditor-General, ibid.

P 69: he accused the minister of constant interference ...: Bernadette Courtney, 'McCully in the right say tourism interests', The Dominion, 2 February 1999.

P 69: he publicly described the portrayal of the payouts ... as hush money as scandalous and absolutely wrong ...: Helen Bain, 'Hush money allegations scandalous says McCully', The Dominion, 11 February 1999.

P 69: he told journalists he was keen to stay on ...: Brent Edwards and Guyon Espiner, 'Board members face sack, PM gives a week's deadline', Evening Post, 28 April 1999.

P 70: advice that recommended 'a much more moderate response' ...: Nick Venter, 'Blooded in battle', The Dominion, 8 May 1999.

P 71: an advertising masterstroke that saw visitor numbers...: Tourism New Zealand, 'Pure as – Celebrating 10 years of 100% Pure New Zealand', 2009.

P 72: he blamed the result on 'the backroom boys of Riley Street' ...: 'Worst campaign "in living memory" – Liberal Party director should resign – Collins Labor landslide', Fairfax Media, 30 March 1999.

P 77: Turnbull, a dedicated student of contemporaneous notes, said that Morrison approached him...: Malcolm Turnbull, A Bigger Picture, Hardie Grant Books, Melbourne, 2020, p 111.

P 78: According to Turnbull, he challenged Morrison's plan ...: Malcolm Turnbull, ibid, p 111.

P 81: Malcolm Turnbull famously declared that the Liberal Party wasn't run by factions ...: Brendan Hills, 'Turnbull challenges the Malcolmtents, while Abbott gets a clap', Daily Telegraph, 11 October 2015.

P 82: the party's more moderate members get together for the Black Hand dinner: Christopher Pyne, The Insider: the Scoops, the Scandals and the Serious Business within the Canberra Bubble, Hachette Australia, Sydney, 2020.

P 85: In August, during an interview with Good Weekend magazine ...: Jane Cadzow, 'The right thing', Good Weekend Magazine, 14 August 2004.

P 86: In late August 2004, John Howard took the bold step ...: Steve Lewis, 'Howard and Latham focus on trust for tight October 9 election – poll choice is truth or dare', The Australian, 30 August 2004.

P 88: 'As far as Labor is concerned, this was a state ...': Cosima Marriner, 'Liberals maintain status quo', *Sydney Morning Herald*, 11 October 2004.

P 89: '[The Liberal Party] seeks membership and support from every section of the Australian community ...': John Howard, address to Liberal Party New South Wales Division State Council, Sydney, 11 December 2004.

P 89: 'This is the best country in the world in which to live ...': Scott Morrison, speech, Sydney, 18 May 2019.

Chapter Four: What the Bloody Hell Happened?

P 92: She publicly confirmed this within days of her appointment, telling the *Gold Coast Bulletin* she had ...: 'Tourism in hands of an unknown', *Gold Coast Bulletin*, 23 October 2004.

P 92: John Witheriff delivered the ultimate insult by asking ...: 'Keech to brief Bailey', *Gold Coast Bulletin*, 26 October 2004.

P 99: Tourism Australia had even anticipated criticism ...: Mike Smith, 'Controversial new ad to woo tourists – Bloody genius or bloody rude', *Daily Telegraph*, 24 February 2006.

P 99: 'It's the great Australian adjective ...': Fran Bailey, speech, Tourism Australia campaign launch, 23 February 2006.

P 99: 'I think the style of the advertisement is anything but offensive ...': John Howard, interview, 23 February 2006.

P 100: translations of the slogan were altered to reflect ...: Simon Canning, 'Shocker or just ocker? Truly blue tourism slogan gets the PM's nod', *The Australian*, 24 February 2006.

P 100: Morrison himself doubled down on the approach ...: Scott Morrison, 'It's just a tourism ad, not a cultural essay needing deep analysis', *The Age*, 2 March 2006.

P 100: According to the research, experience seekers ...: Steve Meacham, 'The selling of Australia', *Sydney Morning Herald*, 25 February 2006.

P 101: 'This is not a cultural essay but a carefully and well-researched campaign ...': 'Kiwis receive the first Aussie invite', *Geelong Advertiser*, 28 February 2006.

P 102: 'How anyone can take offence at a beautiful girl in a bikini ...': Simon Canning, 'Ad is too bloody blunt for the Brits', *The Australian*, 10 March 2006.

P 104: 'I then presented what I considered were three powerful arguments ...': Fran Bailey, 'Bloody hell, here's how we did it!', *The Australian*, 29 April 2006.

P 105: 'I'm convinced that we were successful in reversing the decision ...': Fran Bailey, ibid.

P 108: 'Annual leave stockpiling has critical ramifications ...': 'Saving for holiday of a lifetime', *Daily Telegraph*, 3 May 2006.

P 110: In their final report, the auditors also said a number of industry stakeholders ...: The Auditor-General, *Audit Report No 2 2008–09, Performance Audit, Tourism Australia*, Australian National Audit Office, Commonwealth of Australia, 6 August 2008, p 17.

P 110: 'It is therefore important, particularly ...': The Auditor-General, ibid, p 18.

P 110: the organisation had asked a 'preferred tender' to begin work...: The Auditor-General, ibid, p 21.

P 111: Fischer said in an *Australian Financial Review* piece that he believed Morrison deserved ...: Fiona Carruthers, 'Bloody hell! When ScoMo lost a political knife fight', *Australian Financial Review*, 1 September 2018.

P 111: 'There's been a bit of mystery surrounding it over the years ...': Fiona Carruthers, ibid.

Chapter Five: A Miracle Child

P 114: 'There are babies everywhere,' Jenny later observed ...: Ally Foster, 'Jenny Morrison opens up about 14 year infertility struggle', news.com.au, 31 October 2019.

P 114: Scott Morrison describes the desire ...: Scott Morrison, 'Infertile couples paying a heavy price for Labor', *Essential Baby*, 28 May 2009.

P 114: Jenny has since described parenthood ...: Danielle Messurier, 'PM's wife tells of her pain and "isolation"', *Daily Telegraph,* 31 October 2019.

P 115: 'The feeling of loss at every failed attempt is indescribable ...': Scott Morrison, 'Infertile couples paying a heavy price for Labor', op cit.

P 116: A Danish study of more than 47,000 couples struggling to have children ...: Trille Kjaer, Vanna Alberi, Allan Jensen, Susanne K Kjaer, Christoffer Johansen, Susanne O Dalton, 'Divorce or end of cohabitation among Danish women evaluated for fertility problems', *Acta Obstetricia Et Gynecologica Scandinavica*, January 2014.

P 116: In a separate study conducted in 2009 ...: K Hammarberg, J Astbury, H Baker, 'Women's experience of IVF: a follow-up study', *Human Reproduction*, Volume 16, Issue 2, February 2001, pp 374–83.

P 116: Jenny has said that at times she would be so overcome by grief or anger ...: Ally Foster, op cit.

P 116: 'A lot of things get tested when you go through those sorts of experiences ...': Scott Morrison, *Kitchen Cabinet*, Season 5, Episode 1, ABC TV, broadcast 28 October 2015.

P 116: 'That's the worst thing you can hear when you are in that situation ...': Scott Morrison, *Kitchen Cabinet*, ibid.

P 117: 'Sometimes you can get quite depressed ...': Ally Foster, op cit.

P 119: 'It was just the most bizarre sort of set of circumstances ...': Samantha Maiden, 'Scott Morrison talks faith, politics and creating Lara Bingle', *Daily Telegraph*, 2 August 2013.

P 119: being blessed with a baby reminded him of 'who's in charge': Helen McCabe, 'Scott Morrison: faith and family come first', *The Australian Women's Weekly*, August 2015.

P 119: 'That tells me that God has a very good sense of humour ...': Scott Morrison, Statements by Members: Abbey Rose Morrison, House of Representatives, Canberra, 7 July 2011.

P 120: 'To my wife, Jenny, on Valentine's Day ...': Scott Morrison, Governor-General's Speech: Address in Reply, House of Representatives, 14 February 2008.

P 121: 'It was hard. It was really, really hard ...': Jordan Baker, 'Meet Jenny Morrison, the "unrecognisable" woman behind the PM', *Sydney Morning Herald*, 12 May 2019.

P 121: 'I found myself at the doctor's going, "I'm trying to do everything ...': Miranda Wood and Linda Silmalis, 'Jenny Morrison opens up about her own battles and rallies support for mental health', *Sunday Telegraph*, 5 May 2019.

P 121: 'I learned that it is so important to reach out for help ...': Jane Hansen, 'Perinatal depression affects 1 in 5 new mums, including Jenny Morrison', *Daily Telegraph*, 15 March 2021.

P 123: 'The greatest blessing as a dad is spending time with my girls ...': Miranda Wood, 'The Prime Minister Scott Morrison hits the tools to build daughters a cubby house at Kirribilli', *Sunday Telegraph*, 6 September 2020.

Chapter Six: Cooked

P 130: Perhaps Labor's Anthony Albanese said it ...: Anthony Albanese, media conference on Liberal Party leadership and NSW Liberals, 21 July 2007.

P 131: 'Howard now distanced himself from ...': Andrew Clennell, 'Pending the party's approval', *Sydney Morning Herald,* 28 July 2007.

P 131: 'I spoke to him [Towke] last night ...': Andrew Clennell, ibid.

P 134: 'If there is evidence in relation to ...': Andrew Clennell, 'Vote over Towke's future splits Libs', *Sydney Morning Herald*, 2 August 2007.

P 137: As Christopher Pyne put it ...: Christopher Pyne, *The Insider: the Scoops, the Scandals and the Serious Business within the Canberra Bubble*, Hachette Australia, Sydney, 2020.

P 138: he even described New Zealand as a 'bit of a nirvana' ...: Nick Venter, 'Blooded in battle', *The Dominion*, 8 May 1999.

Chapter Seven: Faith is Personal

P 142: 'I was saying to myself, "You know Lord, where are you ...': Scott Morrison, address to the Australian Christian Churches National Conference, Gold Coast, 20–22 April 2021.

P 142: 'The message I got that day was ...': Scott Morrison, ibid.

P 143: 'My personal faith in Jesus Christ is not a political agenda ...': Scott Morrison, Governor-General's Speech: Address in Reply, House of Representatives, 14 February 2008.

P 145: 'Rightly or wrongly I genuinely believed that I would be pre-empting the victim ...': Brian Houston, evidence given at the Royal Commission into Institutional Responses to Child Sexual Abuse, 9 October 2014.

P 146: 'We are satisfied that, in 1999 and 2000, Pastor Brian Houston and the national executive ...': Royal Commission into Institutional Responses to Child Sexual Abuse, *Report of Case Study No 18: The Response of Australian*

Christian Churches and Affiliated Pentecostal churches to Allegations of Child Sexual Abuse, 23 November 2015.

P 146: The *Wall Street Journal* broke the story after Morrison had arrived …: Vivian Salama, 'Trump, Australian prime minister look to reinforce an at-times strained alliance', *Wall Street Journal*, 20 September 2019.

P 146: Morrison dismissed the report as 'gossip' …: Scott Morrison, doorstop interview, Washington, 21 September 2019.

P 146: he later admitted during an interview on Sydney radio station 2GB …: Scott Morrison, interview with Ben Fordham, 2GB, 3 March 2020.

P 147: When Morrison asks himself what values he derives from his faith …: Scott Morrison, Governor-General's Speech: Address in Reply, House of Representatives, 14 February 2008.

P 148: 'We may be a secular state, but we are not a godless people …': Scott Morrison, contribution to Marriage Amendment (Definition and Religious Freedoms) Bill 2017 – Second Reading, 4 December 2017.

P 150: Murphy has said that while the church is theologically conservative …: John Sandeman, 'When the future PM sits in your pews, Pastor Michael Murphy reflects on ministering to ScoMo', *Eternity News*, 4 October 2018.

P 150: According to the Australian Bureau of Statistics …: Elle Hunt, 'Christianity on the wane in Australia, but Pentecostal church bucks trend', *The Guardian*, 27 June 2017.

P 150: Researchers believe that while Pentecostals tend to support conservative parties …: Pew Research Center, 'Party affiliation among pentecostals in the evangelical tradition', *Religious Landscape Study*, 2014.

P 151: At university, his honours thesis argued that the Christian Brethren Assemblies …: Scott Morrison, 'Religion and society, a micro approach: an examination of the Christian Brethren assemblies in the Sydney metropolitan area, 1964–1989', thesis, University of New South Wales, 1989.

P 152: 'A vote for Labor and the Greens and anyone who represents anti-Christian rhetoric …': Malcolm Sutton, 'Church's pray-for-Scott Morrison federal election email criticised for "dubious claims"', ABC Radio Adelaide, 31 May 2019.

P 153: On social media, progressive trolls likened his hand waving …: 'Morrison hits out at attacks on his faith from "gutless keyboard warriors"', AAP Newswire, 22 April 2019.

P 153: 'It's disgusting. These grubs are gutless …': Scott Morrison, press conference, Melbourne, 22 April 2019.

P 154: 'drunks, homosexuals, adulterers …': Israel Folau, Instagram post, 10 April 2019.

P 154: 'The meanest commentary I've seen in the election …': Joe Kelly, 'Shorten ignites unholy war by targeting Morrison's religion', *The Australian*, 15 May 2019.

P 155: 'Shorten ignites unholy war by targeting Morrison's religion': Joe Kelly, ibid.

P 155: he declared that he did not believe gay people went to hell: Joe Kelly, ibid.

P 155: The electorates that would go on …: Andrew West, 'How religious voters lost faith in Labor: lessons from the 2019 federal election', ABC online, 24 May 2019.

P 156:   It's a label that Morrison has described as 'a bit dated': Scott Morrison, *Kitchen Cabinet*, op cit.

P 156:   'That wasn't necessarily prophetic but something that was informed by our theology …': John Sandeman, op cit.

P 156:   In May 2019, the Pentecostal Prime Minister himself claimed …: Scott Morrison, election night speech, Sofitel Hotel, Sydney, 18 May 2019.

P 157:   'We are called, all of us, for a time and for a season …': Scott Morrison, address to the Australian Christian Churches National Conference, op cit.

P 158:   'I've been in evacuation centres where people thought …': Scott Morrison, address to the Australian Christian Churches National Conference, op cit.

Chapter Eight: I Stopped These

P 161:   Pyne described opposition as a 'special kind of hell': Christopher Pyne, op cit.

P 165:   According to Turnbull, Scott Morrison asked to meet with him …: Malcolm Turnbull, op cit, p 174.

P 166:   Scott Morrison recalls that it was a Sunday afternoon …: Scott Morrison, *Kitchen Cabinet*, op cit.

P 166:   Morrison once described it as like walking on the edge …: Scott Morrison, interview with Michelle Grattan, *The Conversation*, 12 March 2015.

P 166:   Globally, the United Nations High Commissioner for Refugees reported almost no change in the number of people seeking asylum …: United Nations High Commissioner for Refugees, *UNHCR Global Trends 2010*, 2011.

P 167:   seventy-eight asylum seekers who were picked up by the Australian Customs vessel …: Ben Doherty and Katherine Murphy, 'Sri Lankan deadlock continues', *The Age*, 15 November 2009.

P 174:   'If people wanted to attend the funeral service from Sydney …': Phillip Coorey and Kirsty Needham, 'Hockey calls for compassion in funeral row', *Sydney Morning Herald*, 16 February 2011.

P 174:   'I would never seek to deny a parent or a child from saying goodbye …': Joe Hockey, press conference, Sydney, 15 February 2011.

P 175:   'I am disappointed that my successor would take such an approach': Phillip Coorey and Kirsty Needham, op cit.

P 175:   'These are babies who died in the direst of circumstances …': Phillip Coorey and Kirsty Needham, op cit.

P 175:   'Those who were thinking of making the voyage …': Scott Morrison, *Kitchen Cabinet*, op cit.

P 176:   'The timing of my comments over the last twenty-four hours …': Scott Morrison, interview with Ray Hadley, 2GB, 16 February 2011.

P 176:   According to several former colleagues who were present …: Lenore Taylor, 'Morrison sees votes in anti-Muslim strategy', *Sydney Morning Herald*, 17 February 2011.

P 177:   'I'm sure he meant we should engage in a constructive way …': Tony Wright and Michelle Grattan, 'Senior Lib tries to defuse row', *Sydney Morning Herald*, 18 February 2011.

P 177: Between 2008 and 2013, more than 50,000 asylum seekers would arrive ...: Paige Taylor, 'Asylum-seeker boat first to slip through navy's net in two years', *The Australian*, 20 November 2015.

P 177: tried to find a way to block the so-called 'Malaysia solution' ...: Lauren Wilson, 'Offshore deadlock has government getting nasty', *The Australian*, 29 June 2012.

P 179: According to Turnbull, Morrison floated the idea ...: Malcolm Turnbull, op cit.

P 180: But at the first briefing on 23 September, he baffled the attendant media ...: Scott Morrison, 'Operation Sovereign Borders Update', press conference, 23 September 2013.

P 181: Roman Quaedvlieg insists that Operation Sovereign Border wouldn't have been a success ...: Roman Quaedvlieg, *Tour de Force*, Penguin Australia, 2020.

P 184: Quaedvlieg later tweeted a photo of the trophy: @quaedvliegs, Twitter, 20 September 2018.

Chapter Nine: Trust

P 186: Abbott announced a major ministerial reshuffle ...: Tony Abbott, press conference, Parliament House, Canberra, 21 December 2014.

P 188: According to Turnbull, Morrison was already of the view ...: Malcolm Turnbull, op cit, p 235.

P 189: Hockey declared the age of entitlement was over ...: Joe Hockey, radio interview with Alan Jones, 2GB, 2 May 2014.

P 189: he tried to argue that the tax would only really affect high income earners ...: Joe Hockey, radio interview, ABC Brisbane, 13 August 2014.

P 190: Hockey advised people to 'get a good job' ...: Joe Hockey, press conference, Commonwealth Parliamentary Office, Sydney, 9 June 2015.

P 192: Turnbull recalls Morrison suggesting that they commission polling ...: Malcolm Turnbull, op cit, p 238.

P 196: *The Australian* revealed that the Expenditure Review Committee had just approved a cut ...: Greg Sheridan, column, *The Australian*, 23 March 2015.

Chapter Ten: Thirty Newspolls

P 199: since what had been called the 'empty chair' spill ...: Peter Hartcher, 'Abbott ripe for knockout blow', *Sydney Morning Herald*, 14 February 2015.

P 200: Following a heated exchange ... announced his intentions to the media: Malcolm Turnbull, speech, Senate courtyard, Parliament House, Canberra, 14 September 2015.

P 204: But, in early November 2015, the Treasury proposals suddenly appeared on the front page ...: Samantha Maiden, 'PM's plan to cut the debt', *Sunday Telegraph*, 1 November 2015.

P 209: But Morrison was insistent that foreign workers ...: Sarina Locke, 'Federal treasurer says backpacker workers must pay tax, as farm groups worry tax increase will lead to worker shortage', ABC Rural, 2 February 2016.

P 209: 'The Australian people have moved on from all of that …': Scott Morrison, Budget Day Address, Parliament House, Canberra, 3 May 2016.

P 210: Morrison claimed there was a $67 billion black hole …: James Massola, '$67b black hole claim backfires on Morrison – Treasurer admits errors in calculations – Election 2016', *Sydney Morning Herald*, 25 May 2016.

P 210: Morrison retreated somewhat, now claiming that the funding shortfall …: James Massola, '$67b or $32b? Combatants walk with the zombies – Election 2016 – Labor costings – PM on attack', *Sydney Morning Herald*, 26 May 2016.

P 211: the Opposition's so-called 'Mediscare' campaign …: Peter Hartcher, 'Two messages drew blood in the campaign', *Sydney Morning Herald, 2* July 2016.

P 211: As part of the 2016 Budget, the government had introduced a $1.6 million cap …: Ross Gittins, 'Super makeover still leaves many in cold', *Sydney Morning Herald,* 11 May 2016.

P 212: Morrison was roasted by Sydney shock jock Ray Hadley …: Paul Karp, 'Ray Hadley tells Scott Morrison the Coalition may "perish" over superannuation changes', *The Guardian*, 23 May 2016.

Chapter Eleven: Becoming Prime Minister

P 218: Morrison argued against the reform …: Scott Morrison, contribution to debate, Same-Sex Relationships (Equal Treatment in Commonwealth Laws—Superannuation) Bill 2008, Parliament House, Canberra, 4 June 2008.

P 218: 'The language in this bill is seeking to rewrite how we describe marital relationships …': Scott Morrison, contribution to debate, Same-Sex Relationships (Equal Treatment in Commonwealth Laws—Superannuation) Bill 2008, ibid.

P 219: 'Today I have issued a direction to the Australian Statistician …': Scott Morrison, Direction to the Australian Statistician, media release, 9 August 2017.

P 219: told his fellow Australians it was 'OK to say no' …: Scott Morrison (ScoMo), 'A message to my constituents in Cook', Facebook post, Scott Morrison, 18 September 2017.

P 219: On 15 November 2017, the results of the public poll were announced …: Australian Bureau of Statistics, National Results, Australian Marriage Law Postal Survey, 2017, 15 November 2017.

P 221: Morrison would later justify his decision …: Scott Morrison, interview with Leigh Sales, *7.30*, ABC TV, 16 May 2019.

P 222: a proposal to cap the size of the associated deductions …: David Uren, 'Negative gearing cap in the frame', *The Australian,* 13 March 2017.

P 222: when he described Labor's own push to scrap negative gearing …: Scott Morrison, doorstop interview, London, 27 January 2017.

P 223: 'Gary and Michelle Warren are extraordinary Australians …': Scott Morrison, address to the National Press Club, Parliament House, Canberra, 10 May 2017.

P 226: the investigation would provide 'direct and timely assistance' …: Annika Smethurst, 'Banking royal commission: PM urged to consider closer look at industry', *Sunday Telegraph*, 25 June 2017.

P 227: criminal syndicates had run millions of dollars through Australia ...: Charles Miranda, 'CBA faces fines over breaches', *Herald Sun,* 4 August 2017.

P 227: he called it 'a stunt': Samantha Maiden, 'Scott Morrison was the last frontier before the banking royal commission, sources reveal', *The New Daily,* 22 January 2019.

P 228: 'We are writing to you as the leaders of Australia's major banks ...': Stephen Long, 'This letter from the big banks helped shape the royal commission', ABC News online, 5 February 2019.

P 229: 'The nature of political events means the national economic interest ...': Scott Morrison, press conference, Canberra, 30 November 2017.

P 232: 'Of course I want to be prime minister ...': Ben Smee, 'Peter Dutton: "Some leaders fall into the trap of abandoning principles"', *The Guardian,* 7 April 2018.

P 232: 'Down the track I am sure if an opportunity presented itself ...': Scott Morrison, interview with Leigh Sales, *7.30,* ABC TV, 10 April 2018.

P 238: Turnbull announced that Morrison would act as home affairs minister ...: Malcolm Turnbull, transcript, Parliament House, Canberra, 21 August 2018.

P 239: 'I was very grateful when Malcolm invited me to serve ...': Matthias Cormann, press conference, Parliament House, Canberra, 22 August 2018.

P 239: 'This is my leader, and I'm ambitious for him ...': Scott Morrison, press conference, Parliament House, Canberra, 22 August 2018.

P 241: Leaked WhatsApp messages later revealed that Liberal moderates ...: Gareth Hutchens, 'Leaked WhatsApp messages reveal Julie Bishop's leadership bid scuppered by colleagues', *The Guardian,* 26 August 2018.

P 242: 'At the end of the day you are always here ...': Scott Morrison, interview with Annika Smethurst, *Sunday Telegraph,* 25 August 2018.

Chapter Twelve: Nothing to Lose

P 246: 'If you have a go in this country, you'll get a go ...': Scott Morrison, press conference, Parliament House, Canberra, 24 August 2018.

P 248: 'I did tell him I was a rubbish golfer ...': Scott Morrison, interview with Annika Smethurst, *Sunday Telegraph,* 25 August 2018.

P 248: Morrison described her as a 'rock star' ...: Scott Morrison, Blue Room speech, Parliament House, Canberra, 24 August 2018.

P 249: 'She has been an amazing contributor ...': Tom McIlroy, 'Julie Bishop departs frontbench as Scott Morrison assembles new cabinet', *Australian Financial Review,* 26 August 2018.

P 249: forced to resign two-and-a-half years earlier over accusations ...: Ellen Whinnett and Fiona Hudson, 'Chopped Stuey', *Herald Sun,* 13 February 2016.

P 249: she was dumped following a travel rorts scandal ...: Annika Smethurst and Natasha Bita, 'Long Ley off likely for MP', *Herald Sun,* 11 January 2017.

P 250: the lump of coal he waved around in parliament during a bemusing question time performance ...: 'Coal fires Lib attack', *Townsville Bulletin,* 10 February 2017.

P 251: The key advisory role of principal private secretary …: Greg Sheridan, 'Morrison prepares to take his place on the international stage', *The Australian*, 15 September 2018.

P 251: declaring he would relocate Australia's embassy in Tel Aviv to Jerusalem …: David Wroe, 'PM flags embassy move to Jerusalem', *The Age,* 16 October 2018.

P 252: 'Indonesia asks Australia and other countries to continue supporting the Palestine–Israel peace process …': David Wroe, James Massola and Fergus Hunter, with Deborah Snow, 'Indonesia warns on shifting embassy', *The Age*, 17 October 2018.

P 253: his son, Alex, urged Australians to donate to the Labor candidate …: @alexbhturnbull, Twitter, 1 September 2018.

P 253: A snippet of the Philip Ruddock report on religious freedom …: Jewel Topsfield, 'Push for gay pupil rejection', *The Age*, 10 October 2018.

P 253: saw the Coalition vote in favour of a motion by One Nation's Pauline Hanson …: Annika Smethurst, 'Libs' only hope is to learn fast', *Sunday Herald Sun,* 21 October 2018.

P 254: National Party MP Andrew Broad quit in December …: Rob Harris, '"Sugar daddy" MP quits in disgrace', *Courier Mail,* 19 December 2018.

P 255: Morrison quickly announced new laws that would see anyone who contaminated strawberries …: Greg Brown and Richard Ferguson, 'Fruit crisis: PM gets tough with 15 years' prison', *The Australian,* 20 September 2018.

P 257: declare himself 'a prime minister for standards': Staff writers, 'Citizen ceremonies to be compulsory on Australia Day, government says', AAP, 13 January 2019.

P 257: He claimed the vote proved Labor didn't have the 'mettle' …: Katharine Murphy and Paul Karp, 'Scott Morrison suffers historic defeat as Labor and crossbench pass medevac bill', *The Guardian,* 13 February 2019.

P 258: personal income tax cuts to low- and middle-income Australians worth $158 billion …: Josh Frydenberg, Budget Speech 2019–20, on the second reading of the Appropriation Bill, 2 April 2019.

P 258: Frydenberg declared the budget was 'back in the black' …: Josh Frydenberg, ibid.

P 258: the Coalition also promised $285 million worth of one-off payments …: Josh Frydenberg, ibid.

P 259: 'It is crystal clear, at this election, it is a choice …': Amy Remeikis, 'Scott Morrison and Bill Shorten open election campaign for 18 May poll – as it happened', *The Guardian*, 11 April 2019.

P 261: 'Abbott has a strong intellect which I don't think people realise …': Bill Shorten, interview with Annika Smethurst, RAAF plane, 8 May 2019.

P 265: 'You have focused almost exclusively, since your budget reply speech, on health …': Elias Visontay, 'Shorten in testy clash with reporter', *The Australian*, 17 April 2019.

P 267: A subsequent review of Labor's campaign would find that ...: Craig Emerson and Jay Weatherill, *Review of Labor's 2019 Federal Election Campaign*, Australian Labor Party, 2019.

P 271: On polling day, Labor would suffer swings against it ...: Eryk Bagshaw, 'Labor's franking credits blamed for huge swings in booths with older residents', *Sydney Morning Herald*, 21 May 2019.

P 274: 'I have always believed in miracles! ...': Scott Morrison, election night speech, Sofitel Hotel, Sydney, 18 May 2019.

Chapter Thirteen: Aloha

P 276: an unprecedented bushfire season in Australia that would claim thirty-three lives: Victoria State Government Department of Environment, Land, Water and Planning, *Annual Report*, 26 October 2020, p 8.

P 279: In 1974, prime minister Gough Whitlam was on holiday in Greece when ...: David Nason, 'The art of managing disasters', *The Australian*, 10 August 2010.

P 281: Lara Worthington nee Bingle, the model who had fronted ...: @MsLWorthington, Twitter, 18 December 2019.

P 282: She's clearly made a bad judgment call ...: Tom Flanagan, 'ScoMo haunted by 2010 Q&A rant amid holiday outrage', Yahoo News, 18 December 2019.

P 282: a photo was published showing Morrison in board shorts on Waikiki Beach: Samantha Maiden, '"Legend" PM stars in brew Hawaii, as police reduce 13-year-old Izzy to tears over climate protest', *The New Daily*, 19 December 2020.

P 283: 'I deeply regret any offence caused to any of the many Australians ...': Scott Morrison, statement on PM leave, 20 December 2019.

P 284: 'I'll be getting back there as soon as I can ...': Scott Morrison, radio interview with John Stanley, 2GB, 20 December 2019.

P 285: Morrison was photographed with his wife at a bar: Zoe Zaczek, 'Australian tourist who bumped into Scott Morrison as he "sipped cocktails" in Hawaii claims the PM made one VERY dismissive comment about how he should respond to the bush fires', *Daily Mail*, 23 December 2019.

P 288: A number of locals swore at and otherwise abused the Prime Minister: Tita Smith, Kelsey Wilkie and Brittany Chain, 'Pregnant bushfire victim whose hand was shaken by Scott Morrison says it "broke her heart" when he turned his back and walked away from her', *Daily Mail*, 3 January 2020.

P 288: they were the moments that made global headlines: Tita Smith, Kelsey Wilkie and Brittany Chain, ibid.

P 289: 'Whether they're angry with me or they're angry with the situation ...': Scott Morrison, radio interview, 3AW, 3 January 2020.

Chapter Fourteen: A Global Pandemic

P 291: The patient was a man from Wuhan ...: Greg Hunt, 'First confirmed case of novel coronavirus in Australia', media release, 25 January 2020.

P 295: 'The economic impact of closing the border with China seemed monumental …': Greg Hunt, interview with Annika Smethurst, *Sunday Telegraph/Sunday Herald Sun*, 29 March 2020.

P 297: The WHO nonetheless urged governments to 'strike a fine balance …': Tedros Adhanom, 'WHO Director-General's opening remarks at the mission briefing on COVID-19', World Health Organization, 12 March 2020.

P 303: with Sydney's Bondi Beach having to be closed after beachgoers failed to adhere: Michelle Brown and Victoria Pengilley, 'Bondi Beach closed over crowds amid coronavirus pandemic', ABC News online, 21 March 2020.

P 305: She was watching a Sky News UK report: Stuart Ramsay, 'Coronavirus: Italy's hardest-hit city wants you to see how COVID-19 is affecting its hospitals', 11 September 2020.

P 307: He was acutely aware of the economic devastation of pandemics: Dr Steven Kennedy and Matt Comyn, 'Keeping up with JobKeeper: Behind the scenes of Australia's largest ever spending program', episode 23, *Work with Purpose* podcast, 20 September 2020.

P 309: Morrison and Frydenberg fronted the media at Parliament House: Scott Morrison and Josh Frydenberg, press conference, Parliament House, Canberra, 30 March 2020.

P 311: At the time, Morrison told reporters the investment …: Scott Morrison, press conference, Scientia Clinical Research, Sydney, 5 November 2020.

P 312: 'In the case of Australia, enough vaccine …': Christopher Knaus and Nick Evershed, 'Stuffed: how Australia's "unconscionable" gamble on Covid vaccines backfired', *The Guardian*, 10 July 2021.

P 313: 'Partly that is just bad luck …': 'How Australia's COVID vaccine rollout has fallen short and left us "in a precarious position"', Adam Harvey, Sashka Koloff and Nick Wiggins, *Four Corners*, ABC TV, 24 May 2021.

P 314: '3.1 million of the contracted vaccines that we had been relying upon …': Scott Morrison, press conference, Parliament House, Canberra, 7 April 2021.

P 315: He could only simply concede that it would need to be 'recalibrated': Scott Morrison, press conference, Parliament House, Canberra, 22 April 2021.

P 316: a federal government source leaked figures on the slow vaccine rollout: Clare Armstrong, Mitchell Van Homrigh, Georgia Clark and James O'Doherty, 'Australia slow to deliver vital COVID vaccines, figures show', *Daily Telegraph*, 30 March 2021.

P 316: accused Premier Dan Andrews of taking a 'sledgehammer' to the state's education: Dan Tehan, interview with David Speers, *Insiders*, ABC TV, 3 May 2020.

P 322: The winter outbreaks in Melbourne and Sydney led to the federal government announcing …: Scott Morrison, virtual press conference, 28 June 2021.

P 322: 'I don't want an eighteen-year-old …': Stephanie Zilman, 'Queensland's Chief Health Officer rejects Prime Minister's comments on AstraZeneca's COVID-19 vaccine for under-40s,' ABC News online, 30 June 2021.

P 322: The president of the Australian Medical Association …: Dr Omar Khorshid, interview with Michael Rowland, *News Breakfast*, ABC TV, 30 June 2021.

P 322: Days later, finance minister Simon Birmingham …: Helen Sullivan, 'Australia "at back of the queue" for Pfizer Covid vaccines, minister admits', *The Guardian*, 1 July 2021.

P 323: the May and June weekly average …: Dennis Shanahan, 'PM secures faster flood of Pfizer vaccine doses', *The Australian*, 9 July 2021.

P 323: The ghosts of prime ministers past then haunted Morrison …: Laura Tingle, 'Senior business figures turned to former PM Kevin Rudd to intervene in bringing forward Australia's Pfizer vaccine supply', *7.30*, ABC TV, 11 July 2021.

P 323: Morrison's predecessor, Malcolm Turnbull, also chipped in …: Malcolm Turnbull, interview with Patricia Karvelas, *Afternoon Briefing*, ABC TV, 1 July 2021.

Chapter Fifteen: The Women Issue

P 327: Higgins was just a few weeks into a new job as a media adviser …: Lisa Wilkinson, 'Former Liberal staffer speaks up about her alleged rape in Parliament House', *The Project*, Network 10, 15 February 2021.

P 327: She has described a 'culture of silence' within Australia's political parties …: Lisa Wilkinson, ibid.

P 327: It made Higgins 'sick to her stomach' …: Lisa Wilkinson, ibid.

P 327: 'Jenny and I spoke last night, and she said to me …': Scott Morrison, doorstop interview, Parliament House, Canberra, 16 February 2021.

P 329: she claims the Prime Minister's principal private secretary …: Lisa Wilkinson, op cit.

P 329: the ABC published details of an anonymous letter sent to the Prime Minister …: Louise Milligan, 'Scott Morrison, senators and AFP told of historic rape allegations against Cabinet Minister', *Four Corners*, ABC TV, 26 February 2021.

P 330: 'I'm happy to have a prime minister who's been prepared to call out …': Scott Morrison, interview with Barrie Cassidy, *Insiders*, ABC TV, 18 February 2018.

P 331: he told Parliament that protests elsewhere are being 'met with bullets' …: Scott Morrison, Statements on indulgence – March4Justice, House of Representatives, Canberra, 15 March 2021.

P 332: Liberal strategists believe that, during the 2019 election campaign …: Rob Harris, 'Working mums key to Scott Morrison's election win', *The Age*, 28 July 2019.

P 333: The 2021 Budget announced on 11 May saw the government splash billions …: Marise Payne, Anne Rushton and Jane Hume, Women's Budget Statement 2021–22, 11 May 2021.

P 333: By July 2021, polling showed the extent of the damage …: Resolve polling, commissioned by *The Age* and *Sydney Morning Herald*, quarterly data analysis based on surveys conducted in April, May and June 2021, published 6 July 2021.

P 333: A subsequent survey by Newspoll one week later …: Joe Kelly, 'Newspoll: Scott Morrison slides as women turn away', *The Australian*, 11 July 2021.

Acknowledgements

This book was the brainchild of the formidable Louise Adler who, shortly after I resigned from a newspaper job, told me I needed to find something to fill in my days between manicures. She was right, of course. I have never been good at standing still. And then, when I was filling my days with writing this book, Louise displayed an unwavering belief in me that I truly appreciated.

This book required months of research and interviews. I would like to thank Prime Minister Scott Morrison for agreeing to be interviewed on several occasions and for letting me pry into his life. He also allowed me to speak with his friends and foes without too much intervention, even when they dobbed me in for contacting them.

To the current ministers, former prime ministers, former ministers and MPs who agreed to talk to me for this book. I am truly grateful for your insight and time and for trusting me to tell your stories.

A special thanks to the staff at the National Library of Australia for giving me a safe and quiet place to type and for assisting me in finding the most obscure resources.

Thank you to Laura Tingle for her generous support of this book.

Thanks to my clever publishing team at Hachette for your support and continued belief in me. These miracle workers, in no particular order, include the incomparable Louise Adler, the diligent and calm Emma Rafferty, Paul Smitz for his great advice, Luke Causby, Libby Turner, Vanessa Radnidge, Jenny Topham, Bella Lloyd, Ailie Springall and Nic Pullen for (hopefully) preventing another police raid.

To the many editors and journalists who I have worked alongside in Bendigo, Canberra, Sydney and Melbourne. You have taught me so much and I am indebted to you for your guidance and encouragement.

At times, writing this book was a lesson in suffering as I attempted to split my waking hours between my job at *The Age* and an early-morning podcast, as well as maintaining a relationship with my friends, family and husband.

ACKNOWLEDGEMENTS

To my friends and wider family, who I largely ignored for months in order to complete this book, I am indebted to so many of you for your assistance, support and love. To my parents, thank you for the opportunities you gave me and for never attempting to limit what I wanted to achieve.

A special thanks goes to my loyal dog, Merv, for his constant companionship during the writing process. I promise to make it up to you with walks and treats in the future.

And, finally, to my wonderful husband, Byron, who spent the first few months of our marriage doing laundry, cooking dinner and walking the dog so I had the space and time to write. Without your love and support, this book would not have been possible. You may not believe me, but in the future I promise to try and achieve a better work–life balance. I didn't need to see your face to know what you were thinking when, shortly after completing this book, I sent you a text message to say I might be interested in writing another book. It was noted, but may, in the future, be ignored.

Index

INDEX

hachette
AUSTRALIA

If you would like to find out more about Hachette Australia,
our authors, upcoming events and new releases, you can visit
our website or our social media channels:

hachette.com.au
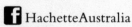 HachetteAustralia
 HachetteAus